HELPING YOUR

HUMAN HORIZONS SERIES

HELPING YOUR HANDICAPPED BABY

by

CLIFF CUNNINGHAM B.Sc. AND PATRICIA SLOPER M.A.

Photographs by Steven Swirkowski
Illustrations by Robert Craven

A CONDOR BOOK
SOUVENIR PRESS (E & A) LTD

ACKNOWLEDGEMENTS

Obviously, a book of this kind owes much to the many people, both professionals and parents, who have a commitment to helping those members of our community who are handicapped. The fact that such a book can be written is, in itself, an acknowledgement of their efforts.

We must thank the many parents who have given us access to their families and homes over the past years. The majority of the ideas in the book have arisen directly from them and their children.

We would particularly like to thank those parents who read the initial manuscript and so tactfully corrected our errors and made many useful suggestions. Similarly, we must thank our colleagues for helpful discussions and comments.

Special thanks go to Professor Peter Mittler for his encouragement and help throughout the whole preparation of the book; to Bob Craven for his illustrations; to Steve Swirkowski for the photographs, and last but certainly not least, Miss Ellen Cullen for typing, layout, retyping, relay-out, retyping, proof reading, retyping!

We would also like to thank the editors of *Child: care, health and development* for allowing us to reprint the case history from an article on parents' needs.

Finally, the opportunity to gain the knowledge and experience to write this book, and at the same time support our families, was provided by grants from the Social Science Research Council and the Department of Health and Social Security.

Cliff Cunningham
Patricia Sloper

We would like to dedicate this book
to our children Barnaby, Oliver and
Tamsin Cunningham and Kristie Sloper
who, above all, taught us that the
books are not always right.

Contents

A*

1: About this book— Its aims and uses

We believe that the fact that you have begged, borrowed, stolen or even bought this book means that you are eager to help your handicapped baby. Or, if you are a professional, that you are hoping to use the book with parents who wish to help their baby. In either case the fact that you believe or hope that the handicapped baby can be helped is the first and vital stage in beginning to help.

We have based the book on our work over a number of years with parents and their mentally handicapped babies—mainly babies with Down's Syndrome (mongolism). Much of what we write has come directly from the parents in the course of helping their own babies.

The book is not meant to be read through once only, but as a source of ideas and information to use as your baby grows and develops.

You will find that many ideas are repeated in different chapters.

This is because the same ideas are used in different ways at different times, and also because we believe that repetition is important for learning.

You will also find that we have used 'he' to refer to the babies, not he and she. This is not because we are male chauvinists but merely because we found it less confusing. Please convey our apologies to your daughters.

Before you plunge into the chapters that tell you what to *do*, we would ask that you read the first chapters about the 'why's and where-fores' of helping.

In this first chapter we will try to explain our purpose in writing the book and some guidelines in using it.

OUR PURPOSE

It is often all too easy to see what our handicapped children *cannot* do; but by observing closely, exactly what they *can* do, it is then possible to see progress that would otherwise have gone unnoticed. This, in itself, is encouraging and stimulating. By breaking down each area of development into the smallest step, we can then help our child towards only the next immediate stage instead of aiming too high and meeting failure and frustration. In this way parents can feel that they are giving the right help at the right time and also see results.

By applying this method of thinking to difficulties as well as to general development, we can learn to identify a potential problem at an early stage, decide exactly what we are trying to achieve and work positively towards that aim.

No one expects miracles, but at least with these guidelines we can feel that we parents can help our children to make progress. We can learn to build on the things they can do instead of perhaps dwelling on the things they might never do.

This was written by a parent who came to a course of evening discussion groups, in answer to the question :

"What did you get out of the meetings?"

She has a son who was $2\frac{1}{2}$ at the time. He was multiply handicapped but the exact cause of this was not known. At the time of the discussion group she was trying to teach him to be more attentive and alert and to manipulate objects.

Her answer expresses, better than we can, what our aim is in this book. If you, as parents of young handicapped children, feel that you can agree with this mother after using the book, we will be very satisfied. If you do not, we can only apologise for raising your hopes and expectations and not meeting your needs.

BEHAVIOUR

In this book we use the word BEHAVIOUR. This does not mean good or bad behaviour but anything the child does, from looking and smiling to speaking, climbing, poking out his tongue or using the toilet. It means things that you *can see* happen, not what you think is happening!

For example : we had one mother who said her child did not sleep as much as babies should and she was very worried. We asked her to keep a daily chart of the time the baby slept for one week. When she added up the hours of sleep she found that the baby did sleep as much as other babies, but in shorter periods. In other words, what was actually happening was very different from what she thought was happening. She was becoming more objective.

SOME GENERAL POINTS

Before getting into the practical work of helping your child we would like to make some general points.

1. All mentally handicapped children are very individual and are very different. In fact there is more difference between two 'handicapped' children than between two 'normal' children. A great deal of confused and unhelpful advice has been offered because people think that all children with Down's Syndrome

(mongolism), for example, are the same. They are not! We have Down's Syndrome babies who can sit up at seven months but others who do not do this until 14 months. 'Normal' babies on the other hand can be expected to sit up between five and nine months : a much smaller difference.

Parents and families are all different. In some there are brothers and sisters, aunts, uncles and grandparents all willing to help and support. In others, parents have to help their relatives to come to understand the problems.

How you can help your child will depend upon the support you can get from friends, relatives and professional people; and, of course, on the nature and degree of the handicap itself.

Because of this we cannot pretend that we are so expert that we know exactly what you should do. Indeed, once you begin to understand your child, you will become the main 'expert' as you will be the one who truly knows him. Therefore you will not find precise recipes of help in this book, you will find guidelines.

You must take these guidelines and experiment with them, try them out and change them to meet the needs of your child and your family. It is only by adapting them that you will discover the special needs of your child, and of course, improve your own expertise.

2. The special help that the handicapped child needs changes as the child grows and develops. But even when he is adult he will still need special help. In this book we have concentrated on the first years of life. You will need to find out more later on. However, there are basic guidelines on how to help which have been worked out from our knowledge of the nature of mental handicap. We have tried to explain these in the first chapters of the book, and hope that you will find them useful, even when the baby has grown into later childhood.

3. An important part of teaching is knowing *what* to teach. Fortunately, even though handicapped babies develop more slowly than 'normal' babies, they usually develop on a similar pattern. This we call normal child development. We use the knowledge of normal child development to tell us what to teach the handicapped baby. The main part of this book is concerned with explaining this development as far as we understand it today. In the future, more information may become available.

This knowledge of normal development is sufficient to plan stimulation for many mentally handicapped children, such as those with Down's Syndrome, who do not have serious damage in specific areas—such as blindness, deafness, physical disorders, epilepsy etc. But parents of babies with these added problems, will need to seek extra advice from specialists (See Appendix Three and Booklist).

4. To teach somebody something you must feel that the person can be expected to learn it, and also feel hopeful that you are teaching it in the best way. If you do not expect him to learn and are not optimistic, then why teach it in the first place? Too many classrooms have become miserable because teachers have lost their belief in the importance of what is being taught. The same applies to parents. If you are going to help your child, you must also be optimistic and expect change. You must have hope and perhaps dreams. But you also need to be realistic. We cannot make the child normal but we can lessen the effects of the handicap. Realistic expectations are those which deal with helping the child to move forward to the next small step in development. Enthusiasm is maintained when you realise that reaching the next step for your child is as great an achievement as passing an examination or winning a race is for other children.

5. Many parents are worried that the amount of time needed to help their handicapped baby will be so great that they will not be able to cope. If the child needs frequent medical treatment, time will be taken up travelling to hospitals or health centres.

However, it is a mistake to think that a lot of time will be taken up teaching the baby. It is not the quantity of stimulation and help that matters, but the quality. Indeed giving constant stimulation may be like giving children large quantities of vitamins; they use what they can and the rest passes through.* It is also possible to overstretch the child by pushing too hard and expecting achievements too soon. If you do this with any child, he soon learns ways of avoiding the teaching. We try to encourage him and lead him gently to new experiences. It is best to treat the handicapped child like a normal child—taking into account his or her special problems. He will develop best in a 'normal' balanced home rather than one which focuses all activities on the handicap. The approach we advise is for the parent to become

* Extreme overdosing with vitamins can lead to hypervitaminosis.

an opportunist. Know what it is you wish to encourage, and then pick up the opportunities to encourage it from the natural every-day activities of the family. You will need time to learn what to look for, and to plan ways of providing the stimulation, but this does not mean teaching a baby for two or three hours a day. Anyway, all young children need time to sleep, eat and join in the general activities of the home, and time for themselves.

6. Last, but not least, there is much truth in the saying that chil-dren develop at their own speed. Mentally handicapped children do need far more help than normal children to keep up their own speed, but no amount of stimulation will push them beyond it. The challenge in helping them is to work out the quality and quantity of stimulation which will maintain their best rate of progress.

To sum up

Don't be afraid to be hopeful, but at the same time try to under-stand that your child is an individual and will have his limi-tations as well as his strengths. We can't all have brilliant chil-dren, and equally we can't all have the brightest Down's Syn-drome child or the most agile spastic child. We have our own children, who are themselves, and we can only try to help them make the most of the potential they were born with and to improve the quality of their life. If they are mentally handi-capped they will probably need and prosper from our help far more than those who are more able.

In this book we will try to show you how to start, by drawing upon our experiences with many parents who have faced the same challenge. But please remember this is a starting point, and you will need to go on from this book and seek more information and advice.

YOU AND YOUR HANDICAPPED CHILD

2: Coming to terms with the handicap

In this chapter we try to report what parents have told us of their feelings about having a mentally handicapped child, and how they coped with them.

The message is: until you come to terms with the handicap you can't really begin to help your baby.

We have never yet met a parent who, on being told that his or her baby is probably mentally handicapped, was not deeply shocked. At first, parents talk of their feelings of helplessness, emptiness and isolation. It is as though the baby they had hoped for and planned for was dead. This often leads to resentment and rejection of the handicapped baby that is there instead: resentment that they have not got the baby they wanted, and rejection, not so much of the baby, but of the idea of the handicap.

It is important to realise that both the baby you wanted and the handicapped baby you have are to some extent imaginary. The one you wanted was only there in your thoughts and dreams. The one that has been born is real enough but it is unlikely that you have at present any clear idea of what the handicap means. All you can do is to use your imagination to create an image of the future child and guess what it will be like. Even if you have known a child with a similar handicap, your child will be different. Much suffering and bitterness can be avoided if you control your imagination and seek out as much accurate information as is available about the handicap and the future problems.

This can be a frustrating task. You will be given much well meaning but inaccurate advice. Even with a condition such as Down's Syndrome, which is a common cause of mental handicap and about which much is known, finding the information is not always easy. In a large proportion of cases of mental handicap the causes are not understood. In seeking out this information you must try to find people who have the relevant experience.

This brings us to another point. Many parents feel angry and frustrated with the doctors who have made the diagnosis. This is a confusion with the anger and bitterness over what has happened to them. Even when they get over this, a new frustration and annoyance builds up when the doctors cannot give them all the information they want, when they are forced to say they cannot do very much—medically—for the child. It is unfair to expect the medical profession to know what is not known, or to know about the development and education of your child when it is not within their field of specialism. Whilst the anger and frustration is understandable, it does not help. Instead, you need to approach the services, which can never be totally satisfactory, as objectively as possible.

Another feeling that the majority of parents experience is guilt : guilt that they could have produced a handicapped child; guilt that they have let down their family; guilt that they may themselves have caused the handicap in some way; guilt that they reject the child, and often wish he or she had not been born, or was dead. These feelings are almost universal, and the best way to overcome them is to recognise that they are natural reactions to the situation, and to talk about them. Talk to close friends, relatives, professionals and other parents. Parents have often told us that so many of the fears, which seemed unconquerable, became unimportant when shared, particularly when shared with somebody who understood and had the relevant information and time to listen.

It is also common to find parents who accept the child but not the handicap. They go from doctor to doctor seeking a miracle, searching for someone who will say this is all a mistake. This seldom, if ever, happens. Others cling to the idea that the child will be a late developer and all right in the end. Some believe that it is only slow speech that is the problem, not permanent damage to the brain. Less obvious are the parents who accept the handicap but not the degree of handicap : the parent, for example, who accepts that the baby has Down's Syndrome but is 'high grade'. You just cannot tell accurately in the first months. Again one can understand these feelings, especially where the baby looks normal and develops well physically; or, as often in the case of Down's syndrome, develops very well for the first six months or more of life. But the sooner you can come to terms with the handicap and accept that the baby will not develop normally, the sooner you can begin to help. As we have so often found, when parents begin to help the child in practical ways, they also find it easier to accept the handicap.

Accepting the handicap often means confronting your own attitude to mental handicap in general, and your whole philosophy of life: the things you prize and value; the things you want out of living. To the painter, blindness in an infant may be more difficult to accept than damage to a limb, to the musician it may be deafness that is most feared. We have met parents who prize their intellectual abilities and find it therefore more difficult to accept mental handicap than parents who make their way in more practical occupations. It is worthwhile examining these values in terms of how they affect what you feel about the handicap.

We use our values to judge other people's lives. When we look at any handicapped person, it is according to our own personal values, at worst we pity them and at best understand their difficulties. But who can judge whether another persons' life is better or worse than our own? Only they know what they value and enjoy. It is important to try to understand their life from their view. Of course, the more skills and abilities you have, the more choices you can make, the more things you can do, the more experiences you can appreciate—that is why we think it is important to help parents to improve the skills and abilities of their handicapped children. But when next you look at your handicapped child with sadness, ask yourself for whom you are sad: for the handicapped child, for the imaginary child you hoped for— or for yourself.

Of course, all this is easier said than done. There are times when the handicap produces tremendous strains on the family. There are some children who are so severely damaged, or whose behaviour becomes so unmanageable as they grow older, that daily life for all concerned becomes intolerable and something has to give. It is difficult to say whether this will happen with a particular baby. We do know that it is less likely to happen in some conditions, including Down's Syndrome, than in others. We also believe that it is less likely to happen where parents have learnt to stimulate and manage the child from his early years. The more able the child is to care for him or herself, the less the strain on the family. Even where it becomes necessary to seek residential care at some later age, you can feel that you gave the child the best you could to fulfil his potential, and we cannot expect more from ourselves or others.

Here are some of the pieces of advice that parents have told us have helped them to come to terms with the handicap.

1. Try to take each day as it comes and do not dwell too much on the future.

2. Get to know your child. Look for those individual ways he has of showing his uniqueness.

3. Try to tackle the situation as a partnership and let the family be involved and give support.

4. Avoid letting the handicapped child become the focus of the family life. Try to keep the organisation and social life of yourselves and the family as close to normal as possible. Do not avoid your friends and relatives.

5. Take the initiative and tell your friends, relatives and neighbours about the child as soon as possible. The longer you leave it the harder it becomes.

6. Do not hide it from other children in the family. This will only cause considerable stress later on. If they are old enough, explain simply that the baby is different, will be slower in growing up and so on. If they are young, talk about it in front of them and as they grow and begin to ask questions answer them honestly.

7. Remember that friends and relatives will take their cue from you. If you are embarrassed and ashamed in talking about the baby, they will act accordingly. They will also believe there is something to be ashamed about and to hide. When this happens, you can lose a great deal of support and help. As one parent told us, "We found a fund of goodwill in our friends and relatives. We needed to harness it and direct it."

8. Also, take your baby out and do not be afraid of people seeing him. On most occasions people are understanding and sympathetic.

9. Get used to the tactless and hurting remarks that people make without thinking. In fact teach them the truth.

10. Try to find out accurate information from people who know.
11. Talk to people, especially other parents of children with similar handicaps. They are usually very helpful.
12. Remember that all the family, and particularly your spouse, will feel upset and irritable. Try to be calm and tolerant with each other.
13. Start to learn how to help the baby, and begin to stimulate him or her as soon as you feel able.

And remember, as time passes and your expertise with the baby grows, this will make it easier to cope both practically and emotionally.

Having a mentally handicapped child is a major upheaval in anyone's life. It will need changes in attitudes and lifestyle. It is a challenge. But it is not without its rewards. Many parents of handicapped children have testified that the child does not just take from the family: he positively contributes to its well-being. As one parent put it: 'Having David has broadened our outlook considerably.'

To end this chapter we include an account by one of our mothers of what happened when her baby girl with Down's Syndrome was born. Other parents who have read it feel that it has helped make them aware that they were not alone in their feelings and fears.

My pregnancy started a lot of soul searching. I wanted the baby very much, but at my age, 38, it seemed pretty late to be bringing up a family. I already had a baby boy, Steven, who was 15 months old, and two boys, one seven and one nine.

My husband longed for a little girl. In my mind I wasn't really bothered.

I was married eight years before I had any children, I had a lot of miscarriages.

On the day Melanie was born, I remember standing outside the locked gate of the maternity wards at the hospital, with one of the ambulance men saying, 'You'll soon have it over with love.'

Melanie, my little girl, was born about 5 o'clock that evening. I had a bit of a rough time and had stitches the same as I had on my other babies.

That was all passed now. I had my little girl and everything had been worth it. I thought of my husband, what he'd say. I was absolutely thrilled to bits. It was funny really, about ten minutes after I had the baby my husband 'phoned and heard about Melanie. My neighbours said he was skipping in the street telling everyone I had a girl.

Everybody seemed to be milling around the labour ward. I saw a doctor looking at Melanie in her cot and she came and said my little girl was lovely. At the time I thought it was funny there being a doctor, but I passed it off as routine.

I went up to the ward, as it was by then nearly visiting time. I couldn't wait to see my husband.

They usually bring your baby with you from the labour ward, but I was told they were really rushed off their feet. As soon as they washed baby they would bring her to see me.

I can't tell you what I actually thought at the time. I was so tired and I thought, she won't be long.

My husband came to see me with my mother. He came up the ward with smiles beaming all over his face. I remember him saying, 'We've cracked it love at last.'

Melanie hadn't been brought to me. It was half way through visiting, I asked the nurse could my husband see baby. She said she would take him up to see baby before he went home.

My husband saw Melanie and came back down to tell me she was lovely and looked the same born as our other children. He went home and time passed. At last they brought my Melanie, she was lovely. She had scratched her face, her nails were that long but to me she was gorgeous. I had a good night's sleep at last.

Melanie slept all night. The next day I felt as if I was walking on air. The doctor came to see me and we were talking about me being sterilized.

Well the day wore on and I felt I was the happiest mum in all the world. Melanie was good and just taking glucose water. I intended to feed her myself like I had done my other babies.

I was on my way to the bathroom to get myself prettied up and have a bath before visiting at seven o'clock. I remember it was round about five o'clock.

On my way to the bathroom the sister came to me and said, 'Mrs J. we are just taking Melanie to the nursery, doctor wants to see her.'

I just passed this off as routine and carried on to the bath-room for my bath. I was really enjoying my first bath after having Melanie. I felt very happy at the thought that it was all over at last.

There came a knock on the door and sister popped her head round to say the doctor wanted to see me.

I knew then there was something wrong. I jumped out of the bath not bothering to dry myself or get dressed. I just put my dressing gown on, and dashed out to see doctor.

There were three doctors round my bed, and sister. I said 'What is wrong?' The specialist spoke to me. 'I've got to tell you your little girl won't be like your other children, she will be a bit backward and she will need all the extra love and understanding you can give her.' I don't know how the word 'mongol' came out, I don't know whether I said it or the doctor did. All I know is that at that moment the roof had caved in on me. I went a bit hysterical, crying, 'There's nothing wrong with her. If you're going off her eyes, the heavy lids, all my other children were born like that and my husband's eyes are like that.' I couldn't think, I'd gone numb all over. The doctor told me to get in bed. It was only then I realised I was wet, and standing in a puddle of water. I wasn't dressed, I just didn't care. Doctor gave me Melanie when I was in bed, rock-ing her, loving her and out loud I was saying, 'I'm sorry, I'm sorry. Oh God it's not true,' but deep down I knew it was. I was fighting for them to say they had made a mistake. It can't happen to me, it only happens to other people. God wouldn't let it happen to me.

They drew the curtains round my bed and the doctor put his arm round my shoulder and he said, 'Well if you think she looks like your husband it might well be she's taking after him,' but all the time I knew he was sort of shaking his head. I said, 'Tell me, what makes you think she is a mongol?' Looking at her honestly I couldn't see a thing wrong with her.

He started to explain. 'You see their muscles are very floppy,' and he demonstrated this by lifting Melanie's arm up and let-ting it drop. As you know, a baby can grip your two fingers and by using their strength they can lift themselves up with a grip like steel. I've had this demonstrated to me many a time on my other babies by the midwives, but Melanie couldn't do this. I went mad crying. I couldn't help myself, it was a sort of despair crying. I heard the doctor saying, 'Tell your husband I want to see him at the hospital in the morning.' Then they left me alone, holding Melanie to me. I was crying, nothing mattered. I wasn't aware there was anybody else in the ward. I knew I had to tell my husband. I was just longing for him to be there.

I got out of bed, put Melanie in her cot and went to phone him. We were on the phone at home. I just told him to come to the hospital as soon as possible. He wanted to know what was wrong, I couldn't tell him over the phone. He was saying, 'What's wrong, is there something wrong with baby, are you all right?' I just said, 'Come as soon as you can,' then I got back on my bed waiting for him.

I felt as if the bottom of my world had fallen out. I didn't know what to say to him, how to put it in words, after him being so thrilled. How do you say it?

Anyhow, I saw him at the top of the ward looking for me and I went to meet him. I don't know whether I walked or ran. I know the tears were streaming down my face and all the other women were looking at me. All I could see was his face, he looked white.

One of the nurses let us go in a little office at the top of the ward. When we got in he put his arms around me and said 'What's wrong, love, why are you so upset?' I'll remember my next words for the rest of my life and the look on his face when I said, 'Melanie, she's a mongol.' Nothing else was said, then for a few minutes I just broke down crying again. Then he said, 'Tell me all that was said,' and I told him everything that the doctor had told me and the fact that he had to go to the hospital the next morning to see him.

I was telling him about all the love and attention she would have to have, and he said she would have got that anyway. He went on to say that no money, or anything in the world would take her from us now.

I don't think I slept five minutes that night.

When my husband went next day to see the doctor, he said, 'You have got the worst thing over now. Nothing will ever upset you or rock your world like this again. Just accepting

your baby how she is, you're well on your way to having a
happy life together."

I came out of hospital. I had told all my friends when they
came to see me. They were upset, but they saw how I was
taking it and they were all right. The person I didn't like telling
was my Mum. Even to this day she won't accept it. My sisters
made a lot of fuss with Melanie, as they still do.

I think that that is the worst part, trying to tell people you're
not worried any more, that it is something to work at to bring
Melanie up as any other little girl.

Melanie was very good. She would sleep, and this was
where I slipped up. I heard somewhere that sleep fed children.
My other children had never slept, so I was thinking it was
wonderful, she would miss a feed and I never bothered. I fed
her as I thought when she was hungry, but you can't do that
with these babies, you have to wake them up and make sure
they have their feeds on time.

Later, Melanie contracted a virus on her chest. I was told
after that these babies suffered with their chests—they soon
get congested. No one had told me.

I don't know to this day if it was my fault in not feeding
Melanie the way I should. Melanie had caught pneumonia. I
wasn't pleased with the way she was responding to the treatment of my doctor. She seemed to take ill over night, so I took
her to the hospital myself. At first they thought she had menin-
gitis. I remember the doctor saying that nothing could be any
worse that what I've told you, but when he said that there was
no holding me. I shook from head to toe. I didn't know what I
had done wrong. My bottles were sterilised and my nappies
were boiled. I thought I'd done everything right. I blamed it
on myself for not waking her up in the night for her feeds. It
was touch and go with her in hospital, I don't know whether
I was standing on my head or feet, every minute I had I would
be with her. I'm sure the nursing staff at the hospital were absolutely fed up with me. In the end she pulled out of it, but the
doctor said he hadn't given her much chance at the time. I
watch her now. I won't let anyone go near her with a cold. I
make sure she's fed at the proper time and she is coming on
wonderful.

We went to the library but there was no literature on mongolism at all. No one came to tell us anything. We asked the doctor if he could recommend anything to us, and he put us on to the Hester Adrian Research Centre, which is the best thing he could have done for us.

A man from the Centre came to the house. He talked for nearly three hours. He made me feel like a proud mum. He had an answer to all our questions. It was a relief to know somebody who could explain what we wanted to know.

They come to see Melanie every six weeks to see how she is developing. They helped her to pick objects up off the table, to use her arms and legs.

I know Melanie has definitely benefitted from her exercises, and they also give you ideas on how to help and exercise her ourselves. I have to fill in charts of any one day a week, what she does every second of the day, whether she sleeps, eats or plays.

We look forward to these visits somehow. Both my husband and I feel as if something is being done for Melanie, that somebody cares, and they are trying to bring these children up to grow up like any other normal child.

I remember my midwife saying to me at one time. 'It's the genes. A normal child has 24 genes, a mongol has 25.'* She said it's like a cake. 'You put the ingredients in for an ordinary cake, but accidentally a little coconut falls in. It's still a nice cake, but it has that little extra.'

Well I think that little extra in Melanie is love. She loves everybody and she is happy and smiling from morning to night-time. She seems to spread happiness all around her—my children adore her.

I fear a little for the future, but you never know in this day and age and with the love of God my little girl will grow up happy and contented for the rest of her life. God Bless.

* This is an example of confused information. Down's Syndrome children have 47 chromosomes whereas normal children have 46 arranged in 23 pairs.

Reproduced from: Cunningham, C. C., and Sloper, P., 1977, Parents of Down's Syndrome Children: Their Early Needs in *Child: care, health and development*, by permission of the editor.

3 : What is mental handicap?

In this chapter we try briefly to explain what mental handicap means—its causes and effects. We think that knowing this will help you to understand why it is so important to stimulate your baby, and also what to teach and how to teach.

We use the words 'mental handicap' with a certain confidence, suggesting we know exactly what it means, We do not. People have been trying for centuries to define it (in England since as early as 1325, the year of the King's Prerogative of Edward II), and it is still debated today. For present purposes two points can be made.

Suppose you measure the height or weight of each person in a group of people. You will probably find that the majority of your measurements will fall within a fairly small range. This range defines the 'normal' height or weight within that group. We can do the same for mental abilities, using tests which measure 'intelligence'. Most people have a test-score or IQ (intelligence quotient) between 90–110, which we define as 'normal'. Those with IQs below 70 are said to have 'subnormal' intelligence.

People with IQs between 70 and 50 usually have difficulties in learning and in developing skills : they usually take a long time to acquire skills, and even once acquired, their abilities are often impaired in some way. However, many of these people can lead relatively independent lives. This range of mental handicap is called mild mental handicap.

Those people with IQs below 50 are said to be severely mentally handicapped. They have severe learning difficulties and usually do not develop the ability to reason in any depth. They often have major damage to the brain or nervous system, or easily recognised genetic conditions such as Down's Syndrome. (This does not of course mean that Down's Syndrome automatically means an IQ of less than 50—Down's Syndrome children and adults may have IQs over 50, in the mildly mentally handicapped range.)

There are also children whose mental ability is so poor that one cannot really measure their IQ. This is usually less than 20, and this range is described as profoundly mentally handicapped. These children nearly always have severe handicaps other than mental.

It must be emphasised that these IQ scores and divisions are not absolute. IQs can change. And all they can measure is specific   abilities at specific stages of development. There are for instance children with IQs of 40–50 who learn to read and write, and others with IQs as high as 60 and 70 have never been able to achieve these skills. So test scores are only relative predictors of potential. It is also important to remember that the IQ does not measure the mental ability a child was born with, but the way in which these abilities have developed to date. Poor stimulation and life experiences will usually depress IQ; a good environment can improve it, at least in the early years.

Thus the IQ is only *one* part of the diagnosis of mental handicap. It is a useful guideline but it must be used with caution.

This brings us to our second point.

Many mentally handicapped people have other problems. They often have added difficulties in physical development, impaired sight and hearing and heart defects. Many suffer from epileptic fits and some from severe disorders in their behaviour : they may be hyperactive, withdrawn or occasionally, aggressive. It is often these added problems which prevent handicapped people from becoming self-sufficient.

Frequently, these added problems are part of the condition which is causing the mental handicap. The Down's Syndrome child, for example, is more likely to have a heart defect than a normal child, and mentally handicapped children with spina bifida have severe physical disorders which affect their mobility, for instance. When we are trying to diagnose and predict a future for the mentally handicapped child, these other problems have to be taken into account. If we understand the cause of the handicap, we *can* use our knowledge of previous cases to diagnose the problems and make some predictions for the future. But unfortunately this is not as easy as it sounds.

CAUSES

In severe mental handicap, the brain, and often other parts of the nervous system, are damaged or markedly 'different'.
This can be caused by either :

(a) a fault in the genetic code or chromosome structure. Chromosomes are complex bio-chemical chains made up of units called genes. They provide the blueprint or programme which controls growth and development. In man, every cell of the body has 46 chromosomes arranged in 23 matching pairs. If for any reason there is more or less chromosome material, a disorder in growth and development is likely to occur. Examples are Down's Syndrome, Patau's Syndrome, Edward's Syndrome, Klinefelter's Syndrome, all caused by extra chromosome material. (For further details see *The Child with Down's Syndrome* by Smith and Wilson, or *Mental Handicap* by Kirman—referenced in the book list.)
or
(b) damage to the brain or nervous system. The growing brain is particularly sensitive to damage, which can be caused by many things. The brain may be starved because there have been problems in feeding the growing foetus during pregnancy, or because the baby has a faulty metabolic system. It may have been starved of oxygen, during a prolonged labour or because the cord strangled the baby at birth.
The brain may have been damaged by disease—the mother may have had German measles during the pregnancy, or the child may have suffered from enchephalitis later in life. It can also have been damaged by physical accident to the head.

Thus the handicap can be determined at the time the egg is fertilised, during pregnancy, at birth or in later life. Depending on when or how it occurs will depend the degree of the handicap, and its particular difficulties.

Some handicapping conditions are so rare that there are very few cases to study. Then the rate of survival among such conditions may be so poor that there are even fewer cases to study. In these circumstances it is difficult to make any predictions about the future, and doctors may be forced to make educated guesses.

This question of what caused the handicap is often of the

utmost importance for parents to understand. Sometimes, to know the cause, seems to help them feel they understand their child better. If they do not know the cause, they find themselves constantly worrying that they were somehow to blame. *But in a large proportion of cases the cause can never really be known, and so there comes a time when the parent must decide that it is unreasonable to keep on looking. To keep blaming oneself and seeking out a cause will only delay or prevent one from starting to help the baby.*

If you find yourself in this situation, all we can say is this: Knowing the cause of the handicap it not vital to helping stimulate and teach your child. The methods we use are the same regardless of the condition—in fact they can be used to help any baby or young child, whether mentally or physically or socially handicapped, or 'normal'.

THE NATURE OF MENTAL HANDICAP

We first discover that a baby is likely to be mentally handicapped in two ways.

Sometimes, we recognise from the child's physical appearance, behaviour or chromosome pattern a condition, such as hydrocephalus or Down's Syndrome, that is known to result in mental handicap.

Always, we find that the baby is not developing as quickly as is expected from our knowledge of babies as a whole. He smiles later, he takes longer to achieve head balance, to recognise mum, to say 'da-da,' 'ma-ma' and so on.

Mental handicap in the young child is shown by slow or delayed development. The less delayed the development, the less is the handicap. It follows that if we can prevent some of this delay through special stimulation, we are reducing the mental handicap.

At this point we must stop and consider two important ideas about mental handicap and about development.

First, handicap and damage to part of the body are not the same thing. The handicap is what happens as a result of the damage. If you lose the sight of one eye, you have 50 per cent loss of your visual system, but this may handicap you hardly at all—unless you are a sportsman, for instance. If you lose a leg, which involves major damage and a fairly serious handicap to your mobility, you can use special aids to reduce the effect of the handicap considerably.

Similarly, with a mentally handicapped child, we cannot repair the damage. But we can use special stimulation to minimise the delay in development—the handicap. We find ways of 'getting around the damage'. Thus we may produce more able babies because we stimulate them, but they will still have the same difficulties in their mental abilities. We will come back to this point later.

Second, when you think about the development of young children you probably have two things in mind. You note, first, the major milestones—such as sitting up, walking and first words— and second, the age at which these occur. Often you will think that because the child has achieved these behaviours early, he or she is going to be a particularly advanced or intelligent child. Unfortunately, this is not the case. These early behaviours are not good predictors of future ability *except when they are abnormally slow*—as in the case of mental handicap. Even then they can be misleading.

We assume that these early behaviours should tell us about future abilities because we feel that they must be closely related to later ones. This is true to some extent : babies who sit early and crawl early usually walk early; but it is not true that babies who walk early necessarily talk early. The parts of the body and brain used for sitting, crawling and walking *are* closely related; all involve muscle strength and coordination and balance for instance. However, talking depends on different skills and areas of the brain. The more behaviours and skills have in common, the more likely they are to help each other. Unfortunately, our present knowledge of how these behaviours and skills work together is incomplete, and we understand little about how they relate to later abilities in learning and thinking.

Let us consider what we *do* know, and how useful this can be in helping our children.

1. The body is made up of separate parts, each having its own job to do but each needing other parts to maintain it at an efficient level. As the baby grows and develops, these parts become more skilled and more specialised.

B

2. Good development is needed in all parts to produce the best overall results.

3. Later behaviours are built upon early behaviours—especially within each specialised area—and so the sooner the early behaviours develop the sooner the later ones can be expected to occur.

4. Specific behaviours are important for other areas of development. For example, when you can sit up you have a different view of the world from when you are lying on your back : you can twist around and look where you want to far more easily; if you can reach out, you can turn around to handle objects, if you drop them you can look to see where they fall. Thus sitting up can change the experiences and stimulation available to you. This new stimulation can now be used to help other areas develop.

5. Most babies have a similar pattern of development. But if a baby has a specific problem, such as blindness, that area of development cannot occur. So we try to find ways of getting around the problem so that other skills that use the visual system to help their development are not held back.

6. We can use this pattern of normal child development to show us what needs to be stimulated in our handicapped babies. It can tell us not only what the behaviour is that we need to encourage, but also when it is needed—what comes before and after it. However, as usual there are complications. As babies get older individual differences among their patterns of development increase. One in ten babies, for example, do not crawl on hands and knees but shuffle on their bottoms. This is a natural healthy pattern for them and we do not need to insist that they crawl before they walk. Normal child development thus provides only guidelines from which to work, and you will often need to adapt them to fit your own child.

7. Many studies have shown that using our knowledge of normal child development to guide the stimulation of young handicapped babies does help them to develop more quickly and more ably. If this help is kept up throughout their childhood, they are able to do things which, years ago, were not thought possible for them.

We must now ask the question 'Why is the development of mentally handicapped children slower than that of other children?'

Development is influenced by two things. One we shall call maturation, the other experience. The maturational part is 'what we are born with'. It is the programme of development that is given to us in the genetic code from our parents. It determines what height we are likely to be, what colour eyes we will have, what our intelligence might be, whether we are likely to be bald, when we are going to reach puberty, and to some extent when we will die. It is like a time-clock which says when certain changes will occur, and sets the basic levels of achievement we can expect. However, for the programme to work it needs experiences from the outside world. And within certain limits, these experiences can alter the programme. For example, people are, on average, taller now than some years ago, and children are reaching puberty earlier. These changes are thought to be due to better nutrition and healthier living, that is to experiences.

The developmental delay found in mentally handicapped children can be thought of as a 'slow clock'. Down's Syndrome babies not only walk and talk later but grow slower: at two years of age they are physically more like a one or one-and-a-half-year-old child. We do not know whether or not we can speed up this 'clock': at present it seems unlikely; but the aspect of development that we can influence is the experience we give to the baby. If experience is necessary to maintain the maturational programme, lack of experience can hold the programme back and this will produce developmental delay or mental handicap. Therefore, we have two handicapping conditions. The first one, or *primary handicap*, is that caused by the genetic abnormality or the damage to the brain. The second one, the *secondary handicapping condition*, is that caused by lack of the necessary stimulation.

Let us consider an actual example from our own research on Down's Syndrome babies. We found that on average the babies to whom we gave special help sat up at about ten months: the earliest was six-and-a-half months and the latest about 15 months. Compare these ages with those given in some studies of Down's Syndrome babies not given extra help conducted a few years ago. These sat up on average at 12 months, the earliest at six-and-a-half months and the latest at 30 months. Normal babies sit on average at six months, with a range of five to nine months between the fastest and the slowest. Now the difference between the normal babies and the *stimulated* Down's Syndrome babies is likely to be due to the primary handicap, and we may never be able to change that. But, the difference between the Down's Syndrome babies who had been given special help, and those who had not, we may conclude to be due to the secondary handicapping condition : in other words, to a lack of the experiences necessary to keep the developmental programme working at its optimum.

This stimulation can actually affect the growth and development of chemicals and cells in the body. Experiments with animals have shown that those which have been well stimulated during early life have more developed brains and different chemical structures from those that have not. They also show more 'intelligence' on various tests (e.g. learning a maze). Other experiments have shown that animals show improved ability to 'pass' the tests if they are stimulated by being handled, or by being given new experiences.

We also know that mentally handicapped children cared for in large institutions, which cannot provide a great deal of individual attention and varied experiences, do not develop as well as those raised in good stimulating homes.

Handicapped children need *at least* as much care and attention as normal children do : and it is our argument that they need more, and of a special kind.

For even when the experiences to stimulate the development programme are available to the child, he may not be able readily to make use of them, because of his primary handicapping condition. We have already noted that to a blind child, visual stimulation is not available, so the development of those parts of his programme that utilise visual stimulation may be inhibited. Now what if the part of the brain which sorts out his various experiences is damaged? This would prevent the information he receives from being *used* to help development and learning.

This seems to be the case with the mentally handicapped. They have a learning difficulty. Not only is their learning slower, it is severely impaired. What they seem to suffer from in particular is an inability to pay attention to the relevant part of the incoming stimulation. They cannot analyse it to see its parts, or synthesise it and see its relationships.

Imagine yourself at a set of traffic lights with a normal child.

The lights turn red—the cars stop. The normal child is taking in all sorts of information about the road, the people and the movement around him; but he suddenly pays attention to the lights and the cars. He notices that the lights turn red, the cars stop : that they turn green, the cars go. Now he can test an idea. Do they always stop when the lights go red? yes, they do. He has analysed the complex situation, found the relevant areas (the lights—the stopping cars), and discovered the relationship between them.

This is what the mentally handicapped child finds very difficult. He sees the same scene, he has the same incoming information, but he misses the conclusion unless *we* can help him. So if we say to him 'Look, what colour are the lights—Yes, red' and 'What did the cars do?'—'Stop'—'Good boy'—'Why did they stop?'—no answer. 'Let's look again. What colour are the lights. . . .'

What we are doing is breaking down the complex situation and directing the child to the relevant cues (parts), then trying to help him put the two together to learn the relationship. If you wish, we are doing the analysing and synthesising—the breaking down and putting together—for him. In this way we can 'by-pass' his learning difficulties and make sure he is making the most of the experiences available. When we teach this way, we find that the mentally handicapped person can learn to do things and can learn about things which are quite complex. It is not the memory which is damaged, but the ability to direct attention, and to abstract, analyse and synthesise incoming stimulation.

This is why we need to use special teaching methods and stimulation to overcome these special difficulties.

CHILD DEVELOPMENT, STIMULATION AND TEACHING

Chapter 4 : The developmental checklist

Chapter 5 : Teaching your baby

Chapter 6 : How to plan your teaching

4 : The Developmental Checklist

This chapter is a list of everyday behaviours which we can see as the baby develops. These behaviours are taken from the many standard baby tests and descriptions of behaviours presently available. The number at the side of an item, e.g. **9m, 18m** *is the average age when babies pass that item on the tests. It is important to realise that these are averages and* that they vary even between different tests. *This is because the development of all babies varies a lot. Also note that the ages refer to when the people who made up the test could first get the babies to show the behaviour: this is not the same point at which the behaviour is well established —which may be some weeks later. So the ages will tend to seem a little early.*

Because handicapped babies develop slowly, the older they get the greater will be the difference between the age of acquiring a new behaviour, and the average age of the normal baby. This can be discouraging, but we feel that the ages are useful all the same. For example, by looking at the time it takes a normal baby to get from one item to the next, you will be better able to work out when to expect new behaviours in your own child.

Go through the tests in the order in which they are written, and tick off all those behaviours that you are sure your baby has acquired; by this we mean things he does nine times out of ten, not things he has been seen to do once or twice.

When you have done this, you should have made three discoveries:

1. The things he is good at now, i.e. his strengths.
2. The things that you are not sure that he can do. These are things that you will have to go away and look at again. This is good practice in learning to observe your child.
3. The next step to be expected in the baby's development. This is what we need to work towards.

B*

If you fill in the checklist every six to eight weeks, and put a date on the last item achieved, you will have both some idea of the progress your child has made, and be able to pin-point areas of difficulty and poor progress which need looking at.

At the end of the chapter we have provided a profile for your general guidance.

1. Read through the lists first to give yourself an idea of the pattern of development, even if your baby is still in the first stages.
2. It may take some time to complete this on your baby. If you wish, start reading Chapter 5 at the same time.

INTRODUCTION

Your baby's development is made up of a series of behaviours which emerge in a certain order. As explained in Chapter 3, both maturation and experience are needed for these behaviours to emerge.

The aim of the developmental checklist is to help you to recognise the point in his development your baby has reached, and identify the experiences he needs to help him develop the next set of behaviours.

This list has been split into four main areas :

1. Physical or Motor Development.
2. First Skills and Mental Development.
3. Communication.
4. Personal and Social Skills.

Within these four sections we have divided the items further into smaller areas—for instance, communication includes hearing, speech, expression and vocalisation.

At the beginning of each section a short explanation of the area dealt with is given. However, we must emphasise here that some behaviours can fall into one or more sections, and all areas of development are inter-related, one affecting the other.

Although the baby's development follows a certain pattern and order there are two variations in this which we feel it is important to understand, particularly when we are concerned with mentally handicapped babies :

1. There are stages in development when the baby does not appear to make much progress for some time—perhaps as long as two or three months. We call these stages *plateaux* and they often occur before certain major items in development. For instance, after the baby reaches the stage of being able to pull himself up to stand holding on to the furniture and to walk with you holding his hands, it is often a long time before he can walk even a few steps on his own. Many parents have commented that at this point it seems as though he will never walk. Similar plateaux occur in the mental development of the baby. Parents may become disheartened at this point, feeling that their efforts in teaching and stimulating the child are having no effect at all. However, nearly every child shows these plateaux in development. In the mentally handicapped baby they are simply longer and therefore more noticeable. If you observe the baby closely, you can often see that although he may not be doing any new things (so you are not getting any more ticks on your developmental checklist), he is practising those behaviours he can already do and becoming more proficient in them. The important thing is to observe the baby, so that you are able to begin teaching new behaviours when he is ready for them.

2. Development is not always an even progression. There are spurts as well as plateaux, and, particularly in the later stages of development, the order of behaviours varies from one baby to another. You may find that as you fill in the checklist you are able to tick off behaviours that are later on the list than some that your baby has not yet attained. This indicates your own child's pattern of development and it need worry you only if all the behaviours that are not ticked fall into one particular category—such as hearing—and thus indicate particular difficulties in one area. If this is the case you will need to seek further help.

DEVELOPMENTAL PROFILE

After the developmental checklist you will find a chart called the developmental profile. Here we have set out the different areas of development and the items that make up these areas in a chart for you to fill in, so that you will be able to see clearly your own baby's pattern of development and the areas in which he is particularly weak or strong.

How to use the profile

The numbers in the little boxes on the chart refer to the item numbers in the developmental checklist, the headings at the side are the sections of the checklist, and the months across the top are the ages referred to in the checklist. So if you look at the section headed ADAPTIVE on the chart, there is a sub-section 'Manipulation', and under three months there is a box numbered 15. If you look back to the checklist you will see that this refers to item 15 in the Adaptive section—'manipulation—fingers one hand with the other when he is lying quietly'.

As you tick off items on the checklist, colour in the box on the chart for each item that you have ticked (you may find it helpful to use different colours for different areas of development). When you have filled in a number of items you will see that a pattern is beginning to appear—the areas of development where the baby is strong are coloured in, while those where he is weaker are still blank. You will see which areas are affected by plateaux and where development is uneven, where you need to try to give particular help to the baby and where your teaching has begun to show marked effects!

Finally, before you rush for a pen to begin ticking and colouring there are three things we would like to mention:

1. A practical point

When you are working with your baby it is important that he feels safe and supported. When observations are to be made of the baby lying on his front or back, lie him on a firm surface such as a blanket or his changing mattress on the floor. When he is sitting, make sure he feels secure but also that he has enough freedom to move his arms and legs and head. Imagine you are sitting on the end of a flagpole—you are likely to be very careful how you twist around, reach out and so on. A baby who is not too good at sitting and does not feel secure may feel like this!

2. Materials

In order to assess your baby's development on these checklists you will need the following equipment:

(a) A ring about four inches (10 cm) in diameter and half an inch (1 cm) wide, attached to a piece of string.

(*b*) A small rattle—small and light enough for the baby to hold easily.

(*c*) A small bell.

(*d*) Ten wooden or plastic one-inch (2·5 cm) cubes, preferably brightly coloured.

(*e*) A pegboard—a piece of wood with six holes drilled into it with six round wooden pegs about half an inch (1 cm) in diameter which fit easily into the holes.

(*f*) A formboard—a board with a circle, a square and a triangle cut out of it, and blocks of these shapes which fit into the appropriate holes.

At the end of the book you will find some suggestions for making these items, and some diagrams which may help. (Appendix 2).

You do not need all these items immediately; you can begin to fill in the checklist before you have them all.

3. A warning
In our experience, when mums and dads fill in the checklist they frequently disagree. Please see this as a positive indication of where you can improve your observation rather than as a battle as to who is right.

Remember, it is *not what you think the baby can do* that matters but *what you can see happening*.

PHYSICAL OR MOTOR DEVELOPMENT

This list of behaviours is broken into two parts :

1. Those that involve movements of the whole body, such as sitting and walking. These are called gross motor movements.
2. Those that involve the use of the arms and the hands for reaching out, grasping and touching things. These are called fine motor movements.

Of course it is not only the hands that develop fine motor movements : the muscles of the eyes have to develop precise coordination, and so do the mouth, the lips and the face muscles in order that we can chew without biting our tongues, and speak and communicate clearly. These aspects of fine motor development, and their importance in the development of language and social skills, are dealt with later.

The most noticeable thing about motor development in the young child is the gradual growth in his control and coordination of the parts of his body. When you look at a baby a few weeks old lying on his back, you will notice that if he moves an arm, the other arm and his legs move at the same time. In other words any movement he makes involves all the parts of his body. If you look carefully you may even notice that as he smiles he often reaches up with his hands. Only gradually do the parts of the body come to be used independently of each other—the baby can use his arms without kicking his legs, he can use one arm instead of both, kick one leg instead of both together, and eventually he can use his fingers separately.

The development of coordination and control is based upon growth and experience. As the baby gets stronger he becomes more able to use his muscles to control his body. But the skilled use of these muscles will also depend upon exercising other senses : to hold your head steady, to sit and walk all need the sense of balance; to reach out accurately and pick up an object you need to coordinate the sense of vision with the arm movement.

Therefore, the brain has to develop plans or programmes which coordinate information from the senses, such as balance and vision, with information from the muscles to produce skilled actions. The pattern of gross motor development starts with building up strength in the neck muscles so that the head can be lifted. Gradually this skill is linked with balance, so that the baby can hold his head and turn it and look around.

About this time the baby is also learning to control the muscles in the shoulder and upper back, so he can begin to sit with support and reach out, albeit not very accurately. As the coordination and control move down the back to the hips and along the arms to the hands, the baby will start sitting independently and at the same time reaching and picking up objects.

The next stage is to develop coordination and control in the legs for crawling and walking. By now the baby will usually have enough strength in his legs to support his weight. In the same way as control spreads down to the hands and fingers, it spreads down to the feet and toes—don't forget that your toes, especially your big toe, are very important in walking.

Our experience suggests that mentally handicapped babies have difficulty in coordinating the muscle areas and the sense areas, and that this causes delay in their motor development. For this reason we have emphasised in the training programme not just activities that strengthen the muscles, but activities that encourage this coordination.

GROSS MOTOR

1m. (1) When baby is lying on his back, put your hands against his feet. Tick if he pushes against your hands. ☐

1m. (2) Hold baby in a sitting position. Tick if he holds his head up momentarily. ☐

1m. (3) Lie baby on his front. Tick if he makes crawling movements with his arms and legs. ☐

1m. (4) Lie baby on his back. Tick if he can roll part way to the side. ☐

1m. (5) Hold baby in standing position, press the sole of his foot against a hard surface. Tick if he makes little walking movements. ☐

1m. (6) Hold baby in a standing position. Tick if he extends his legs as if to support himself. ☐

1m. (7) When baby is lying on his back, awake and alert, touch and tickle him. Tick if he makes large jerky movements of his arms and legs. ☐

1½m. (8) Lie baby on his front. Tick if he raises his chin off the mattress a few times. ☐

1½m. (9) Hold baby in a sitting position. Tick if he holds his head up a few times. ☐

1½m. (10) When baby is lying on his back, pull him to a sitting position by holding his arms. Observe the position of his head—at this stage it lags considerably behind his body. ☐

2m. (11) Hold baby up against your shoulder and, without supporting his head, observe how long he can hold his head up. Tick if it is about 15 seconds. ☐

2m. (12) Lie baby on his front. Tick if he can roll part way to the side. ☐

2m. (13) Lie baby across your knees on his front so that his head is not supported. Tick if he can bring his head up. ☐

2m. (14) Hold baby in a sitting position without supporting his head. Tick if he can hold it erect for most of the time, although it is unsteady and makes a bobbing movement. ☐

2m.   (15)   Pull baby to sit by his hands. Tick if he is beginning to use his neck muscles and bring his head up. There will still be some lag.   ☐

2m.   (16)   Lie baby across your knees on his back without support for his head. Tick if he can bring his head up nearly in line with his body.   ☐

3m.   (17)   Lie baby on his back. Tick if he waves his arms together and can bring his hands from his side into his middle over his chest and chin.   ☐

3m.   (18)   Tick if he also kicks vigorously with his legs, usually alternating and occasionally together. ☐

3m.   (19)   Hold baby against your shoulder without support for his head. Tick if he can hold his head steady when you sway him from side to side.   ☐

3m.   (20)   Hold baby in a standing position. Tick if he can take a little weight on his legs briefly. He then sags at the knees.   ☐

3m.   (21)   Place baby lying on his side, and observe if he can roll on to his back. Do not tick if he just flops back by accident.   ☐

3m.   (22)   Lie baby on his front. Tick if he can raise his chest up off the floor or mattress on his elbows, forearms or hands.   ☐

3m.   (23)   Hold baby in a sitting position. Tick if he can hold his head steady with a straight back (except in the lower part) for a minute or two.   ☐

3m.   (24)   Pull baby to sit by his hands. Tick if his head only lags slightly behind.   ☐

3m.   (25)   Lie baby on his back. Tick if he can lift his head slightly off the mattress.   ☐

3m.   (26)   Lie baby on his back. Tick if his head is now not turned to the side but kept mainly in the middle.   ☐

4m.   (27)   Lie baby on his back, lean over and put your hands around him ready to lift him. Tick if he tenses his body ready to be lifted.   ☐

4m.   (28)   Tick if he can roll from his back to his side. ☐

4m.   (29)   Tick if he can sit propped up in his chair for 10–15 minutes.   ☐

4m.   (30)   Tick if he can sit with only slight support—your hand supporting the lower part of his back but not all his back. ☐

4m. (31) Hold baby in a sitting position. Tick if his back is straight and firm and his head steady, although his head may wobble when he is shaken. ☐

5m. (32) Pull baby to a sitting position by his hands. Tick if his head does not lag behind his body. ☐

5m. (33) Lie baby on his back. Tick if he can lift his head and shoulders off the mattress. ☐

5m. (34) Hold baby upright, then sway him back and forward, left and right. Tick if he can now balance his head and hold it steady. ☐

5m. (35) Hold baby in a standing position. Tick if he can bear most of his weight on his legs. ☐

5m. (36) Tick if he can roll from side to side. ☐

5m. (37) When lying on his front, can he raise his head and chest and support his weight on his forearms or the palms of his hands? ☐

5½m. (38) When sitting in his chair, is his body now straight, not bent over? ☐

5½m. (39) Sit baby on floor and spread his legs at an angle of 50°. Talk to him and capture his attention. Then release hold and tick if he sits for a moment without support. ☐

5½m. (40) Can he sit propped up in his chair for 30 minutes? ☐

5½m. (41) Lie baby on his front. Tick if he pushes his chest and upper part of his abdomen off the couch and takes his weight on his hands, not his forearms. ☐

5½m. (42) Tick if he can roll from back to front and front to back. ☐

5½m. (43) When lying on his back, does he stretch out his arms to be picked up when you bend over him to lift him? ☐

5½m. (44) Lie baby on his back. Tick if he can pull himself up to sit by holding on to your thumbs. Be careful not to pull him up. ☐

6m. (45) Tick if he sits without support for one minute or more. ☐

6m. (46) Hold baby in a standing position on a hard

surface. Tick if he takes his weight on his feet and bounces up and down actively. ☐

6m. (47) Hold baby in a standing position. Tick if he moves his feet in stepping movements. ☐

6m. (48) Lie baby on his front. Tick if he draws his knees up in crawling position. ☐

7m. (49) Lie baby on his front. Tick if he can turn his body round 180° for a toy out of reach. ☐

7m. (50) Hold baby in a standing position. Tick if he can stay in that position for a few seconds, holding on to your hands only. ☐

8m. (51) Tick if he is able to get into a crawling position, on his hands and knees (in trying to crawl, he may go backwards). ☐

8m. (52) Tick if he can sit steadily without support for 10 minutes or more, lean forward to reach something and then straighten himself without falling over. ☐

8m. (53) Tick if he can pull himself up to a standing position holding on to your thumbs, but without any further help from you. N.B. Baby must do the pulling himself. ☐

8m. (54) Tick if he moves around by rolling. ☐

9m. (55) Tick if he sits alone steadily for long periods. ☐

9m. (56) Lie baby down. Tick if he can pull himself up to sit, perhaps by using the bars of his cot or sides of his pram. ☐

9m. (57) Lie baby on his front. Tick if he can rock or pivo around, scoot backwards and turn round when he is left on the floor. ☐

9m. (58) Tick if he crawls by pulling himself forward with hands, ☐

or

sits and hitches forward or sideways. ☐

9m. (59) Tick if he can go over on to his front from a sitting position, and back up again. ☐

9m. (60) Tick if he can pull himself to standing position by the rail of his cot or on the furniture. ☐

10m. (61) When he is standing holding on to furniture, tick if he can lift then replace one foot. ☐

11m. (62) Tick if he can turn himself round when sitting on the floor. ☐

11m. (63) Tick if he gets around by:
(*a*) creeping or crawling: now crawls on hands and knees or hands and feet. ☐
(*b*) sitting and hitching. ☐

11m. (64) Tick if he can walk with both hands held. ☐

11m. (65) Tick if he moves sideways, standing holding on to cot rail or furniture. ☐

11m. (66) Tick if he can stand alone without support for one minute or more. ☐

11m. (67) When baby is standing, tick if he lowers himself to sit instead of flopping. ☐

12m. (68) Tick if he rises to sitting position from lying down without pulling himself up on anything. ☐

12m. (69) Tick if he walks with one or both hands held. ☐

12m. (70) Tick if he walks on hands and feet like a bear. ☐

12m. (71) Tick if he takes three or more steps without support. ☐

13m. (72) Tick if he climbs on to a low ledge or step. ☐

13m. (73) Tick if he walks without help—several steps. ☐

13m. (74) Tick if he can stand up without having to pull himself up—when lying down, he first rolls on to his front then gets up. ☐

14m. (75) Tick if he kneels on floor or chair, without support. ☐

14m. (76) Tick if he walks sideways several steps when pulling a toy. ☐

15m. (77) Tick if he creeps up stairs—hands and knees. ☐

15m. (78) When he is walking, tick if baby can start off and stop himself. He cannot yet go round corners or stop suddenly without falling. ☐

15m. (79) Tick if he walks backwards several steps pulling toy. ☐

18m. (80) Tick if he walks around carrying a doll or ball. ☐

18m. (81) Tick if he begins to be able to jump with both feet off the floor. ☐

18m. (82) Tick if he sits down himself on a small chair. ☐

18m. (83) Tick if he creeps backwards down stairs *or*

occasionally bumps down a few steps on buttocks
—facing forward.   ☐

18m. (84) Tick if he walks up stairs with one hand held or
gets up and down stairs holding rail (no help). ☐

18m. (85) Tick if he walks fast; at this stage he runs stiffly,
eyes fixed on the ground 1–2 yards ahead, and
cannot continue round obstacles.   ☐

18m. (86) Tick if he walks well with feet only slightly apart,
starts and stops safely.   ☐

18m. (87) Tick if he seldom falls when walking.   ☐

18m. (88) Tick if he stands on one foot while holding your
hand (he usually does this first when getting
dressed and undressed).   ☐

18m. (89) Tick if he stoops and picks up toy from floor
without falling.   ☐

21m. (90) Put a large ball on the floor and show baby how
you kick it. Observe if he can kick it himself
without falling, after your demonstration.   ☐

21m. (91) Tick if he can throw a ball to you when you ask
him.   ☐

21m. (92) Tick if he can get down off an adult-sized chair
without help.   ☐

24m. (93) Tick if he can stand on one leg briefly without
holding on.   ☐

24m. (94) Tick if he kicks a large ball without a demonstration.   ☐

24m. (95) Tick if he can jump off a low step—both feet
together.   ☐

24m. (96) Tick if he walks up and down stairs easily (may
use rail), and can be trusted on stairs alone. ☐

24m. (97) Tick if he runs well without falling, stops and
starts easily and avoids obstacles.   ☐

24m. (98) Tick if he can squat to rest or play with something on the ground, then get up without using
his hands to help.   ☐

FINE MOTOR

1m.   (1)   Place a rattle in baby's hand—tick if his hand clenches on contact with the rattle, even if he drops it immediately.   ☐

1m.   (2)   Baby's hands are usually closed, but if they are opened, tick if he will grasp your finger when you touch his palm.   ☐

2m.   (3)   Tick if he holds on to a rattle that is placed in his hand for a few seconds.   ☐

3m.   (4)   Tick if he is beginning to clasp and unclasp his hands together.   ☐

4m.   (5)   Tick if he holds a ring or cube when it is placed in his hand.   ☐

4m.   (6)   Tick if his hands now remain open for about half the time.   ☐

4m.   (7)   Place a one-inch cube in his hand. Tick if he holds it using his fingers against the palm of his hand (not yet using thumb).   ☐

4m.   (8)   When he is holding an object, tick if he resists if you try to take it away.   ☐

5m.   (9)   Hold out a rattle or ring to baby's hand. Tick if he is now able to grasp it voluntarily.   ☐

5½m.   (10)   Tick if he grasps a one-inch cube using his thumb as well as his fingers to hold it.   ☐

6m.   (11)   When baby is holding a rattle or other object, observe whether he turns his wrist when he is moving the object. If he does, tick this item.   ☐

6½m.   (12)   When baby is sitting on your knee, or in his chair, at the table, place a small object the size of a currant in front of him on the table. If he reaches for the object, rakes the table with his whole hand and contacts the object, tick this item.   ☐

8m.   (13)   Tick if he can grasp a one-inch cube using his thumb against his forefingers.   ☐

8m.   (14)   Tick if he can pick up an object the size of a currant or a piece of string. (Does not need to be a neat pincer of finger and thumb.)   ☐

9m. (15) Tick if he can release a toy against a firm surface. He cannot yet drop it voluntarily. ☐

9m. (16) Tick if he picks up an object the size of a currant quickly, using thumb and fingers. ☐

10m. (17) Tick if he picks up an object the size of a currant using his thumb and forefinger only. ☐

11m. (18) Tick if he can roll a ball to you. ☐

11m. (19) Tick if he throws objects instead of dropping them. ☐

13m. (20) Tick if he can grasp two cubes in one hand. ☐

15m. (21) Tick if he picks up crumbs quite skilfully. ☐

18m. (22) Tick if he tries to turn doorknobs. ☐

21m. (23) Show him how you put your middle finger against your thumb, and ask him to do this. Observe whether he can do it in imitation of you. ☐

24m. (24) Show him how to put your little finger against your thumb and ask him to do this. Observe whether he can do it in imitation of you. ☐

24m. (25) Cross your feet and ask child to do the same. Observe whether he can do this in imitation. ☐

MENTAL DEVELOPMENT

In the next three sections we shall be listing behaviours on which the child's mental development is built. This does not mean that motor development is not involved in this process, but we feel that by treating mental development separately we can build up the most detailed and useful picture for teaching the baby. You will also find that we have broken down mental activity into three areas: personal—social behaviour, communication and adaptive behaviour—and that these areas are all broken down into smaller ones. By breaking down these complex areas into smaller ones we can begin to pinpoint the child's daily behaviour.

As we found in the motor area, the first stage involves developing and practising the basic skills of the senses. For example, at first the baby learns to focus on objects held about six to eight inches (15–20 cm) from his eyes. He also begins to follow slow moving objects but this following is rather jerky. Gradually the baby learns to follow smoothly, and sees objects at longer distances. The next stage is to coordinate the senses: for instance, if you hold an interesting object in front of the baby and attract his attention to it, first he can look at it with his *eyes*, then he can use his *arms* to reach out for it and finally his *hands* to grasp it. In doing this last, he has to coordinate his sight and movement in order to reach and pick up the object.

However, these skills in themselves are not sufficient for further development. *It is the use of the skills to do things* that is important, so it is the mental activity which controls the use of the skills that we need to examine at this point. For example, having learnt to use his eyes in the first few weeks of life, the baby begins to search people's faces, paying attention to the different parts. At first the young baby will smile at an oval shape the size of a face, even if the parts are drawn on it and jumbled up. Soon he will do this only if the eyes are in the correct position; and then, a little later, the nose and mouth. The baby has built up a mental picture of a human face—its order and consistency. At this stage he will smile at any face. But he soon moves on to discover that mum's face is special. The baby visually recognises mum. Having identified mum, he can now watch her appear and disappear. This experience gives him the opportunity to begin to learn the same phenomenon about other objects: that is, that they disappear and appear again. He can also now learn about the special relationship he has with mum : he feels secure in her presence, he learns what to expect from her, and because he knows the difference between mum and other people, he can learn that they may not treat him in the same way as she does. Soon he understands these differences so well that he begins to show fear when strange people appear, and will turn to mum for support and security.

In a similar way he develops his hearing until he recognises familiar noises; he learns to see and feel the difference between objects; he learns what objects are used for—a cup you drink from, a pencil you draw with and so on. What the baby is doing is learning how to use his skills to build up mental images of people, objects and places, and a set of expectations about these which can then be used to direct his behaviour in future situations—in other words, he learns to adapt his behaviour appropriately, which is what mental activity is really about.

ADAPTIVE BEHAVIOUR

In this section we are concerned mainly with behaviours to do with learning about objects—first, with development of the skills needed to explore the objects; and second, with learning about the uses of objects.

For each behaviour we have tried to give a title which indicates the main mental activity that we think it is developing. By looking at these titles and the behaviours that go with them, we hope you will be able to see not only the actual behaviour but also the underlying mental activity, and use this knowledge to plan your own child's stimulation.

Visual discrimination
The use of the eyes.

Manipulation
The way in which the baby uses his hands to manipulate objects.

Reaching
The development of the ability to reach out towards an object.

Grasping
The ability to pick up and hold the object.

Attention span
A young baby can attend only to one object at a time at first, but his attention is gradually extended so that he attends to two then three objects. He also becomes able to direct his attention to things for longer periods of time.

Permanence of objects
For the very young baby, out of sight is out of mind—he cannot understand that something can still exist when he cannot see it, so if he drops his rattle he does not look for it. Gradually he begins to look for things he has dropped, and then for a hidden toy etc. With this his *memory* develops and he can begin to find things after longer delays.

Exploration
Exploration and examination of objects is an important way in which the baby learns about his world.

Relation of objects
The development of baby's ability to use two or more objects together, e.g. to bang two cubes together.

Problem solving
This is the baby's ability to see the relationship between objects and to use his understanding of the relationship, e.g. a toy is attached to a piece of string—the baby cannot reach the toy but can pull the string to bring the toy to him.

Imitation
Baby's ability to imitate your actions—an important stage in learning.

Discrimination
The baby gradually learns to see the differences between objects and then to use each object appropriately. At first he will play with all objects in much the same way : for instance, a doll is treated in the same way as a rattle, and both objects are exam-

ined, chewed, etc. But later the baby can *discriminate* between the two. He will probably show a preference for one rather than the other and treat them differently. He will begin to look at pictures in a book instead of trying to chew the book, he will throw a ball, ring a bell. Later he will begin to see the differences between shapes in using simple jigsaws.

Eye/hand coordination

This skill follows reaching and grasping, and relates to the baby's ability to perform fine motor movements such as building with cubes, and using a crayon.

ADAPTIVE

1m. (1) Tick if baby turns head to same side when his cheek is touched. ☐

1m. (2) Place a cloth over baby's face when he is lying on his back—observe whether he reacts to this in any way, either by making more or less movement than before. Tick this item if you see any reaction. ☐

Visual

1m. (3) When baby is lying on his back, dangle a ring or rattle over him about 6–8 inches (15–20 cm) from his eyes. At this stage he will look at it only when it comes into his line of vision. ☐

1m. (4) Tick if baby looks at your face when you bend over him and his activity lessens. ☐

1½m. (5) Dangle the ring 6–8 inches (15–20 cm) from baby's eyes and move it *very slowly* from side to side. Tick this item if he follows it several times with his eyes.* ☐

1½m. (6) Observe whether baby's eyes follow you when you walk back and forth within easy view. ☐

1½m. (7) Move the dangling ring very slowly back and forth from his chest to his forehead several times, about 6–8 inches (15–20 cm) above him. Tick this item if his eyes follow it several times. ☐

1½m. (8) Move the dangling ring very slowly in a circle about 12 inches (30 cm) diameter above baby's eyes. Tick this item if he follows the movement in both the upper and lower halves of the circle, even though his eyes may not follow it continuously. ☐

1½m. (9) Observe whether baby turns his head freely to look at the surroundings, either when being carried or when lying on his back. ☐

2m. (10) When baby is lying on his back, prop his head at each side with pillows so that his face is

---

* At first his eye movements will be jerky.

held upward. Lean over him to attract his gaze upward, then slowly move the ring from the side of his vision to the centre, first on one side then on the other at about 12 inches (30 cm) from his eyes. Tick this item if he turns his eyes to the side to look at the ring as it moves inwards. ☐

2m. (11) Try this item with a friend whom your baby does not know well. Ask the friend to gain baby's attention, then step aside. Mother should then bend over him and talk to him. Tick this item if he shows, by any change of expression, that he recognises you. ☐

3m. (12) As baby is lying on his back, hold a long pencil by one end so that it is about 6–8 inches (15–20 cm) from his eyes and in line with his body from head to chest. Move it slowly back and forth, and tick this item if his eyes follow the pencil through more than one movement. ☐

3m. (13) Sit at a table with baby on your lap. Pull an object slowly across the table top (it is easiest to do this if the object is attached to a piece of string, so that you can be sure baby is watching the object and not your hand). Tick this item if baby follows the movement of the object by turning his head. ☐

3m. (14) Place a piece of paper over baby's face when he is lying on his back. Tick this item if he reacts by vigorously turning his head. ☐

Manipulation

3m. (15) Tick if he fingers one hand with the other when he is lying quietly. ☐

3m. (16) Place the ring in baby's hand. Observe whether he waves it about, moves it in front of his face to look at it, tilts it back and forth or performs any other manipulation with it. ☐

Visual

3m.   (17)   Tick if baby is now very alert visually, and particularly preoccupied by nearby human faces.   ☐

Visual/hearing

3m.   (18)   When baby is lying on his back, prop his head at each side so that it is in a central position, being careful not to block his ears. Hold a bell in one hand and a rattle in the other about 8 inches (20 cm) apart in front of him. Gently shake one, then the other, to make a soft sound. Continue to do this a few times, leaving several seconds between shakes for baby's eyes to move from one object to the other. Tick this item if baby's eyes move back and forth between the bell and rattle at least 3 times in response to the sound of each.   ☐

Visual

3m.   (19)   Hand regard: tick if baby often watches movements of his own hands.   ☐

3m.   (20)   Observe whether baby glances at a rattle in his hand.   ☐

3m.   (21)   Tick if he can fix his eyes on an object about 2–6 feet (1–2 metres) away from him.   ☐

3m.   (22)   When baby is seated on your lap at the table, or in his chair with the table in front of him, place a one-inch cube on the table directly in front of him. Note whether he clearly and directly looks at the cube.   ☐

4m.   (23)   When baby cannot see you approach, touch him from behind and note whether he turns his head.   ☐

Manipulation

4m.   (24)   Tick if baby now feels objects deliberately with his hands.   ☐

4m.   (25)   Tick if baby plays with a rattle placed in his hand for long periods (more than one minute). He cannot yet pick it up if it drops.   ☐

Visual

4m.   (26)   When baby is seated in his chair or on your lap, hold a spoon vertically by the tip of the handle so that it is about 2 feet (60 cm) from his eyes. Then move it *slowly* around to his side, and return to the other side across his line of vision, several times. Tick if he turns his head to follow the spoon to each side. ☐

Reaching

4m.   (27)   When baby is sitting or propped in his chair, dangle the ring within easy reach. Tick this item if he reaches in the direction of the ring. ☐

4m.   (28)   Tick this item if baby grasps the dangling ring. ☐

4m.   (29)   Tick if when holding the ring he takes it to his mouth. ☐

4m.   (30)   Tick if he can get hold of a rattle placed on his chest. ☐

4m.   (31)   Tick if he reaches and touches a toy placed on the table top in front of him. ☐

Manipulation

5m.   (32)   Tick if he likes to crumple paper. ☐

Reaching

5m.   (33)   Tick if he reaches and picks up a cube. ☐

Grasping

5m.   (34)   Place one cube in each of baby's hands. Tick this item if he grasps both cubes and holds them for 3 seconds or more. ☐

Manipulation

5m.   (35)   Tick if he likes to bang objects on table. ☐

Reaching

5m.   (36)   Tick if he reaches persistently for a cube or toy just out of reach. ☐

Manipulation

5m.   (37) Tick if he plays with string—picks it up, chews it, manipulates it.   ☐

5m.   (38) Tick if he can transfer an object from one hand to the other.   ☐

Attention span

5m.   (39) When baby is holding a cube, place a second one on the table within easy reach. Tick if he reaches for the second cube, even if he does not grasp it.   ☐

Reaching/grasping

5m.   (40) Tick if he can pick up a cube from the table top in front of him, neatly and directly.   ☐

5m.   (41) Tick if he grasps a dangling ring and pulls it down against resistance.   ☐

Reaching

5m.   (42) Tick if he clutches at a dangling ring held above his line of vision.   ☐

5m.   (43) Tick if he reaches for an object with both hands and grasps it with the nearest hand.   ☐

Permanence of objects

5½m.   (44) When baby drops a toy and it lands noisily, tick if he begins to look to see where it has gone.   ☐

5½m.   (45) Tick if he can pick up a cube that he has dropped on to the table.   ☐

Attention span

5½m.   (46) When baby is holding two cubes, place a third cube in front of him. Tick this item if he looks at the third cube immediately, although he may drop the others at this stage.   ☐

Reaching

6m.   (47) Tick if he reaches with one hand for an object.   ☐

Attention span
6m.   (48)   Observe whether, when he is holding the
                      ring, baby manipulates it and looks at his own
                      movements with it for some time.   ☐

Exploration
6m.   (49)   Tick if he manipulates the bell, plays with it
                      and shakes it deliberately.   ☐

Attention
6m.   (50)   Tick if he looks immediately at interesting
                      small objects within 6–12 inches (15–30 cm)
                      and stretches his hands to grasp.   ☐

Problem solving
6½m.   (51)   Dangle the ring by the string, then place it on
                      the table out of baby's reach, extending the
                      string towards him so that he can easily reach
                      the end of it. Observe whether he pulls the
                      string and draws the ring towards him. He
                      may pull the ring accidentally at first, then
                      purposefully later. Tick this item if he secures
                      the ring in any way.   ☐

Attention span
6½m.   (52)   Tick if he maintains his hold on two cubes
                      when a third is presented to him (as in
                      item 46).   ☐

Permanence of objects
7m.   (53)   Tick if he looks for a dropped toy when it is
                      definitely dropped from table to floor.   ☐

Imitation
7m.   (54)   Beat on the table with your hand and note
                      whether baby imitates you.   ☐

Problem solving
7m.   (55)   As in item 51, note whether baby secures the
                      ring by deliberately pulling it to him with the
                      string.   ☐

c

Touch
8m.   (56)   When touched or pinched, tick if baby looks at the part touched.   ☐

Permanence of objects
8m.   (57)   Place a favourite toy on the table and half cover it with a cloth. Tick if baby picks up the object.   ☐

Relation of objects
8m.   (58)   Tick if baby manipulates two objects at once: for example, bangs two objects together.   ☐

Reaching
8m.   (59)   Tick if baby secures key or peg with one and same hand five times out of six—shows hand preference.   ☐

8m.   (60)   When baby is sitting in his chair, cover his face with a cloth. Tick if he removes the cloth.   ☐

Imitation
8m.   (61)   Tick if baby bangs a spoon on table in imitation of you.   ☐

Attention span
8m.   (62)   When he is holding two cubes, offer him a third. Tick this item if he gets hold of the third cube as well as the other two.   ☐

Visual attention
9m.   (63)   Tick if baby watches activities of adults, children and animals within 10–15 feet (3–4 metres) with eager interest for several seconds at a time.   ☐

Permanence of objects
9m.   (64)   Place a small toy on the table in front of baby, and cover it with handkerchief while he is watching. Tick if he removes the handker-

chief to find the toy, and looks at or picks up the toy. ☐

Imitation
9m. (65) Tick if he rings a bell in imitation of you. ☐

Relation of objects
10m. (66) Tick if he removes a cube from a cup. ☐

Discrimination of objects
10m. (67) Place a book with a plain cover in front of baby, and place a cube or match-box on top. Tick if he picks up the cube or match-box. ☐

10m. (68) Place a rattle and small doll on table about 6–8 inches (15–20 cm) apart and note which one the child picks up. Repeat this three or four times, changing the position of the doll and rattle. Tick if child picks up the same object three times. ☐

10m. (69) Tick if he plays with a book not as any object, but looks at the individual pictures on the page. May touch or try to pick them up. ☐

Manipulation/exploration
10m. (70) Tick if he pokes fingers in small holes. ☐

Relation to objects
10m. (71) Tick if he plays at pulling or dangling a toy by a string. ☐

Manipulation
10m. (72) Tick if he pokes objects with forefinger. ☐

Permanence of objects
10m. (73) Place a small interesting toy under a cup or tin while baby is watching. Tick if he removes tin deliberately and picks up the toy. ☐

Imitation

10m.   (74)   Imitates actions—do various actions yourself and observe whether baby imitates them, e.g. (1) click two bricks together; (2) hit a cup with a spoon; (3) beat a tin or drum with a stick.   ☐

Relation of objects

10m.   (75)   Tick if he is beginning to put objects in and out of containers.   ☐

Instructions/imitation

10m.   (76)   Place a cube in a cup then take it out and hand it to baby. Ask him with words and gestures to put it in the cup. Tick if he places the cube in or over the cup.   ☐

Relation of objects

11m.   (77)   Tick if he can place one object on top of another—a book on a book, a brick on a book etc.   ☐

11m.   (78)   Tick if he plays with cup, spoon and saucer and puts them together as they are normally used—that is cup on saucer and spoon in saucer.   ☐

Gesture

11m.   (79)   Tick if he points with first finger.   ☐

Imitation

11m.   (80)   Scribble with a crayon on a piece of paper in front of baby; then give the crayon to him. Tick if he makes any attempt to mark the paper.   ☐

11m.   (81)   As baby is looking, place a toy in a small box and put a loose lid on the box. Open the box and take out the object, then put it back in the box and replace the lid. Hand the box to the baby and say 'Get the. . . .' Tick if baby is able to take the lid off at least twice.   ☐

Permanence of objects/memory
12m.   (82)   Tick if he looks in the correct place for toy
                   that has rolled out of sight.   ☐

Permanence of objects/exploration
12m.   (83)   Tick if he drops toys deliberately and watches
                   them fall to the ground.   ☐

Manipulatian
12m.   (84)   Tick if he uses both hands freely, though he
                   may show preference for one.   ☐

Imitation
12m.   (85)   Push a toy car slowly along a table or the floor
                   in front of baby. Push it to him and indicate
                   that he should push it. Tick if he pushes the
                   car with its wheels on the floor or table.   ☐
12m.   (86)   Show baby how to stand a toy dog upright,
                   then place dog lying on table in front of baby
                   and indicate that you want him to stand it up.
                   Tick if he imitates your action and stands the
                   dog up.   ☐

Visual
12m.   (87)   Tick if out of doors he watches movements of
                   people, animals, cars etc. with prolonged,
                   intent regard.   ☐

Memory
12m.   (88)   Tick if he recognises familiar people ap-
                   proaching from 20 feet (6 metres) away.   ☐

Relation of objects
12m.   (89)   Tick if he puts small objects in and out of cup
                   in play.   ☐

Eye/hand coordination/discrimination
12m.   (90)   Tick if he will hold a pencil as if to draw on
                   paper, and will use the pencil a little.   ☐

Permanence of objects

12m.   (91)   While baby is watching, wrap a cube in a tissue or cloth, making a loose bundle. Tell him 'Get the block'. Tick if he unwraps or shakes it deliberately in order to find it.   ☐

Eye/hand coordination

12m.   (92)   Tick if he will try to put a small object the size of a currant into a bottle. At this stage he does not usually succeed. ☐

12m.   (93)   Build a tower of cubes (three or four), then give the cubes to baby. Tick if he tries to build a tower or put one on top of the other, even if he fails to do it.   ☐

Imitation/manipulation

13m.   (94)   Scribble on a piece of paper. Hand the crayon to baby and tick if he scribbles vigorously.   ☐

13m.   (95)   Tick if he now shows a definite preference for one hand rather than the other—observe which hand he uses most often to grasp when you offer objects to him.   ☐

Attention span

13m.   (96)   Demonstrate as item 76 but tick if he puts three or more cubes into the cup. You may need to bring his attention to each cube in turn.   ☐

Visual discrimination

13m.   (97)   Using your formboard, show baby how to put a round disc in a round hole. Give him the disc—tick if he puts it in the correct hole.   ☐

Eye/hand coordination

14m.   (98)   Tick if he scribbles spontaneously when given crayon and paper, with no demonstration.   ☐

Problem solving

14m.   (99)   Place a toy behind a piece of glass or other transparent material. Tick if baby reaches round the glass to get the toy.   ☐

Visual discrimination

14m. (100) Place formboard in front of baby and give him a round block. Tick if he places it correctly without a demonstration. ☐

Attention span

14m. (101) Demonstrate as item 76. Tick if baby puts nine cubes in the cup. You may bring attention to cubes once or twice but not for each cube. ☐

Eye/hand coordination

14m. (102) Using your pegboard, place pegs in the board in front of baby. Remove all the pegs and put them on the table. Point to the pegs and holes saying: 'You put them in.' Tick if baby puts one peg in the board, two or more times. ☐

14m. (103) Tick if baby builds tower of two cubes after demonstration. ☐

Manipulation

15m. (104) Tick if he holds two cubes in one hand. ☐

Memory

15m. (105) Tick if baby can now remember for a short time where he has left toys. ☐

Eye/hand coordination

15m. (106) Tick if he is able to take lids off and put lids on small boxes—you can demonstrate this first. ☐

Problem solving

15m. (107) Put a small object such as a currant inside a transparent cylinder-shaped bottle. Give the bottle to baby saying: 'Get it out.' Tick if he removes the object from the bottle deliberately (not if it falls out by chance) without any demonstration from you. ☐

Manipulation
15m.   (108)   Tick if he can hold four cubes in hands at once.   ☐

Attention span
15m.   (109)   Tick if he stands or sits at windows and watches events outside intently for several minutes.   ☐

Visual
15m.   (110)   Tick if he follows with eyes the path of a cube or small toy swept vigorously from table.   ☐

Eye/hand coordination
17m.   (111)   Tick if he builds tower of three cubes after demonstration.   ☐

Problem solving
17m.   (112)   Put a toy out of reach of baby on a piece of paper or cloth. Tick if baby pulls the paper or cloth to get the toy.   ☐

Visual discrimination
17m.   (113)   Put the formboard with a circle, square and triangle in front of baby with the blocks in position. Take them out and place them between the board and the baby, so that each block is opposite its own hole. Tell him to put them in. Tick if he places a block correctly.   ☐

Attention span
18m.   (114)   As item 102, but tick only if baby puts all the pegs in the pegboard without you having to urge him on.   ☐

Eye/hand coordination
18m.   (115)   Tick if he will build in play with boxes, bricks or other materials.   ☐

Discrimination
18m.   (116)   Draw a straight vertical line on a piece of paper in front of baby. Give the crayon to

baby saying: 'See you do it.' Repeat this if necessary. Tick if baby makes a definite stroke on the paper rather than a scribble. □

Visual
18m. (117) Tick if baby points to distant interesting objects out of doors. □

18m. (118) Roll a small ball the size of a golf ball across the room at 12–15 feet (3–5 metres) away from baby, making sure that you have his attention on the ball first. Tick this item if he watches the ball as it rolls, and follows it with his eyes. □

Eye/hand coordination
19m. (119) Tick if he builds tower of four cubes, after demonstration. □

19m. (120) Tick if he will attempt to unscrew the top on a small bottle. □

Memory
20m. (121) Place two identical cups in front of baby. Put a sweet or an interesting toy under one cup, then slowly change the position of the cups around twice. Ask baby to find the sweet or toy. Tick if he succeeds in his first choice of cup. □

Discrimination
21m. (122) Make a vertical line on a piece of paper with a crayon, as in item 115. Note if baby makes a definite stroke. Then scribble on the paper. Give baby the crayon saying: 'Now do this.' Tick this item if baby definitely changes from a stroke to a scribble. □

Visual discrimination
21m. (123) As item 113. Tick only if baby places all the shapes correctly. □

c*

Imitation

21m. (124) Fold a square piece of paper in half once. Give baby another piece of paper the same as yours, and ask him to fold it. Tick this item if baby turns one edge of paper in an attempt to fold it, even if he cannot make a definite fold. ☐

Eye/hand coordination

21m. (125) Tick if he builds a tower of five or six cubes. ☐

Memory

21m. (126) Place two identical boxes in front of baby. Place a small toy under one box then put a piece of paper in front of the boxes for 3 seconds. Tick if baby goes for the correct box when you remove the screen and tell him to find the toy. ☐

Eye/hand coordination

24m. (127) Tick if he builds tower of six or seven cubes. ☐

24m. (128) Tick if preference for one hand is now well developed. ☐

24m. (129) Tick if he can pour water from one cup to another without too much mess. ☐

Manipulation

24m. (130) Tick if he can turn a doorknob and unscrew a lid. ☐

Imitation

24m. (131) (1) Tick if he imitates making a brick or toy walk. ☐

(2) Tap a pencil at the rate of one tap per second. Give baby a pencil and tick if he imitates the timing of your tapping. ☐

Imitation/attention span

24m.   (132)   Put ten cubes on the table. Place four in a row, saying: 'Look how I make a train . . . etc.' Push the train across the table making suitable train noises. Give baby the other cubes and say: 'You make one, make a train. . . .' Tick if baby puts at least three cubes in a row and pushes them.   ☐

Discrimination/matching

23+m.   (133)   Take three pictures of objects or animals that the baby knows. Put them in front of him and then hand him a picture which matches one of the three. Ask him to 'put it on the same'. Tick if he can match all three.   ☐

23+m.   (134)   Tick if he can match three circles and three squares. Use white paper cut into circles and squares, and proceed as in item 133.   ☐

23+m.   (135)   Tick if baby can match four colours. Use pieces of coloured paper all the same shape, and four boxes. Put a red piece in one box, a blue in another, yellow in another, green in another, and as you demonstrate to baby say: 'Look, the red ones go in here, the blue ones in here . . . etc.' Tick this item if he can correctly match four colours. (The boxes should each be of the same colour as the paper, or all the same neutral colour).   ☐

PERSONAL—SOCIAL

This list of behaviours is concerned with the development of personal skills important for the eventual attainment of independence—feeding, dressing, etc. Because much of the social behaviour between baby and parents takes place during these activities, we have included social skills in this section. In the last section —Adaptation—we were concerned with what babies do to things. In this section we are concerned with *what babies do with people.* Another part of what babies do with people is communication, and this is dealt with in the next section. You will see, however, that social skills are closely related to communication, so some communication behaviours are noted in this section.

The items of behaviour are listed under the following headings, most of which are self-explanatory.

1. Feeding

2. Mouth
We have included this in this section because the way the baby begins to find and use his mouth is closely linked with feeding skills. When he begins to put things into his mouth he can begin to do this with food such as biscuits and therefore start finger feeding himself.

3. Social, communication and emotional behaviour (see Chapter 10)

4. Anticipation and expectation
The baby's recognition of similar social situations and his reactions to them.

5. Play (see Chapter 11)

6. Dressing

7. Toilet

8. Washing

PERSONAL—SOCIAL

Feeding
1m.   (1)   Tick if he sucks well, opens mouth and
                      searches when breast/teat is taken away. ☐

Mouth
1m.   (2)   Tick if he can put his hand to his mouth. ☐

Social
1m.   (3)   When you feed him or talk to him, tick if he
                      looks at your face and quietens his move-
                      ments, and begins to watch your face.   ☐
1m.   (4)   Tick if he stops crying when picked up.   ☐
1½m.   (5)   Tick if he gazes into your eyes for long
                      periods.   ☐
1½m.   (6)   Tick if baby smiles at you when you lean
                      over him smiling and talking to him and
                      touching him gently.   ☐
2m.   (7)   Tick if he enjoys his bath.   ☐

Anticipation
2m.   (8)   Tick if he shows excitement at start of
                      picking up, feeding, etc.   ☐

Feeding
3m.   (9)   Tick if he fixes eyes unblinkingly on mother's
                      face when feeding.   ☐
3m.   (10)   Tick if he recognises feeding bottle and
                      makes eager welcoming movements as it
                      approaches his/her face.   ☐

Social
3m.   (11)   Tick if he responds with obvious pleasure to
                      friendly handling, especially when accom-
                      panied by tickling and vocal sounds.   ☐

Play
3m.   (12)   Tick if he pulls at his clothes.   ☐

Feeding

4m.   (13)   Tick if he tries to hold bottle.

☐

Anticipation

4m.   (14)   Tick if he is beginning to react to familiar situations—showing by smiles, coos and excited movements that he recognises preparations for feeds, baths, etc.   ☐

Social

                          Tick if he:

4m.   (15)   reaches for familiar persons;   ☐

4m.   (16)   is friendly to strangers;   ☐

4m.   (17)   gets a little cross when someone stops playing;   ☐

4m.   (18)   resists adult who playfully tries to take toy or doll;   ☐

4m.   (19)   is aware of a strange place—may startle, look around;   ☐

5m.   (20)   stops crying when talked to;   ☐

5m.   (21)   is now aware of strangers and shows some reaction.   ☐

Mirror

5m.   (22)   Hold a mirror in front of baby so that he can see his own face, and observe his reaction. Tick at this stage if he smiles at his image or approaches it in any way.   ☐

Washing

5m.   (23)   Tick if he splashes in bath.   ☐

Feeding

                          Tick if he:

$5\frac{1}{2}$m.   (24)   holds bottle;   ☐

$5\frac{1}{2}$m.   (25)   drinks from a cup when it is held to his lips;   ☐

$5\frac{1}{2}$m.   (26)   begins to hold cup.   ☐

Social
Tick if he:

5m.   (27)   shows fear of strangers and is 'coy'; ☐
5m.   (28)   imitates a cough or sticking out tongue. ☐

Mirror
$5\frac{1}{2}$m.   (29)   Tick if he smiles and vocalises at his own image. ☐

Play
Tick if he:

$5\frac{1}{2}$m.   (30)   likes frolic play—being held high, swung up and down etc.; ☐
$5\frac{1}{2}$m.   (31)   occupies himself unattended for about 15 minutes. ☐

Mouth
6m.   (32)   Tick if he takes everything to his mouth. ☐

Anticipation/expectation
6m.   (33)   Tick if he reaches for and looks at your hands when you stop clapping them. ☐

Social
6m.   (34)   Tick if he shows a defensive reaction to your attempts to take a toy away from him—he holds it firmly. ☐

Feeding
Tick if he:

$6\frac{1}{2}$m.   (35)   takes solids well; ☐
$6\frac{1}{2}$m.   (36)   chews; ☐
$6\frac{1}{2}$m.   (37)   feeds self with a biscuit; ☐
$6\frac{1}{2}$m.   (38)   keeps lips closed when offered more than he wants. ☐

Social
$6\frac{1}{2}$m.   (39)   Tick if he tries to establish contact with a person—he may cough or shout or wave his arms to draw your attention to him. ☐

Mirror
6½m.   (40)   Tick if he reaches and pats his reflection.   □

Feeding
7m.   (41)   Tick if he drinks from a cup—may be a feeding cup with a spout—and holds it a little by himself.   □

Social
7m.   (42)   Tick if baby is now actively seeking contact with people.   □

Feeding
8m.   (43)   Tick if he shows dislike for some foods.   □

Social
8m.   (44)   Tick if he reaches out for people and demands attention.   □

Play
8m.   (45)   Tick if he enjoys peek-a-boo.   □

Feeding
          Tick if he:
9m.   (46)   holds, bites and chews a biscuit;   □
9m.   (47)   tries to grasp spoon when being fed.   □

Social
          Tick if he:
9m.   (48)   shows fear of strangers—clings to known adult and hides face;   □
9m.   (49)   pulls your clothes, hands or hair to attract attention;   □
9m.   (50)   throws body back and stiffens in annoyance or resistance.   □

Play
          Tick if he:
9m.   (51)   shows toy in hand to adult, though he cannot give it yet;   □

9m.   (52)   plays peek-a-boo himself—pulls cloth over his head and off again. ☐

Feeding
10m.   (53)   Tick if he discriminates among foods and has likes and dislikes. ☐

Dressing

Tick if he:
10m.   (54)   pulls off hat; ☐
10m.   (55)   holds arm out for sleeve, foot for shoes; ☐
10m.   (56)   pushes arm up through sleeve. ☐

Social
10m.   (57)   Tick if he drops objects deliberately so that you have to pick them up. ☐

Play
10m.   (58)   Tick if he moves about independently and explores new places. ☐

Feeding
11m.   (59)   Tick if he finger feeds himself: picks up bits of food with his thumb and forefinger and puts them in his mouth. ☐

Social

Tick if he:
11m.   (60)   now gives a toy to adult and releases it; ☐
11m.   (61)   gives affection—may kiss or hug you. ☐

Feeding

Tick if he:
12m.   (62)   drinks from a cup with little assistance—may be a feeding cup. ☐
12m.   (63)   holds a spoon. He cannot yet use it alone, but may attempt to spoon feed himself awkwardly. ☐

Mouth
12m.   (64)   Tick if he takes objects to his mouth less often. ☐

Social

Tick if he:

12m.	(65)	is apt to be shy; ☐
12m.	(66)	demonstrates affection to people he knows well, and may kiss on request; ☐
12m.	(67)	likes to be constantly within sight and hearing of adult—usually mother. ☐

Communication

12m.	(68)	Tick if he points with finger at objects he wants to handle, or which interest him. ☐

Dressing

Tick if he:

13m.	(69)	tries to help—puts arms into coat, steps out or into pants; ☐
14m.	(70)	pulls off socks and unfastens shoes etc. ☐

Play

Tick if he:

14m.	(71)	plays rolling ball, pushing little cars along; ☐
14m.	(72)	marks with pencil or crayon for about 15 minutes. ☐

Feeding

Tick if he:

15m.	(73)	no longer uses a bottle; ☐
15m.	(74)	picks up cup, drinks, and puts it down; ☐
15m.	(75)	holds spoon, brings it to mouth and licks it, though he cannot yet prevent it turning over; ☐
15m.	(76)	chews well; ☐
15m.	(77)	can manage all his food without help, even if he is still very messy. ☐

Mouth

15m.	(78)	Tick if he now seldom takes toys to his mouth. ☐

Play
15m.   (79)   Tick if he appears to be interested in books—
                      pats pictures, may kiss picture of animal. ☐

Dressing
15m.   (80)   Tick if he tries to pull up pants or pull vest
                      or jumper down over head.   ☐

Toilet
15m.   (81)   Tick if he indicates wet pants—he may
                      point, wriggle, make a certain noise.   ☐

Social
15m.   (82)   Communication—tick if he shows you what
                      he wants by pointing and vocalising.   ☐

Play

                      Tick if he:
15m.   (83)   begins to imitate mother in domestic tasks
                      sweeping, cleaning;   ☐
15m.   (84)   is physically restless and very curious.   ☐

Feeding

                      Tick if he:
18m.   (85)   hands an empty dish to you, without letting
                      it turn over;   ☐
18m.   (86)   manages a spoon with very much spilling. ☐

Dressing
18m.   (87)   Tick if he attempts to dress himself without
                      success.   ☐

Toilet

                      Tick if he:
18m.   (88)   has attained bowel control;   ☐
18m.   (89)   indicates toilet needs by restlessness and
                      vocalisation.   ☐

Social

                      Tick if he:
18m.   (90)   likes to sit on your knee and look at a book
                      for several minutes;   ☐

18m.   (91)   plays with other children and gets along with them.   ☐

Communication

18m.   (92)   Tick if he sometimes uses words to make his wants known, and then demands the objects he wants by pointing, accompanied by loud urgent vocalisations or words.   ☐

Emotional behaviour

18m.   (93)   Tick if he alternates between clinging and resistance.   ☐

Play

Tick if he:

18m.   (94)   fetches or carries familiar objects, messages etc.;   ☐

18m.   (95)   briefly imitates actions, e.g. reading book, kissing doll;   ☐

18m.   (96)   plays contentedly alone, but likes to be near adult;   ☐

18m.   (97)   explores surroundings energetically.   ☐

Feeding

21m.   (98)   Tick if he handles cup or glass well—lifting, drinking, replacing.   ☐

Social

Communication. Tick if he:

21m.   (99)   asks for food and drink in words (not necessarily very clear);   ☐

21m.   (100)   pulls person to show something.   ☐

Play

Tick if he:

21–24m.   (101)   shows social play—for example, puts a watch to his ear and to yours, rolls a ball, chases etc.;   ☐

21–24m.   (102)   engages in simple make-believe activities— e.g. he wraps up a doll and puts it to bed, pretends to feed doll etc.   ☐

Social

2 yrs.+   (103)   Tick if he will listen to short stories whilst looking at pictures in a book.   □

Feeding

2 yrs.   (104)   Tick if he chews competently and can manage most sorts of food.   □

Toilet

2 yrs.+   (105)   Tick if his bowel control is complete, and he has bladder control by day.   □

Dressing

Tick if he:

2 yrs.+   (106)   pulls on simple garment—socks, mittens or hat;   □

2 yrs.+   (107)   helps actively in dressing or undressing (pulls off blouse, pulls on jersey etc.).   □

Washing

Tick if he:

2 yrs.+   (108)   can wash and dry his own hands;   □

2 yrs.+   (109)   tries to brush own teeth.   □

Toilet

Tick if he:

2 yrs.+   (110)   is dry at night if lifted;   □

2 yrs.+   (111)   has bladder control with occasional lapses during day. Tells need to go to toilet fairly consistently.   □

Social

Tick if he:

2 yrs.+   (112)   defends his own possessions with determination, though as yet he has no idea of sharing;   □

2 yrs.+   (113)   is jealous of attention shown to other children.   □

Emotional

2 yrs.+   (114)   Tick if he has tantrums when frustrated, but his attention is easily distracted.   □

COMMUNICATION

Communication is simply the process by which information is transmitted from one person to another. It may then be acted upon by the receiver which may provoke a further response.

Information can be transmitted in many ways—by hand gestures, facial expressions, body gestures or poses, cries, vocalisations, or in the most complex form, by language.

We shall briefly describe the stages of communication development leading to language. We hope this will indicate how language is built upon earlier behaviours, and so emphasise the importance of these. More details are given in the practical guidelines.

1. From the moment a baby is born he is sending out signals, in cries, facial expressions, gestures and even wriggles of his whole body. His signals are picked up by you, and you interpret them, giving them meanings such as 'he is hungry, tired' etc. You then act in response to the signal—feed him, put him to bed. Communication is a two-way process, from the very beginning.

At first you will learn to distinguish between the cries which indicate contentment and those that indicate discomfort. You will hear the cry of hunger, the cry of 'boredom', the sharp cry of pain or fear.

2. By reacting to these 'cries' appropriately, you begin to teach the baby that his cries produce certain results or pay-offs. The more consistent your reactions to the cries are, the more likely he will learn the association.

The baby is also making noises other than cries, such as hiccups, coughs, squeals and using various gestures and expressions. By imitating these, and reacting to them as though they have meaning, you further help the baby to learn the pay-offs, or consequences, of his communication behaviours.

3. To send out sound signals, and to receive them, you need command over certain mechanisms. You need to control breathing, vocal chords and later tongue and lip movements; and you need to be able to hear.

Babies are usually born with the ability both to make noise and to hear. They need to develop these, by making an ever wider and more controlled range of noises and by hearing and *listening* to more distinct sounds. (Do keep in mind that hearing is not the same as listening. In *listening* we deliberately direct our attention to sounds.)

Crying, sucking, licking, swallowing, chewing, twisting lips, using the tongue all help to practice and develop the muscles and mechanisms which we need to produce controlled sounds. Therefore, feeding and chewing are important for speech.

4. By three or four months of age, most babies have started to make a range of sounds such as cooing, chuckling, and a few vowel sounds. They have also started to look for the source of sounds with their eyes and to react to hearing a voice.

5. Soon the baby begins to make lots of little sounds (babble), often to himself, and listening to himself. He learns to recognise mum's voice, and special noises such as his food being prepared.

This babble also begins to take on a rhythm and expressiveness. He is beginning to pick up the intonations and stresses of speech. You can tell from this vocalisation whether he is excited, happy, cross etc.

He also becomes more able to look for the source of sounds by turning his head, and he can hear and listen to quieter sounds.

6. He enjoys being talked to and 'talks' back with babble. He is beginning to understand the meaning of what is said to him. At this stage he does not understand the words, he picks up the meaning from the tone of voice and expression used. He can tell if mum is cross, happy, impatient etc. He will also use the gestures and facial expressions of the people speaking to him to get at the meaning.

7. By seven or eight months the baby is putting sounds together, such as 'da-da.' He is also happy when you copy his sounds and will then repeat them.

His range of sounds gradually increases as he uses them in sing-songs, and playing 'sound games' with others who copy him, and soon he is directing his sounds and shouts at you to get attention. At this stage he is really beginning to understand how to use sound to communicate.

8. Gradually these sounds become more like recognisable words. His first words are very closely related to his immediate world, such as keep coming up in every-day use, e.g. 'mum-mum.' By using the word and getting a consistent response, he builds up its meaning, and by about 12 months of age he can usually say

one or two words meaningfully. He also has long 'conversations' consisting of apparently random sounds, with the occasional clear word.

9. Between 12 and 24 months he begins to build up his vocabulary. This comprises (a) the number of words he recognises and understands, but may not be able to say; and (b) the words he can say.

The words he recognises are not just single words, but also *short* phrases and instructions such as 'clap hands', 'give me a kiss'. At first the words he says are single words, usually connected with a person or object, e.g. Mummy, David, cup, drink. He then develops words about actions or events, e.g. 'gone'.

The small child's one word can often indicate a sentence. For example, he says 'mummy' meaning 'where's mummy?' or 'mummy come here', and you can tell which he means from the way he says it—just as you could tell the meaning behind his first cries as a baby.

10. By the end of the second year he begins to put two words together, e.g. 'ball gone,' or such short common sentences or phrases as 'give me', 'where is it?'

It is clear then that the early stages of communication are vital for later language development: they should be seen as links in the chain just as important as the words themselves. So each of the many skills that come together to build communication should be stimulated when you are trying to teach a child to speak.

This section of the checklist is divided into the different areas which help language and is designed to help you to pinpoint important behaviours at various stages.

We have broken it down under the following headings:

1. Vocalisation
All the sounds the baby makes.

2. Hearing and listening
Responding to sounds and attending to the differences between them.

3. Expressive behaviours
Facial expressions and gestures.

4. Communication
All movements and sounds which the baby uses to try to affect your behaviour.

5. Comprehension
The development of the baby's understanding of your speech, gesture and expression.

6. Speech
Using recognisable words meaningfully.

Remember, the headings indicate the main part of the behaviour, though the behaviour may be made up of several parts.

COMMUNICATION

Vocalisation

Tick if he:

1m.   (1)   makes some sounds, such as when crying, hiccupping, coughing or sneezing; ☐

1m.   (2)   cries when hungry or uncomfortable; ☐

1m.   (3)   makes small throaty noises. ☐

Hearing

1m.   (4)   Tick if he stops whimpering on hearing a soft voice (except when screaming or crying during feeds or when hungry). ☐

1m.   (5)   When the baby is busy waving his arms or wriggling, make a tapping noise or crumple some grease-proof paper. If baby then makes less movement—tick this item. ☐

1m.   (6)   Tick if baby startles in response to a sudden loud noise—stiffens, quivers, blinks, screws eyes up, extends limbs, fans out fingers and toes, or cries. ☐

Expressive behaviour

1m.   (7)   Tick if baby looks at you, though vaguely and with only a little eye-to-eye contact (gazing into your eyes). ☐

Vocalisation

2m.   (8)   Tick if he makes simple vowel sounds—ah, eh, uh. ☐

2m.   (9)   Look straight into the baby's face and smile, talk and touch him very lightly. Tick item if baby smiles and makes any vocalisation. ☐

Hearing

2m.   (10)   Ring a bell (gently) about 6–8 inches (15–20 cm) away from his ear but out of sight. Look for change in baby's facial expression, also quieting of movement or turning of head. ☐

Note: Responses at this age are not always

consistent. If you do not get a response *fairly soon*, try changing the sound *or* repeat again later.   □

Expressive behaviour

2m. (11) Tick if baby has alert expression, baby directly and definitely looks at you—a lot of eye-to-eye contact.   □

When you approach baby and before you touch him, talk quietly and smile. Observe if:

3m. (12) *Vocalisation:* baby coos, chuckles, crows, laughs or squeals with pleasure;   □

3m. (13) *Listening:* he quiets down or looks for and smiles on hearing voice;   □

3m. (14) *Expressive:* his face brightens at sound of your voice.   □

(N.B. Do not expect these reactions if baby is very sleepy or very excited or distressed.)

Hearing and listening

3m. (15) Observe whether baby begins to search for sound. When baby is lying quietly on his back, make sure you are out of sight and ring a bell or shake a rattle. If the baby turns his eyes and/or moves his head from side to side as though trying to find the sound, tick this item.   □

Vocalisation

4m. (16) Tick if baby develops a 'proper' giggle or laugh—a distinctive chuckle.   □

Hearing and listening

4m. (17) Support the baby in a sitting position. Ring a bell (or make some other sound) about 6–8 inches (15–20 cm) from his ear. Make sure the sound source is at the same level as ear and eyes and just behind the head. Tick if baby turns his head toward source of sound.   □

Expressive behaviour

4m.   (18)   Tick if baby begins to show excitement in response to various events or people: he waves arms, opens eyes wide, and often pants.   ☐

Vocalisation

Tick if he:

5m.   (19)   starts to put two sounds together, such as 'ah-goo';   ☐

5m.   (20)   begins to show feelings—pleasure, displeasure, eagerness or satisfaction—in vocalisations.   ☐

Vocalisation/Communication

5m.   (21)   Tick if he starts to vocalise to people *before* they talk. Also starts to vocalise to toys.   ☐

Vocalisation

Tick if he:

6m.   (22)   uses vocalisation (shouts and screams) to show anger and frustration;   ☐

6m.   (23)   begins to pronounce 'm' sound;   ☐

6m.   (24)   says syllables such as 'ba', 'da', 'ka';   ☐

6m.   (25)   begins to babble (that is, makes a string of noises such as 'a-ga, a-ga');   ☐

6m.   (26)   makes 'm-m-m' sound in crying.   ☐

Hearing and listening

Tick if he:

6m.   (27)   shows that he can tell difference between familiar and strange noises;   ☐

6½m.   (28)   is interested in producing sound from an object—ringing bell, banging and tapping. (Be sure that it is the sound that interests the baby, and not the shaking and banging movement.)   ☐

Comprehension

6m.   (29)   If you show you are cross or pleased (by tone of voice and facial expression), tick if baby reacts appropriately. Observe whether this happens:

(a) mainly to your tone of voice, ☐

(b) mainly to your face expression, or ☐

(c) equally to both. ☐

6½m. (30) Tick if he responds to his own name. ☐

Vocalisation

Tick if he:

7m. (31) makes four or more different sounds; ☐

7m. (32) combines syllables 'da-da', 'ba-ba'; ☐

7m. (33) imitates sounds. ☐

Comprehension

7m. (34) When you say 'no', tick if baby shows some comprehension by stopping or pausing in whatever he is doing. ☐

Vocalisation

8m. (35) Tick if baby produces singing tones. ☐

Listening

Tick if he:

8m. (36) listens to tick of watch at ear; ☐

8m. (37) listens to conversations. ☐

Vocalisation

Tick if he:

9m. (38) says 'da-da', 'ma-ma', 'ba-ba' or 'ga-ga' etc.; ☐

9m. (39) babbles tunefully, repeating syllables in strings, e.g. ma-ma-ma-mam; ☐

9m. (40) tries to imitate sounds playfully: coughs, brr's or blowing raspberries. ☐

Communication

Tick if baby:

9m. (41) babbles and vocalises directly at you as though trying to communicate; ☐

9m. (42) shouts to attract attention, then listens, then shouts again if not attended to. ☐

Comprehension

9m.   (43)   Tick if he responds to simple and familiar words such as 'bye-bye', 'dance', 'where's ...', by a physical gesture, looking for the object etc. (Be careful not to use gesture yourself when testing this, lest the baby respond to your gesture rather than the words.)   ☐

Vocalisation

10m.   (44)   Tick if he says one word with meaning: such as 'daddy', 'der' meaning there, etc.   ☐

Communication

10m.   (45)   Tick if he shakes head for 'no'.   ☐

Listening

11m.   (46)   When music is being played or you are singing to the baby, tick if he will try to sing as well.   ☐

Comprehension

11m.   (47)   Tick if he will show the appropriate gesture to match a familiar nursery rhyme. (Note: when you teach this you use the gesture; but when you test this item it is the baby who shows the gesture, not you.)   ☐

Vocalisation

Tick if he:

12m.   (48)   babbles loudly, tunefully and incessantly— when alone he often babbles on and on and on;   ☐

12m.   (49)   imitates one or two words. (This does not mean that the baby pronounces words perfectly.)   ☐

Comprehension

12m.   (50)   Tick if he shows a better comprehension of a number of words. If asked 'where is' daddy or some familiar object, he will look to the person or object, or point, very quickly. Providing baby is paying attention, no repeats of the question should be necessary. □

Vocalisation

13m. (51) Tick if he jabbers with expression. Baby makes a long string of varying noises which sound like conversation but have no real words in them. □

Vocalisation/imitation

13m. (52) Tick if he says two or three words with meaning. □

Vocalisation

14m. (53) Tick if he says four or five words with meaning, including names of people or objects. □

Communication

14m. (54) Tick if he uses gestures and vocalisations to make you understand what he or she wants. Often this starts at meal time. □

Comprehension

Tick if he:

15m. (55) points to familiar persons, animals or toys, when asked to do so; □

15m. (56) understands and obeys simple commands (shut the door, give me the ball, get your shoes); □

15m. (57) knows some parts of his or her body—points to nose when asked: 'Where is your nose . . .'. (again, be careful not to use gesture when testing this); □

17m. (58) obeys simple command, e.g. 'give it to mummy', 'give dolly a kiss', 'stroke pussy'. □

Vocalisation

18m. (59) Tick if he uses five or more words. □

Vocalisation/imitation

18m.   (60)   Tick if he frequently imitates a stressed word, or the last word said to him. ☐

Speech

18m.   (61)   Tick if he conducts long babbled conversations, with some clear words and much expression. ☐

Comprehension

Tick if he:

18m.   (62)   will point to a familiar picture, e.g. car, dog, ball, in a picture book (note—you need a page with three or four objects on it, so that child has to select the picture); ☐

18m.   (63)   knows two or three parts of own body, and can show *one* part on a doll (note—mum's body usually comes before own body and own body comes before doll); ☐

19m.   (64)   will name one or two pictures of familiar objects when asked (note—use books with one object per page). ☐

Speech

19m.   (65)   Tick if he begins to combine two words spontaneously (e.g. 'ball gone', 'there daddy', 'there pussy' . . .). ☐

Vocalisation

21m.   (66)   Tick if he can name six or more familiar objects, such as ball, cup, spoon, doll, dog, shoe, on demand. ☐

Vocalisation/imitation

Tick if he:

21m.   (67)   repeats two or three sentences, such as 'where is it'; ☐

21m.   (68)   repeats two out of four words in a sentence, e.g. 'get your coat on' and child says 'get coat' or 'coat on'. ☐

Comprehension
21m.   (69)   Tick if he brings familiar objects on request, e.g. 'get teddy', when they are not in sight. ☐

Speech
Tick if he:

21m.   (70)   combines two or three words spontaneously; ☐

21m.   (71)   uses 'I', 'me' or 'you' in speech.   ☐

Communication
21m.   (72)   Tick if he tries to tell you about what he is doing, or to name things immediately around him.   ☐

Vocalisation
2 yrs.+   (73)   Tick if he says 20 words clearly.   ☐

Speech
Tick if he:

2 yrs.+   (74)   can say a three-word sentence;   ☐
2 yrs.+   (75)   refers to himself by name;   ☐
2 yrs.+   (76)   joins in nursery rhymes and songs.   ☐

Communication
2 yrs.+   (77)   Tick if he asks for things at table by name. ☐

Comprehension
Tick if he:

2 yrs.+   (78)   comprehends and asks for 'another' or 'more';   ☐
2 yrs.+   (79)   listens to stories.   ☐

D

DEVELOPMENTAL PROFILE

PERSONAL - SOCIAL	1	2	3	4	5	6	7	8	9	10	11	12	13	14	15	18	21	24
Feeding	1, 2		9, 10	13	24, 26, 25	35, 37, 36, 38	41	43	46, 47	53	59	62, 63			73, 76, 74, 75, 77	85, 86	98	104
Mouth	3, 5, 4, 6	7	11	15, 16, 17, 18, 19	20, 27, 21, 28, 22, 29	34, 39, 40	42	44	48, 50, 49	57	60, 61, 64	65, 67, 66, 68			78			
Social		8	12	14		33		45	51, 52	58					82	90, 92, 91, 93	99, 100	103, 112, 113, 114
Anticipation						33												
Play					30, 31				51, 52				71, 72		79, 83, 94, 84	95, 96, 97	101, 102	
Dressing and Washing					23					54, 56, 55			69	70	80, 87			106, 107, 108, 109
Toilet															81, 88	89		105, 110, 111

COMMUNICATION	1	2	3	4	5	6	7	8	9	10	11	12	13	14	15	18	21	24
Vocalisation	1, 3, 2	8, 9	12	16	19, 21, 20	22, 25, 31, 23, 26, 32, 24	33, 35		38, 40, 39	44		48, 49	51, 52	53	59	60	66, 67, 68	73
Hearing	4, 6, 5	10	13, 15	17		27, 28		36, 37			46							
Expressive Behaviour	7	11	14	18														
Communication					21				41, 42, 45, 43		47	50		54			72	77
Comprehension					29, 30		34								55, 57, 56	58, 62, 63	64, 69	78, 79
Speech															61		65, 70, 71	74, 75, 76

Columns for Months 15, 18, 21, 24 appear under the heading DEVELOPMENTAL PROFILE (continued).

DEVELOPMENTAL PROFILE

MOTOR DEVELOPMENT

Months 1 – 4

Category	Month 1	Month 2	Month 3	Month 4
Gross Motor (a)	1, 6, 2, 7, 3, 8, 4, 9, 5, 10	11, 14, 12, 15, 13, 16	17, 22, 18, 23, 19, 24, 20, 25, 21, 26	27, 30, 28, 29, 31
Fine Motor (b)	1, 2, 3		4	5, 7, 6, 8

ADAPTIVE

Category	Month 1	Month 2	Month 3	Month 4
Visual (c)	3, 10, 4, 8, 5, 9, 6	11, 12	12, 19, 26, 13, 20, 17, 21, 18, 22	
Attention Span (d)				
Discrimination (e)				
Manipulation (f)			15, 16, 24, 25	27, 30, 28, 29, 31
Reaching (g)				
Grasping (h)				
Eye-hand Coordination (i)				
Permanence of Objects (j)				
Memory (k)				
Exploration (l)				
Relation of Objects (m)				
Problem Solving (n)				
Imitation (o)				

DEVELOPMENTAL PROFILE (continued)

Months 5 – 14

Category	5	6	7	8	9	10	11	12	13	14
Gross Motor (a)	32, 39, 33, 40, 34, 41, 35, 42, 36, 43, 37, 44, 38	45, 46, 48	47, 49	51, 53, 52, 54	55, 58, 56, 59, 57, 60	61, 63	62, 65, 64, 66	68, 70, 69, 71	72, 73, 74	75, 76
Fine Motor (b)	9, 10, 11, 12			13, 14	15, 16, 17		18, 19		20	
Visual (c)					63			87	97	100
Attention Span (d)	39, 46, 48, 52, 50			62	63				96	101
Discrimination (e)						67, 68, 69		90	97	100
Manipulation (f)	32, 37, 35, 38				70, 72			84	94, 95	
Reaching (g)	33, 41, 47, 36, 42, 40, 43			59, 60						
Grasping (h)	34, 40, 41									
Eye-hand Coordination (i)			53					90, 92, 93		98, 102, 103
Permanence of Objects (j)	44, 45			57	64	73		82, 91, 83		
Memory (k)								82, 88, 83		
Exploration (l)	49					70				
Relation of Objects (m)				58		66, 71, 77, 78, 75, 89				
Problem Solving (n)	51		55							
Imitation (o)	54			61	65	74, 76, 80, 81, 85, 86, 94, 95				99

DEVELOPMENTAL PROFILE (continued)

Months 15 – 24

Category	15	18	21	24
Gross Motor (a)	77, 78, 79	80, 82, 84, 86, 88, 81, 83, 85, 87, 89	90, 91, 92	93, 94, 95, 96, 97, 98
Fine Motor (b)	21	22	23	24
Visual (c)			123	
Attention Span (d)	109, 114	113		132, 133
Discrimination (e)			122	134
Manipulation (f)	104, 108			130
Reaching (g)				
Grasping (h)				
Eye-hand Coordination (i)	106, 111	115	119, 120, 125	127, 128, 129
Permanence of Objects (j)				
Memory (k)	105		121, 126	
Exploration (l)				
Relation of Objects (m)		112		
Problem Solving (n)	107			131
Imitation (o)			124	132

5 : Teaching your baby

Teaching is the art of getting someone to learn. Learning has taken place when someone can do something they could not do before. So anything that helps someone learn something new can be called teaching.

Seen like this, we are all teachers. We all help each other and our children to learn. Many of the things we write about in this chapter you will already be doing. However, by thinking about them we hope you will begin to realise their importance and to use them more effectively.

A word of warning: teaching is a skill. Think about other skills you have acquired—learning to knit or to drive a car. At first you had to go through each little action slowly and carefully. Often you had to tell yourself what to do, and to check constantly that it was correct. Gradually you began to blend each practised bit together, so that the whole action became quicker and smoother. At last the skill became 'automatic' and you could stop practising and concentrate on the best use of the skill.

It is the same with teaching. It will take time and patience. You will need to keep analysing how it is working, why it is not working.

This chapter is about the everyday things we do with babies and children which help them to learn. Chapter six is about specific ways you can analyse tasks and plan the way you will teach.

As parents you provide four major things which help your child to learn and develop.

1. A learning environment
This is the world around the child, and all the things in it which provide experience.

2. Models of behaviour

When you do something—even something ordinary like switching on the light or talking to someone—you are providing a model which your child can copy or think about.

3. Encouragement and motivation

This is something which we all need and seek out. Children particularly want the attention and approval of their parents.

4. Interactions, instructions and information

Every day you are interacting with the baby, doing things with him, telling him things and showing him how things work.

You have only to look around your home and think of the things that your child comes into contact with or can see or can hear, to realise how much stimulation is already available. Now think of the things you have said or shown him, the cuddles, smiles and 'good-boys' you have given him.

During the next two or three days try to look at the four areas through your baby's eyes. What can he see or hear when in his pram, his cot, on the couch? Can he see what you are doing? How do you talk to him? When do you smile at him, cuddle him?

Take a new look at your home and ask yourself what opportunities it is providing for the child.

We shall now discuss a number of ideas connected with the four areas. They have been selected from many research studies and our own experience as of great importance in the development of *all* young children. The first chapter will deal with some general points about the four areas and the young child, and the second with the teaching procedures you can use to help.

THE LEARNING ENVIRONMENT

You can recognise good learning environments in two ways:

First, they provide opportunities for a variety of stimulation.
Second, they are organised and have a sense of order.
Let us look at the first point and some examples.

Variety

(a) The baby or physically handicapped child who cannot move around is often placed in the same cot or on the same couch—lying on his back so all he can see is the ceiling. The result is a low level of stimulation. You need to prop him up, move him to different rooms and different positions.

(b) A number of homes have a very high level of noise. Radios and television are on, other children laughing and shouting and so on. Often we turn up the radio to drown out the noise from the street or the children playing. This high level of noise masks the variety of noises, and so one gets poor stimulation again. What is needed is not silence, but a level of noise which allows the child to hear particular ones and to hear changes in noise, e.g. the telephone, fridge humming, dog barking. You will then need to draw his attention to these changes.

(c) Many people make the mistake of thinking that the baby or handicapped child does not 'get much' from trips outside the home. This is wrong. All children profit enormously from going on trips—shopping, days out, visits to the zoo or museums or places of interest, holidays and so on. Many parents have told us, in surprise, how much the child developed when they went to spend a few days with relatives, or how he said two new words when they went to the zoo. Changing the environment can be very stimulating indeed to any child and, of course, to the parent.

(d) Children raised in homes where there are plenty of things to do, toys to play with, magazines to cut up, look at or just tear, and paper to draw on, always seem to be happier and more developed than those who do not get this variety but, for example, watch the television all day. (This does not mean you should not let a child watch television, only that television should be used as one source of stimulation only.)

Organisation, order and consistency

Imagine that every time you went to the kitchen nothing was in the same place as it was the time before. The things that go together—pots and pans, cups and plates, tinned foods, fresh foods—were all mixed up and placed at random. Life would be bewildering, and extremely difficult. Now imagine the young child, who has yet to learn about order and what things go with what other things, faced with a similar chaotic picture.

Now think about the mentally handicapped child, who takes

much longer to learn than the normal child, and has not got the same ability to cope with complex situations.

So one needs to create a learning environment which has some order and organisation, though not too rigid an order. The degree will depend upon the level of the child's development and his needs. Organisation is clearly necessary in any case if you are to maintain the home and your family life yet find the time to provide special stimulation for the handicapped child. Any new baby brought into the home means re-organisation, and if you can plan new routines from the start you will find it easier to keep them up.

Routines. The first problem is to establish the *baby's routine.* All children vary. They have different sleep patterns; are more hungry at some feeds than others; are particularly lively and energetic at different times. You will need to adapt your patterns as the child changes and develops. Many handicapped children become too dependent on strict routines and order and show a great deal of frustration when they change, so it is useful to establish routines and then to teach the child to be flexible afterwards by altering parts of the routine a little at a time.

Fitting in with the child's *daily rhythms* is important. For example, it is not very useful to expect the child to sit quietly on your knee and concentrate on a picture book or building with bricks at the time of day when he is most energetic and wants to be tossed about or rolled around.

You may find, like a number of our parents, that because you have other children who need your attention, you get little time to work with the handicapped child alone. One solution is to establish a routine whereby you spend time with the child when the others are in bed, and then let him sleep later in the morning. In the case where father does not come home until late, this strategy may be especially necessary when you are working on physical development and need another pair of hands. Particular patterns will depend on the situation of each individual family, but some thought given to the organisation of time in this way will be time well invested.

Access to toys. Organisation also includes how you arrange the toys and objects that the child will play with. Usually this becomes more important as the child becomes more mobile and starts getting his own toys.

We have found that storing all toys in a single large toy box usually means that the small toys end up at the bottom and the large ones at the top. The young child cannot reach the bottom, and so he always plays with the same toys from the top. A cupboard or set of shelves with the toys kept in certain places is far better. Or you could select and keep out a range of toys which you feel are helpful at each stage of development.

Much of this book is about the way to select toys* to meet the stage of development the child has reached, and to encourage the next step forward. But it is very important for children to be able to go back to old and familiar toys, to have time to 'mess about' with them in ways that they have enjoyed, and to find new things to do with them. Therefore, when you organise the 'toys for today', make sure a few of the old favourites are around as well.

Another point can be made about new toys. Children are attracted by something new and usually want to play with it immediately. But sometimes the new object is so 'new' that they seem wary of it. (In our experience this frequently turns out to be a present bought by Grandma at Christmas, and the child's refusal to be 'delighted' causes embarrassment all round!) When a new toy is presented to a child, it is important to give him time to explore it and mess about with it, before expecting him to use it as we adults think best. Opportunity for this first exploration may involve simply leaving the toy around and letting the child look at it whilst playing with other things. It can be several weeks before he takes notice of it and begins to use it.

Consistency and order. A sense of order and consistency is also important in a different way.

When born, a baby has potential for learning but no knowledge of the world about him. Much of the early years will be spent in learning that things in his world are orderly and consistent. A square, for example, is always a square, a ball is round and will roll. He also needs to learn about cause and effect. If

* By toys we do not mean only the brightly coloured things from toy shops, but anything the child plays with, from old socks to cardboard boxes.

D*

you switch on the light you usually get light, if you touch the fire you get burnt.

Less obvious are the rules of how to live with people. Children need to know that if they do something today and are not punished, they will be able to do it tomorrow and not be punished. They need to learn that their parents work to a consistent set of rules, that the behaviour of other people is to be relied on and that it ties in with their own behaviour : when someone says 'hello' and smiles, they say 'hello' or smile back, and when they smile the other person smiles.

Therefore, if they are to develop a sense of confidence in dealing with their world and especially to explore it, children need to know what to expect and, whenever possible, why to expect it. Again, this learning will take longer for the handicapped child. He will need more repetitions and very precise models of behaviour to learn from. He especially will need consistent responses to his actions.

Many of the behaviour problems we find with mentally handicapped children result from inconsistency in our reactions to them, and from failures to show them exactly what we expect and why we expect it.

We cannot emphasise this need for consistency too much. As one parent told us, 'It is one of the most difficult things to do as parents—you have to start as soon as possible. These babies seem to find it difficult to see that what we do is consistent and so we have to work harder to make sure that what we do really *is* consistent'.

MODELS OF BEHAVIOUR

Anyone who has spent some time with young children soon realises how much they learn by watching and listening to other children and their parents, and then copying the behaviour. Almost anything we do acts as a model for the child to imitate. We have all see the obvious imitations : the child mimicking a favourite television character, or the way father eats his dinner; or, more bizarre, the little girl standing at the toilet because she has seen her father or her brothers use it that way. But if we are to use this ability to help the child to learn, we must realise just how important a learning strategy it is, and in mentally handicapped children we often have to help them to develop it fully.

Some people believe that the baby of a few weeks old has already begun to imitate. As you talk to the baby you will notice small mouth movements, not smiles, as though he is copying your own mouth movements. A little later, when the baby is a few months old, facial expressions appear as if he is surprised or happy or puzzled, and again they seem to occur in response to yours. If you look into a mirror and pull faces you can begin to analyse them into separate parts: for example, expressing surprise, the eyebrows are usually raised, the eyes are wide open and the mouth is open and round. Facial expressions are used a lot in communication, and so they are important. If the child can learn to imitate them, he is ready to go on and learn when to use them appropriately. Remember that the mentally handicapped child is less able to spot the important parts of an action—the cues. To help him we need to make them more obvious, more intense, make them last a little longer and repeat them more often. We need to make sure that our smiles are big and full, our raised eyebrows are really raised and our mouth movements and words are clear and sharp.

By the time the baby is using his hands to do things, imitation becomes more obvious. You clap your hands and the baby claps his. You bang the rattle and the baby bangs the rattle. If the handicapped child does not do this of his own accord, you need to teach him to copy. You will need to take his hands and pat them together for him. This is showing him a clear model of what you want. As his hands touch you give him a big smile and say, 'good—clap hands'. What you are doing is teaching him to imitate, so that when you later want to teach skills such as holding a pencil and copying a circle he already knows how to model his actions on yours.

Imitation also includes *you imitating* the child. This is something that young babies enjoy, and is probably one of the most important ways to begin to stimulate and play with them, so we would advise you to take every opportunity to copy your baby —especially his expressions and vocalisations. (See Chapter 7 p. 156.)

TURN-TAKING

Whenever we interact with another person we take turns. For example, they speak, then we speak. If we do not stick to the rules in this way, the interaction suffers.

Turn-taking starts in the first months of life, when babies begin to 'coo'. They 'coo' and stop, we 'coo' or talk back, then they start again. Learning this turn-taking is vital for learning how to interact with people. But the handicapped baby is slow to respond. Please remember this, and keep telling yourself to *give him time*. If you have talked to the baby or tickled him, and expect a response, before you make up your mind that it will not come and repeat your behaviour, count slowly to three—the reaction often appears.

Let's move on to an example at an older age. You hold a rattle in front of the baby to stimulate a reach. Nothing happens. Before shaking it to get him interested, provided he is looking at it, wait a little longer. If nothing happens then, shake it, and if there is still no reach bring his hand up to the rattle. Do not just give up and stick it in his hand.

Many parents and even teachers do not understand the importance of giving the child time to take his turn in responding. They ask a question, and before the child can think up an answer they interrupt and tell him, or repeat the question in another way. What is worse, people often seem to give the brighter child longer to respond than the less able child. If they did not expect the less able child to know the answer, why did they ask the question?

Eager parents and teachers who want the child to show he can do something—who expect the child to be able to do it— also tend to jump in too soon. We must give the child *time to persist*, to try to find the answer. If he has tried to place the jig-saw piece in upside down and it is not fitting, provided he is still trying, or has put it aside to use another piece, do not interrupt. Only when he is truly stuck give him a prompt.

If you keep interrupting and showing him how to do something, he will learn it quite quickly. But will he learn to persist? Will he learn to concentrate for longer? Will he learn to make his own decisions by solving problems for himself?

It is not easy to know when and when not to interrupt, but it is worth thinking about and working on.

One behaviour which is very helpful in showing us when to interrupt is 'referent looking'.

REFERENT LOOKING

Remember back to when you were last out in the company of a close friend or spouse in a group of strange people. You started to state an opinion which you were not sure they would agree with. You probably glanced at your spouse more often than usual. Depending on his or her expression, you felt more or less sure of what you were saying—you might even stop talking. In these 'looks' you were referring to your spouse—seeking some non-verbal comment on what you were saying. This is referent looking.

Let's take the example of a small child doing a jigsaw puzzle. He places a piece correctly. He looks up at mum as though to say, 'look how well I've done'. If he catches mum's eye she will usually say 'very good', or smile. She interprets the child's referent look as meaning he wants some approval. However, he may be stuck with a piece and look up at mum. This time she is likely to interpret the look as meaning 'is this the right way?' in which case a nod is sufficient; or it may mean 'come and help me'; or on the other hand, he may be putting it in wrong deliberately and his look may mean 'what are you going to do about it?'—the well known 'testing out mum's reactions and present level of patience game' which we have all come to love and hate!

Referent looking then can be :

  (a) a request for reward and approval; or
  (b) a request for information and assistance.

It is certainly a very common and useful means of communication and well worth observing, especially in a child who has difficulties in communicating with words.

It is also used in another way. If you have known a child at the stage of development when he is afraid of strangers, you will have seen it. A stranger comes near and the child glances at mum to see if everything is O.K. Even at a slightly earlier age, this kind of referent looking is important. If on a shopping trip you left the pram outside the shop so that the child could see you, he was happy—as long as he could keep referring to you by looking into the shop he felt safe and secure and would carry on looking confidently about him at the strange sights and people. But if you moved behind one of the shelves, the shriek was ear shattering.

Again, mentally handicapped children, particularly those with a very severe problem, may not develop referent looking spontaneously, or may not use it very well. By being aware of it and looking for it yourself, you will be in a position to respond appropriately and so encourage its development.

When children are blind they obviously do not have this tool. We have not had enough experience of blind children to know whether they develop an equivalent physical gesture, but if your child is visually handicapped it is worth looking to see if certain gestures seem to work like referent looking for eliciting approval or assistance.

Whilst talking about looking behaviour, we would like to bring your attention to *eye-pointing*. Before babies can use their arms to point, they indicate interest with their eyes, so you will need to observe their looking behaviour to guide you to the things that particularly interest them. This is especially important in the case of physically handicapped and cerebral palsied children who cannot use their arms very well. For these children you also will need to arrange your teaching so that the child can show you things by eye-pointing.

LOVE AND CARE

Basic needs

Regardless of the disability and degree of handicap, all children need and respond to love and care. They need to learn about these, as much as about any other aspects of this complex world we live in. They need to feel safe and secure.

A baby learns first through the handling which we give him in the first weeks of life, when feeding, changing and playing with him. He needs to 'get to know' one or two adults, to get used to being handled by them. He soon begins to recognise the face and voice of an adult—usually his mother—then of others.

If the child is handicapped and has difficulty in learning these things, and even more difficulty in showing that he has learnt them and can respond, we need to be patient, and to look for very small signs to show that a relationship is growing.

Again, we build up this secure and loving relationship by being consistent in our response to the baby.

Crying and attention

We will all respond to the baby who is hungry or uncomfortable. We soon learn to know what the cries and vocalisations mean. However, we often hear the cry for attention and feel that we should not respond to it in case we teach the child to cry out for every little thing. Much advice on babies argues that we should ignore these early cries for attention, lest we spoil the child. This is not really true.

Imagine the young baby awake in his pram or cot, staring at the dull ceiling. He will cry because he wants some stimulation, something to happen.

This need for stimulation is as great, and as important to the development of the child, as the need for food.

Adult subjects placed in experimental environments where all stimulation has been removed or reduced to a very low level, soon become very disorientated, emotionally disturbed and frightened. Indeed, isolation is one of the first steps in 'brain-washing' techniques. We all need stimulation—the baby's cries for attention are his way of letting us know.

When we respond to these first vocalisations or 'calls for attention,' we are also teaching the child something. First, we are teaching him about cause and effect: he shouts and cries—we appear. Second, we are teaching him his first lessons in communication: that certain types of vocalisations produce certain reactions in us. Some recent studies with young children have shown that when mothers do respond to these cries for attention and take the appropriate action, the child at one or two years of age is *less* likely to be one who is always shouting and screaming for what he wants. This happens only if we respond appropriately and try to teach him how to let us know what he wants without screaming.

Many mentally handicapped babies do not cry as much as other babies. They do not cry for food, or because they are uncomfortable, or for attention. We think of them as 'good' babies but, by not crying, they are getting less stimulation and attention. As parents we need to compensate for this. We have to plan a routine so that they are given plenty of food, attention and stimulation.

Confidence and exploration

By providing the child with loving care and attention, we help to give him a safe and secure base—confidence. From this base he can start to explore the strange, complex and exciting world he finds himself in. Thus by the age of two the 'normal' child will have started to develop a *sense of trust* in his parents, his world and, most importantly, himself.

He also starts to test this trust, just as he tests out all learning situations. How often have we heard, or said, that our children are no trouble at the neighbour's house, yet at home there is a constant battle? This is because you do not 'test out' people that you do not know, whose reactions you are unsure of. The child has a fairly good idea of the rules and standards that his parents work to, and the sort of behaviours that are most likely to 'get them going'. This testing out is wearing, but must be seen in the same way as other activities: it is an exploration of the breadth of the relationship, of the flexibilities needed in interacting with other people, and, of course, it represents the beginnings of independence. It is also a sign that the child is learning.

Protection and overprotection

Love and care, then, involves more than just giving. A mother of a child who had an incurable disease summed it up like this:

Loving is not sloppy and sentimental. It is objective and sometimes one has to be hard. When our child was dying we had to learn to keep treating her as normally as possible. We could not plan for the future but had to make each day full and worthwhile. Loving and learning is for the moment as well as tomorrow. It would have been so easy just to love her and do everything for her—but this would really not have helped her. She would have vegetated and become less of a person. Even when she was in pain we made her do things for herself and so still be a unique person.

Whenever a child is ill or handicapped we are in danger of overprotecting him, of smothering him and not allowing him to live his life to the full. This is natural—it comes from our love and our compassion. But we do need to be aware of the dangers and to give our love and care in such a way that it helps him to grow and develop into as independent a person as possible. After all, the competent and well developed child is the one who is able to leave the parent and make a life in the world. We have to try to be as objective in the use of our love and care as in any other aspect of our teaching.

OVERDOING THE TEACHING

The amount of teaching you do at one time is important. The simple rule is that it is better to do a little at a time often, rather than a lot at one time. You teach a little at a time because this way :

You do not tire the child.

You also do not lose his interest easily.

And you do not give him too many different bits of stimulation which might confuse him. When this happens he will have great difficulty relearning something he has got wrong, because he is having to 'unlearn' one pattern of behaviour at the same time as learning another.

If you observe the child closely and get to know the behaviours he uses to show you he is tired or fed up, you will soon learn when to stop, or when to change to a new lesson.

1. Switching
Switching from one activity to another demands care. We said earlier that it is important not to jump in and interrupt the child's play without observing the child carefully first, and choosing an opportune moment. This is because mentally handicapped children often have difficulty in switching their attention from one activity to a new one. When changing activities, try to make it a smooth change, giving the child time to adjust himself. Another approach is to give him a short rest—about 30 seconds to a minute—and just chat or cuddle him. Then start the new activity.

2. Bombardment
In our eagerness to help the child we often bombard him with assistance, talking to him and showing him what to do. Remember that when you have learnt a skill, it seems easy so you do everything much more quickly than if you are still learning it. Do not bombard the child with too much help and information, especially a mentally handicapped child, whose major difficulty is in sorting out complex incoming information.

3. Losing interest
When you miss the end of a film that interests you, you may find that it keeps coming back into your mind afterwards. Somehow by not fully completing the experience, you were left in a state of high interest. On the other hand, suppose you work in a choco- late factory. At first you devour the free samples, but by the end of the week you don't want to see another chocolate : your inter- est in chocolate has totally disappeared. Similarly, with the child who is fascinated by light switches and is always playing with them, one approach might be to let him go on switching them on and off, on and off, until he has had enough, his interest in switches is exhausted, and hopefully he looks for other activities.

If, therefore, you stop an activity *before* you have totally satisfied yourself with it, you are likely to be interested in doing it again at a later date. On the other hand, if you are kept at the activity until your interest is totally used up, you are less likely to want to do it again. When you are teaching your child, *stop while it is still fun*. Then it should again be fun when you repeat it.

INITIATIVE

One of the big differences between many mentally handicapped babies and normal babies is in the degree of initiative they show in doing things for themselves. Many handicapped babies give the impression that if you did not get them going, they would simply lie and do nothing. So it is very important for you to learn to take the initiative for such a baby. However, if you *always* take the initiative and direct the baby's activities, you will smother any initiative he does have, and certainly not be helping him to learn to direct his own activities or make his own decisions. If the mentally handicapped child and adult is going to be able to direct his own life and make decisions for himself—to the best of his ability—we have to make initiatives for him, but also take every opportunity to encourage him to use his own. One of the hidden aspects of overprotection is *not allowing* the child to use his initiative and to make decisions. For example, one can encourage the young child to choose which clothes he wants to wear—explaining, where necessary, whether it is an appropriate choice or not. And one can reward a small baby's initiative in choosing a new toy, trying a new strategy with an old one, or crawling to a new part of the room, by showing him you are pleased and by allowing him to explore further.

GETTING AROUND A PROBLEM

Remember that it is often more useful to remove a problem for the time being, than to try to teach a solution. For example, one can use zip or velcro fasteners instead of buttons; slip-on shoes instead of buckles or lace-ups; polo-neck sweaters instead of shirts and ties.

Problems frequently arise because the child does not have the necessary skill to cope with the task and is not ready to learn—his development is not sufficiently advanced. Therefore we have to think of a way around the difficulty until the child is ready to learn. A nappy or diaper is a device to get around the soiling problem until the child is able to learn to use the pot or toilet.

However, we do not accept that this will always be the case, but look for signs that suggest the child is ready to learn the new skill.

STRESSING THE CUE

In Chapter 3 we noted that a major problem of mentally handicapped children is in paying attention to the relevant cue, e.g. the colour of the traffic lights when the cars were stopping. We have constantly to help them to *direct their attention*, to take notice of the cue. With babies and young children we often need to stress the cue by making it stand out. We can do this in two ways:

First, make sure that there are not too many other cues around to confuse or distract the baby's attention from the important one. For example, use one or two toys at a time and make sure others are out of the way; instead of using a lot of words in the instructions, use just a few relevant ones; with a jigsaw, start by fitting in one or two pieces not the lot.

Second, emphasise the important cue. For example, in teaching the baby to look at the rattle rather than shake it, make sure it is visually attractive—and stands out, perhaps by using one with moving parts and bright stripes and colour contrasts.

ENCOURAGEMENT AND MOTIVATION

If you look up the word *motivation* in a dictionary you will find a definition such as 'that which initiates action', the motive for doing something. So you can only know if someone is motivated by observing his actions or behaviours. If he approaches someone or something—that is if he takes the necessary action to come in contact with someone or something—we can assume he is motivated toward that someone or something.

Before you can learn about anything you need to approach it—to make contact. If you want to learn how to switch the light on, you will need to make approach behaviours towards the light switch. These behaviours are looking at the switch, extending an arm, leg, head or nose to the switch, touching the switch and pressing it. The motivation comes before the behaviours. Unless you are motivated, you will not make these actions.

The motivation could have arisen from within you : you saw this object on the wall and your curiosity was aroused, you approached it to find out what it does. It could be that your attention was drawn to it when you saw someone else touch it. If the light went on at the same time, you may have asked yourself "If you push that, does the light go on?" You were motivated to find an answer to your question. It could be that you were bored (unstimulated) and the only object around was the light switch so you sought stimulation by exploring it.

Or the motivation could come from outside you. Someone indicated to you that if you approached the switch you would get a reward. *A reward is simply anything that will make you approach something*—try it out, do something, act upon something.

Handicapped children often have little motivation from inside. They seem to lack curiosity, they do not approach things, or set up little 'I wonder how, or I wonder why . . .' speculations of their own. In this case we will need to motivate them—to encourage approach behaviours from the outside.

Let us take the light switch as an example. Assuming that the child can crawl or walk, we can start by attracting his attention to the switch. We tap it and say 'look'. If he does not come over to the switch (approach it), we switch it on with a very exaggerated movement, and when the light comes on we make a big surprised and happy face. Here we are providing two channels to motivation : one is the light going; the second is the pleasure you have got from it.

If the child still does not approach the switch, we will need to think of something else to motivate him. We can take a favourite toy, such as a teddy, and make teddy push the switch. The child may then approach the switch to get teddy. We may also resort to offering him one of his favourite foods or drinks. If he approaches the switch we give him a little of the food or drink for coming over. Then we press the switch again (model), and if he presses it we would give him some more reward. If he does not press it, we take his hand and guide him to the switch and help him press it (a prompt)—then we reward him and repeat the sequence until he was doing it well by himself.

The problem with using food or drink rewards to motivate the child, is that we have to fade them out. You cannot spend your life giving out sweets for every little action. Therefore, it is best to use these types of reward as sparingly as possible. Fortunately, most handicapped babies will have *some* curiosity and motivation, and will also do things to get approval (smiles, cuddles and 'good-boys') from mum and dad.

As we said earlier, it is very important to encourage the child to use his own initiative, to make his own choices and to explore. And the first step towards initiative is motivation—'that which initiates action'.

But how can we encourage and develop initiative and motivation?

We have discussed some of the things necessary to encourage initiative and motivation in earlier sections. However, they are so important that they will stand repetition.

Security and confidence
Children will explore and approach new objects and situations only if they feel confident in themselves. They develop this confidence by having a secure base from which to work. This base develops out of the happy relationship established with the parents, and particularly out of the knowledge of order and predictability in things that happen. This predictability comes from *consistent* response to the actions the child performs.

Access
To initiate actions and explore you need access to things. Toys should be so organised that the child can reach them easily, and select them for himself. If he cannot get to things by himself, they must be brought to him. If he is mobile he must be allowed to get to things—within reason. For example, if you are stopping him from going into the garden because it is dirty; from going near the fire and the television plugs because they are dangerous; and from touching ornaments and cupboards because they will break, you are really training him not to use his curiosity and initiative.

Of course, there are very good reasons why a child must be prevented from doing certain things, and children need to learn the rules of what not to do as well as what to do. But you need to reach a balance. Using a fireguard, putting locks on cupboards with special objects in them, removing the breakable treasures from reach, will get around many problems. Later, when the child is more aware, you can begin to teach him not to touch certain things.

Novelty

Most people are attracted by something new and different. If on the other hand it is so different that we cannot fit it into our scheme of past experiences, we may be a little apprehensive or even frightened of it. Therefore, though new things and situations are necessary to motivate the child, we must make sure that they are not too different from past experience.

We can extend this idea into a very important tool for learning. If we do something that we have done many times before— pick up a familiar rattle and shake it, for instance—we have an expectancy of what will happen : it makes a noise, it has a certain weight and feel. However, if something happens that does not quite fit our expectations, we are surprised. We look at the object with a new interest, we are motivated to discover more about it. In other words, it is when a *mismatch* occurs between what we expect and what happens that we begin to learn new things.

We might even go as far as to say that learning occurs only when our expectations are not met, and something new and novel is found. The baby who has learnt to grasp and shake his rattle will learn very little from repeating this constantly. But if we give him a new rattle which is slightly different from the old one, he can try to find out whether it works the same way. If he shakes it and it does make a noise, he has learnt to apply his old skill (shaking and listening) to a new object. If the noise, feel and weight of the rattle are different from his expectation, he may be motivated to explore it further, or to try out his shaking strategy on other objects.

Therefore, new things help to motivate the baby and also help him to extend his learning—to adapt old skills and knowledge to new situations. He learns that it pays to explore.

This is very important learning indeed. Always plan to extend learning to new things and situations, making sure that they are not too new to prevent the old skill and knowledge being applied but new enough not quite to fit the old expectations.

Success

If you tried to do something and kept failing you would give up. After a while, if you kept failing at enough things, you would stop trying new things altogether, and generally become less interested, exploratory, curious and motivated. Success is the reward for wanting to do something, or for predicting the outcome of some action and achieving it. Often handicapped children and babies can see what they want to do but because of their disability, they fail. The effect of this is that they become less confident and more apathetic.

It is important that we plan for them to succeed. The next section will discuss how we can do so.

To sum up

The important things to remember about teaching your baby are :

1. To provide a good *learning environment* you need :

   (a) *Variety of stimulation*
   (b) *Organisation and order.*

   Try to establish the baby's *routine*, then introduce *flexibility* gradually. Provide easy *access* to toys, and order and *consistency* in the child's world so that he learns to know what to expect and why to expect it.
2. Young children learn a great deal by *imitation*, so you need to think about your *models of behaviour*. Remember that it is more difficult for the mentally handicapped child to see the important cues in actions, so you will need to *emphasise your actions more* and *teach him to imitate.*
3. Give the baby *time to respond* and *time to persist*. Don't jump in too soon. Use your observation of *referent looking* to help you to see when to interrupt.
4. Every baby needs *love and care. Consistency* in your response to the baby helps him to build up a secure relationship. Cries for attention are cries for stimulation and need a response. Help the

baby to build up confidence, and be aware of the dangers of overprotection.

5. It is easy to *overdo the teaching*. Remember to do *a little at a time*, don't *bombard* the baby with too much information, give him time when *switching* from one activity to another, *stop while it is still fun*, encourage him to use his own *initiative*; and remember that sometimes it is necessary to *get around a problem* for the *time being*.

Make sure that you *stress the relevant cues* by keeping the number of things to attend to small, and by intensifying the important cues.

6. You need to encourage and develop *initiative and motivation*. There are four things to remember in order to do this—the baby needs:

(i) *Security and confidence*.

(ii) *Access to toys* and *opportunity for exploration*.

(iii) *Novelty*—he learns from a mismatch between what he expects and what happens. New things, which are not too far beyond his range of experience, will interest him.

(iv) *Success*—it is important to plan for the baby to be successful in what he is doing so that he does not become less motivated through constant failure.

6 : How to plan your teaching

Two essential rules of teaching are :

1. *Work from the known to the unknown*; start with something the child can do and work to the next stage that he cannot do.
2. *Know exactly what it is you are trying to teach.* If you don't know what you want the child to do, how can he know what it is you want him to do?

To meet these rules is not easy. You have to start by observing your child closely and finding out his strengths and weaknesses. Whenever you are unsure of what to do or your teaching is not working, stop and observe.

WHAT TO TEACH

The first stage in observation of the baby is to go through the developmental checklist. This will direct you towards the areas you need to work on. Having pinpointed what the baby can do, and the next step in the developmental progression, you will need to observe in detail the child's behaviours when he is playing on his own, and also to set up little test games.

From these observations you should make a short list of things he can do, and the things he needs to learn next. It is also useful to look ahead a little and get some idea of where these behaviours are taking you.

Let us take the example of a Down's Syndrome baby, who might be anything from 7–12 months of age, and look at the kind of first list we might make (see p. 124).

As you see, even in this preliminary list, considerable detail is needed. We also note the next small step in development. But even these steps are too big for the detailed planning of a teaching programme, and in later chapters you will find a number of examples of planning the teaching of smaller steps.

You will also note that we have a 'how to teach' column. When you are making your list you will often have ideas about how to teach, so make a quick note in this column to remind you when you work out your teaching plan.

To make the list, you can start either with 'things he can do' or with 'things to do next'. Often you will find that it is only as you write down what you think he needs to do next, that you realise what he needs to be able to do before he can take the next step. For number 12 on the chart, for example—finding half-hidden objects—you see that what he needs to be able to do is not only to reach but also to sit and to look for hidden objects in other situations. As you learn to analyse in this way, you begin to get a good idea of how many skills in development fit together and help each other. You will also be less likely to make the mistake of concentrating on just one area, instead of looking at the whole development of the baby.

None of us is very good at first at observing our own children : observation is a skill that needs constant practice. So if at this stage you think that this is all rather complicated and time-consuming, don't worry. You are just learning the skill and will need to take it slowly. Once you get into the way of doing it you will not spend so long on the lists. Soon, in fact, many parents find they can do without listing in detail, except when they come across a particularly difficult problem. In later chapters we have tried to give plenty of practical models to work with.

HOW TO TEACH: INSTRUCTION

We have already made a number of general points about how to teach. We have noted the importance of a happy relationship, of finding the right time to teach particular activities, of not doing too much at one time or bombarding the child with stimulation, of giving him time to respond, and of accentuating cues.

Table 1

THINGS HE CAN DO	TO DO NEXT	HOW TO TEACH
1. Balance his head	Complete	
2. Pull himself almost to a sitting position holding on to your hands. (No head lag)	Pull up completely by self	(i) Keep pulling up (ii) Lying on stomach—pushing up
3. Sit with slight support	Sit for one or two seconds without support	Practice sitting; use high chair and support cushion
4. Rolls from back to side	Roll over on to stomach	Use toys to encourage rolling over
5. Reach up and grab suspended objects when on his back	Finished but still need to practice	
6. Reaches out and grasps suspended objects in line of vision when sitting on your knee	1. Pick up objects off table 2. Grasp objects held above line of vision	
7. Uses his thumb and fingers in grasping cubes and largish toys	1. Use thumb and forefinger 2. Pick up smaller objects with thumb and fingers	
8. Supports weight on legs for several seconds	1. Support weight for longer time 2. Begin to bend knees and straighten up again	Bouncing on knees and standing on floor
9. Can hold an object for a long time	Bang objects	Show him how to bang; use range of objects and physical prompts
10. (i) Takes objects to mouth (ii) Chews biscuits and solids (iii) Drinks from cup	1. Start feeding self with biscuit, crust 2. Begin to hold cup	Put favourite biscuit in hand. Take it up to his mouth

THINGS HE CAN DO	TO DO NEXT	HOW TO TEACH
11. Turns head to sounds	To make sounds for self by banging, shaking different objects	
12. (i) Plays peek-a-boo (ii) Pulls cloth off mum's face (iii) Looks for object fallen out of view (briefly) (iv) Can pick up objects off table (v) Sit in high chair with support	Find an object half hidden, or hidden under cloth	1. Keep play peep—but stay hidden for longer time 2. Cover objects held in hand (a) noisy (b) silent object 3. Half cover favourite toy on table 4. Play at noisy objects disappearing under table then reappearing

There are three teaching procedures which you will need to use when teaching any skill. They are modelling and demonstration, shaping, and prompting and cueing.

1. Modelling and demonstration

We have already discussed modelling, but it is worth emphasising. After you have observed the child, and decided on the task you want to teach, always start by giving him a clear and precise model. This is how you tell him what it is you want him to do. Always make sure that you have his *attention* when you show him the model.

2. Shaping

Let's imagine the potter making a jug or vase. He starts with a lump of clay and the first step is to get it rounded and centrally balanced in the middle of the wheel. The next step is to make a small hollow in the middle by raising the sides. Next he gradually brings up more clay from the middle and base to raise the sides higher. The pot is slowly taking shape. Soon he will begin to develop the type of vase he wants. He has been shaping the vase by a series of small steps, each new one building on the one before. To be able to shape a vase you need to know what each step is, and how it is built into the next step. You have to have a plan or programme for each vase or jug.

Behaviours and skills are the same. Each is made up of small steps fitting together in a given way. We need to analyse each skill, break it down into its parts and work out a plan for teaching it step by step. Then we shape it up. Turn to Section 3 and study some examples of these plans set out step-by-step. If in making the vase the potter has not completed one step thoroughly, the vase will collapse or turn out differently from the way it was planned. It is the same in shaping behaviours. Each step must be *sufficiently mastered* to allow the next step to be built on to it.

3. Prompting and cueing

Often, even after we have demonstrated to the child the step we want him to learn, he still finds it too difficult. To make it easier for him, we use prompts. For example, if we are teaching reaching and the child does not reach up for the object, we take his elbow and encourage him to bring his arm up. If we want the child to grasp an object, we try to stimulate a grasp by touching his hand, fingers or palm with the object : If this does not work, we put the object in his hand, then mould his fingers around it —this is the prompt. If we are teaching him to step forward and he does not move his feet, we take his foot and move it for him.

The important thing about using a prompt is to use it only when necessary, and to fade it out as soon as you can. Fading it out is simply using less and less of the prompt. In walking for example, you may need to grip the foot firmly at first and move it forward. Gradually you have to use less strength as the child learns to step. The last stage of the prompt might be just tapping the back of the heel.

Remember, always try to get the behaviour *before* you use the prompt and always use the smallest prompt possible.

Prompting can also be an 'attention getter', or a reminder of what to do. If you are teaching the child to complete a jig-saw with round and square shapes, for example, you would first give him a jigsaw with two shapes only. Let him explore and play. If he does not complete it, you take out each shape and, making sure he is watching you, put them back in the jig-saw. You then hand him the round one, leaving the square in place. If he does not put it in the hole, but sucks it, taps it or throws it, you get his attention and tap the hole—this is a visual prompt—saying 'put it in'. If this fails, you go back to a physical prompt and guide his hand until he puts the piece in the hole. Then you say 'good boy' and give him a cuddle.

Let's consider an older child who is naming objects in a picture book. You know he can say 'doggy' or something equivalent, and so when the picture of the dog appears you say 'what is it?' If he does not respond—and remember to give him time to pat the dog, stroke it, and so on—you might give a verbal prompt by saying 'd———'. (If on the other hand 'dog' was a new word, you would first give him a model by saying very clearly 'dog' while he was watching your lips).

Again, the thing to remember is not to use prompts unless you need to, and to *fade* them out as quickly as possible.

You probably use prompts and cues all the time without knowing it. And prompts that we are unaware of can be misleading. As an example, one of us was trying to teach some mentally handicapped children to match pictures of objects and shapes. Sitting opposite a child, he placed two pictures on the table. He then held up a third, which was the same as one of the two on the table, and said 'Show me the same'. The child had to point to the matching picture. He found, much to his surprise, that the children all learnt to match the pictures very quickly, and could even match difficult letter shapes and abstract drawings. Finally, practising what he preached, he started to observe the children more closely. He noticed that before they pointed to the picture they would first look at him. If he was looking at them, they often did not respond, but if he looked down at the pictures they pointed to the one he was looking at—sometimes even leaning towards!

There are three morals to this tale :

(i) Mentally handicapped children may have learning difficulties but they are not stupid !

(ii) Always try to observe and analyse what is happening when you are teaching.

(iii) Plan the use of prompts and cues to aid the learning—but do not let them become so established that the child will not respond without them. This is a particular hazard with prompts that you are not aware of.

A common illustration of this last point arises in teaching an everyday activity—in teaching a child to put his coat on. You hold up the coat, and the child puts one arm into one arm of the coat. Then you take the coat around the back ready for the other arm, and take hold of this second arm and guide it into the armhole. This is a physical prompt. Because one is usually in a hurry to go out when putting on the child's coat, it is a great temptation to keep up this prompt. But if you do so, what you are teaching the child is simply to stand and wait until you put his arm in the coat! One day, when it does dawn on you that he should be able to get his second arm in the coat by himself, you find that you need to *undo* the 'stand and wait' training (which by then is well practised) before the training of the new behaviour can start.

There is another pitfall involved in teaching a child to put on a coat that is worth mentioning here. Because the child is so much shorter than you, the temptation is to hold the coat up high for the second arm, so that the child has to bring his arm *up* into the coat. Now try putting a coat on yourself, and observe how you get the second arm into the coat: you bring your arm *down* into the coat around the back—a movement totally different from taking the arm up and pushing out. Because we have not worked out the correct sequence of small steps used in putting on a coat, we may have spent months or even years teaching a totally inappropriate behaviour! To a slow learning child, unlearning a 'wrong' behaviour takes as long as learning a new behaviour.

There is one final thing that it is useful to know about prompts and cues: we can begin to build up a set of cues which can be used across various teaching situations. For example, if we teach the baby to respond to the cue 'look' whenever we say it, we can use it to attract his attention in many teaching situations. The way we teach this is to take an object which we think the baby will like and hold it up just out of his vision. We then say 'look' or 'look John', loudly and clearly. If he does not turn to look, we repeat the cue, and at the same time turn his head towards the object (a physical prompt). We hold the object between our face and the baby's, and when he is looking, say again 'look', shake it and give it to him. If we get into the habit of doing this to attract his attention, he will gradually learn to look when we call 'look'.

Other useful general cues are 'show me' (meaning 'point to'), or 'give me'. These are also helpful when teaching language.

Cues and actions. It is useful to think of cues as signals for action. The telephone rings (cue), you pick it up (action); the child looks at you with a frightened expression (cue), you reassure him by smiling, speaking or picking him up (action); your stomach rumbles (cue), you look for food (action); you see the cup of tea (cue), you pick it up (action). In other words, anything can be a cue if it is followed by an action.

The actions or behaviours which follow a cue are not haphazard. They are usually expected and predictable, that is, they are appropriate for the cue. You do not expect someone to eat with a pencil or try to write with a spoon. Seen like this, much of our learning about the order of the world involves fitting the appropriate action to the cue.

But how do we find out which action fits the cue? We do this by taking note of the *consequences*.

Consequences follow an action. They can be pleasurable or unpleasurable. If they are pleasurable and rewarding, we are likely to seek them out—we will want to learn about the cues and appropriate behaviours which result in pleasurable consequences. If, on the other hand, the consequences are not rewarding but punishing, when we see the cue we will search for behaviours and actions to avert the consequences. If the consequences are neither rewarding nor punishing we will probably not fit the action to the cue at all.

If it is the consequence of our action that helps us to associate the appropriate action to the cue, then the sooner the consequence follows the action the more likely we are to fit them together. In the case of shaking a bell or using a pencil, the consequences are immediate. But often the consequences are not so obvious, *or* they do not give the child sufficient reward by themselves. When, for example, we are trying to teach the child to use the potty or toilet, the fact that he performs may not be particularly rewarding for him. However, if we reward him with our approval (cuddles, smiles or 'good boys') *immediately* he performs, he is more likely to repeat the action in future. When we reward him, we are doing two things : we are making the consequences of his actions pleasurable; and we are telling him that that is the correct and appropriate action. If our approval is

E

not sufficiently rewarding, we may need to look for something else : sweets, or a favourite toy to play with.

ORDERING THE TEACHING STEPS

Once we have worked out the sequence of steps or stages in a task, we need to ask what order to teach them in. It would seem commonsense to say from the first to the last; but this is not always the case.

Let us start with a simple task for an older child : teaching the writing of a capital B. We can think of this in three stages :

(i)   Draw the straight line—I.
(ii) Draw the top loop—P.
(iii) Draw the bottom loop—B.

This sequence follows the way most people form the capital B. To complete the task the child has to do three things. However, we can also teach this way :

(i)   We give the child the incomplete shape **ℬ** and he has to complete it with a straight line.
(ii) When he can do this well, we give the child **ℬ** , and he completes two steps to form the B.
(iii) Then we present an outline **ℬ** , and he completes all three steps.

In this plan the child only has to do *one new* step each time, and he always ends by *completing* the task. Therefore, we are rewarding him for both the individual steps and for completing the task. If we can assume the child is really motivated to write a B, then by always ending up with the capital B, we are utilising his interest.

Let us look at a dressing task. To put on our pants or knickers we :

(i) Pick them up and check that they are the right way around, e.g. the label is towards us or the front panel of the underpants is facing away from us.
(ii) Hold them at the side, step in with one leg, and pull up— not too far, making sure that the foot is through and clear of the pants.

(iii) Step in with the other leg.

(iv) Pull the pants up to the waist. Often we need to reach around the back and pull them up—they get stuck under the buttocks, especially if the hands have been placed too near the front and centre. Then we straighten the top.

If we teach this task in sequence (i)–(iv), the child has to take at least four different steps to complete the task. He is likely to meet many setbacks and failures, and so the whole task tends to be unsatisfying. If he wants to 'do it himself' and have the satisfaction that he has done it, then we need to plan the teaching to give him this reward.

We can do this, again, by working backwards through the steps, starting with the last step of pulling up the pants. This can be made easier by having them high up the legs at first, and then making him pull them further and further.

In this example it is worth noting also that for the young child, the last step is probably the easiest, and will come earliest in his development. Once he can stand and stoop a little, he can pull the pants up around his waist. Gradually, as he gains balance and coordination, he can stoop, stand on one leg and step into the pants.

Of course, there are always alternatives to every plan. In this task, if a child finds balancing on one leg difficult, we can teach him to sit down, then put the pants on over the feet, pull up to the knees, and then stand and complete the task.

When you have analysed a task to teach, ask yourself whether you can teach it backwards, so that the child always ends up completing the task. In this way you will capitalise upon the child's satisfaction *in doing it himself*, without having to go through a long series of stages.

Working backwards through a plan can also be useful for another reason. If you have a plan of action that contains many simplified steps, using prompts and cues, by always starting with the simplest step you may be going over ground with which the child is already familiar, and so you may be able to build on his own initiative.

As a simple example, let's assume that you have a new toy for the baby, which demands knocking pegs through holes using a hammer. The behaviour you want (your objective) is that the

baby picks up the hammer and knocks the pegs into the holes.
You may :

(i) Place the hammer in his hand.

(ii) Hold his hand and hammer, and bang it on the pegs. This would be the prompt and also the model.

(iii) Release the hand—i.e. remove the prompt—and let him bang it himself.

(iv) Place the hammer and toy within reach and encourage the baby to bang the pegs.

But if, instead of teaching from (i)–(iv), you start with (iv) and simply give the baby the opportunity to hammer, he may soon discover for himself what to do *or* he may already know what to do. If he has used hammers to bang with before, or played banging on drums and tins, he may transfer this behaviour to the new toy. Obviously it is better for this to happen—for him to learn to discover and explore, and to transfer his learning to new situations—than to be taken through the programme. Of course, if after several minutes or opportunities he is still not using the toy, and if you have not observed him banging other toys, then you go through the plan.

Finally, let's take a more complicated example. The baby wakes at night and cries. Your objective is for him to go back to sleep as quickly as possible—assuming he is not ill or in discomfort. There are several things that you can do and we can put them in a sequence of steps :

(i) Put the light on in his room, pick him up, take him downstairs until he is quiet or goes to sleep, or take him to your own bed.

(ii) Put the light on, pick him up, and walk around talking to him, looking at things, etc.—but do not take him out of the room.

(iii) Pick him up and cuddle him, walk about, talk to him—but do not put the light on.

(iv) Pick him up, cuddle him, talk quietly—but do not walk about or jog him up and down.

(v) Sit by the side of the cot or bed, stroke his head or back and talk gently—but do not pick him up.

(vi) Bend over the cot or bed, stroke him—tell him to go to

sleep gently—but do not talk too much or settle down yourself.

(vii) Stroke him and tell him to go to sleep.

In each step the behaviour you want is for the baby to quiet down and go back to sleep. If you start with step (vii) and then work backwards, giving yourself a reasonable amount of time before going back to the next step, you will have a chance of finding the least disruptive step each time. If you always take the baby downstairs, then you are not only providing an opportunity for him to wake up, but also a possible reward : being downstairs may be more exciting than being in bed.

Of course, it is up to you to decide whether it is more rewarding for you to go through the plan in the hope that you will teach the baby to stay in bed and go to sleep, *or* whether it is more rewarding for you to let him come down or take him into bed.

The problem with the latter course of action is that, whilst he may 'grow out of the behaviour' and sleep through the night—especially when he goes to school and is tired—you risk that he may in fact learn *not* to go to sleep or not to stay in bed.

If you decide to try the backward-working plan :

(*a*) Listen to the baby's breathing as you sit by the cot. This will give you an indication of when he is settling and dropping off to sleep, so that you can decide when to creep out.

(*b*) Try to find out what soothes the baby best—stroking his head, his belly, rubbing his back or gently stroking his cheek. Each baby will have his own preferences, and;

(*c*) If you have got the baby working to this plan, so that you do not usually need to go back more than two or three steps, you will be better able to decide whether he is unwell or particularly upset on those nights when it does not work.

A final point on sleeping. It often helps to establish a routine (plan) which you put into action just before the child goes to bed. For example :

(i) 'Time for bed in five minutes.'

(ii) 'Here's a little drink—bed soon.'

(iii) 'Have you got teddy—he must be tired.'

(iv) 'Switch off the TV.'

(v) 'Say night-night to. . . .'

(vi) 'Come on—off we go—bye-bye everyone.'

Each step in this plan acts as cue or signal to the next step, and gradually brings the child to the final behaviour of going to bed. In this case the order of the steps is crucial. They are deliberately placed in a *consistent* sequence. The first step is a long way from the act of going to bed, and so the child is so much the less likely to react unfavourably. Gradually the behaviour is brought a little closer. Of course, if the child is not ready for bed, i.e. is not tired, you will have problems—usually after he has got to bed. Similarly, many young children can get 'over-tired' and start to become active and excited. This too will cause problems. You need to pick the timing, and learn to observe the child for the signs that he is getting pleasantly tired.

Having said all this, there is no guarantee that any strategy will work with every child. But provided you are consistent, a programme such as we suggest can help reduce 'bed-problems' with many children.

To sum up so far

1. We must work out *exactly* what it is we want the child to learn. This should be a piece of behaviour which we want the child *to be able to do* after our teaching that he could not do before.

If you have chosen the behaviour correctly it should be :

(*a*) Something the child needs to learn and which has some use in his everyday activities.

(*b*) Something you can expect him to learn in the next few days or weeks. Not next month or year !

(*c*) Something you know that he is ready to learn, and for which he has already acquired all the behaviours needed to build it upon.

2. You should have a plan of the very small steps which make up the behaviour.

3. You should have placed them in an order which makes sense, and then decide whether it is best to teach them forwards or backwards. Also you should note any steps the child already knows.

4. You should have a good idea of the materials, toys, situations which will help him learn the behaviour.

5. You should have an idea of the prompts and cues you might use.

6. You should know what the consequences are for the child, and what rewards you may need to use.

An example of this type of plan is given at the end of this chapter.

At first, when you are teaching yourself the skill of teaching your child, you should always choose small and simple behaviours to aim at, and make a thorough plan—write it down. You need to try to make sure that *you* will succeed. If you succeed you are more likely to try again. But please do not give up. *All parents are very capable of becoming skilled teachers of a handicapped child, but it does take time and application.*

IF YOU FAIL

Even the best of teachers and parents meet failure. The child does not progress, the behaviour is not learnt. Too often we blame this on the handicap.

It is so easy to say he behaves in certain ways because he is handicapped, or he cannot learn it because he is handicapped. This may sometimes be true. But more often we fail because our planning and teaching did not match the child's abilities. If you blame failure on the handicap you may stop teaching. If you stop teaching, there is no chance of maintaining progress at its best level.

From our experience, failure to meet aims arises from two main sources.

1. The step-size in the learning plan was too large. In other words, we expected the child to learn too much at one step, or to learn more quickly than he was able. Usually we find that we have not broken the behaviour down into small enough steps, or that we have not been building upon skills which have already been well mastered. For example, we try to teach the child to put small pegs in a pegboard without first finding out whether he can hold a small peg, twist his wrist, look at a small hole, place an object in a container, or fit a large peg in a large hole.

So, when things are not going well, check your plan and look for smaller steps.

2. The consequences and rewards of the behaviour were not sufficient, or were even punishing. The child was not interested in performing the act; or, because the step-size was too big, he was failing and so soon learnt to avoid the teaching.

Always ask yourself, is he interested, what is the reward for him, what is he getting out of it?

Two other things are worth noting.

Sometimes the child is progressing, but the progress is so small you do not notice it. When this happens, all you can do is try to find a better way of measuring. For example, you may be trying to teach the child to reach out and grab the rattle you hold in front of him. You know the child looks at the rattle and you know he can reach and grasp. You have tried different rattles, and also cuddles and smiles, to make it rewarding; but he still reaches only occasionally and you have to keep prompting him. When this happens you may need to start to count how often he reaches without the prompt.

To do this you will need to set up a little test. Each day at the same time, present him with the rattle and encourage him to reach for it without prompting. Give him a certain amount of time to reach—say ten seconds—and if he does not do so, wait for a few seconds, then try again. Repeat this for ten presentations of the rattle and keep a score of how many times he reached. After several days you will be able to look at your record sheet and see if he is, in fact, reaching more often.

Sometimes, even when we have tried all this, we still do not find progress. If this happens, and only when we have tried everything we can think of to help, we may have to conclude that the child is not ready to learn the new behaviour. That is, the maturational part of the child's development has not advanced sufficiently. Because we know so little about the early development of mentally handicapped babies, we can never be sure that this is the case. But our experiences do indicate that handicapped babies can get stuck at certain stages in development, and that we cannot do much to bring them on until they are ready. For example, with many Down's Syndrome babies, we have found that we can get them to walk with help quite quickly, but that they then take an unexpectedly long time to reach the next stage of standing alone, and then taking one or two independent steps. This does not mean they are not developing, only that we cannot *see* development. After all, walking with help and walking independently means developing and coordinating our sense of balance with our muscle system, and so these periods of getting stuck may simply be periods of further preparation. However, parents do often say that babies get stuck, then suddenly they *can* do it. The danger in these 'getting stuck' times is that *you* become anxious and frustrated—so you stop helping. Try to understand the problem, and do not blame yourself for the apparent lack of progress.

If you really think the baby is stuck and you cannot find a way of making the learning easier, then leave this task and concentrate on another area which does seem to be moving forward. But do not give up. Every few days, do a little probe. Test to see if he is still stuck, and when you think you detect some change in the baby's response try your teaching plan again. (Don't just wait until he can do it.) After all, if he can do it, you do not need to teach.

E*

STAGES OF LEARNING

In this final section we will look at teaching children skills from a different angle. You will recognise many of the ideas already discussed in the chapter.

The learning of a new skill can be thought of as passing through four stages :

1. Acquisition.
2. Proficiency.
3. Maintenance.
4. Generalisation.

Acquisition

This is the stage of developing or acquiring the skill to the point that one can complete the action with some regularity.

Learning or acquiring a new skill has already been discussed in detail. But let us look briefly at a new example : the skill of eating with a spoon. We can break this up into five small parts :

1. Grasp the spoon appropriately from table.
2. Take spoon to dish.
3. Scoop food from dish.
4. Bring food to mouth.
5. Get food from spoon—in mouth.

(Repeat sequence from 2.)

Each part of the whole skill is itself a skill, which needs to be acquired before it can be used and *blended* together into the whole action. Each part must be taught thoroughly. To do this we will need to use prompts and models. In this particular example the prompts are physical. For example, we take the baby's hand and mould it around the spoon to grasp, scoop the food, bring it to the mouth, remove the food from the spoon by dragging against the upper lip, and bring the spoon down again to the bowl. Once the baby is doing this we begin to fade the prompt by (i) holding the wrist, (ii) moving down to the forearm, (iii) holding the elbow, (iv) just occasionally touching the elbow or correcting the action.

With an older child you can train the skill all at once, but with a baby you may find that he will learn some part, e.g. 2 and 4, quite easily, but others, such as 3 and 5, he may not be ready for.

You can train each part separately, then blend them together. When the baby can complete a part of the skill *or* the whole skill, with occasional prompting, you can accept that he has learnt it. He will still make quite a mess, however—occasionally missing the plate, or not getting all the food off the spoon—so the skill is not yet smooth and efficient.

This brings us to the next stage :

Proficiency

He now needs to strengthen the new behaviour and become 'skilled' in its use, by regular practice. We no longer need prompts, except occasionally to keep him going. But we may need to use more rewards. When you first learn a skill it is new and exciting. The novelty itself is rewarding. But once you have got the idea, and merely need to practise, it can become tedious —especially if you are hungry and know that mum can feed you quicker than you can feed yourself. Apart from being insistent, you will often need to be very pleased *each time he completes* the action : that is, gets the food in his mouth. 'Oh good boy, you did it *all by yourself*'. You can emphasise his independence. You may need to make sure you use some of his favourite foods at this time.

Beware. It is often at this stage that a new difficulty arises. He can do it—but won't do it. If you are going to help him, you will need to look at *the reward*. Often you will find that you have actually taught him 'won't do' because :

(i) You did not make sure that he had fully acquired the skill before you jumped on to the proficiency stage.
(ii) You tried to make the step to 'feed independently' but instead of always insisting he did it himself, you tended to take over, either because he got cross and refused *or* because he was so slow you got impatient.

If you took over when he got cross, you have *rewarded* his cross behaviour. Therefore, he will have learned to do this, again and again.

If you took over when *you* got cross—you *punished* him for performing the skill, and you also taught him that he had failed. Therefore, he will have learned not to try.

In both cases you *prevented* him from having the *practice* he needs to become proficient.

Of course, life isn't so simple. If baby is very hungry and is not yet very proficient you may need to give him the first few spoonsful to take the edge off his hunger. Often you will need to give him the last two or three spoonsful as well because he is not hungry enough to want to eat more—but always wait at this point until he has really stopped feeding himself, and he is *not* demanding to be fed.

The next stage after gaining proficiency—and closely related to it—is maintaining the behaviour.

Maintenance
This means not allowing the new behaviour to disappear for lack of use. Most behaviours will be maintained because they are needed in other new behaviours, e.g. grasping is used in play, feeding, dressing. Feeding skills are maintained because the child needs to eat regularly and using fingers—that is for gooey food— is not very efficient or acceptable. But if a baby moves on from soft to solid or lumpy foods, which can most easily be handled by the fingers, the spoon feeding skill could disappear. So you need to plan for the maintenance of the behaviours learnt, and also to make sure that you insist the child does them for himself. There are often long periods between the development of preliminary behaviours and other later ones : using words, for example, is built upon 'babbling', linking up sounds, and sing-song noises; but it can take a long time for the mentally handicapped child to get to the words themselves, so you need to keep the 'babbling' going, through games, and not allow it to disappear.

Most skills are maintained because they bring rewards from the environment. If you get dressed you can go out, if you walk you can find interesting new things, if you can feed yourself you can satisfy your hunger. You need to think about the reward for the child in the behaviour, and to link the two together as much as possible.

Generalisation
Once you have learnt a new behaviour and are quite proficient, you need to learn to use it in different situations. Once you can

feed yourself sticky foods with a spoon, you need to generalise the skill to other foods, such as cornflakes and soup. When you have learnt that you can drink from a two-handed blue cup, and have an idea of what cups are, you need to generalise this to other cups of different shapes and sizes, cups with one handle and so on.

This is an important step, and you should ask yourself how you can help the child to use his skills in new ways and so get the most out of them. Using new objects and toys in play is particularly useful for doing this. It will also help to maintain the new behaviour.

To sum up
When teaching your child new behaviours and skills, always check that you have thought about :

1. How you are going to teach it—acquisition.
2. How you are going to practise it—proficiency.
3. How you are going to keep it going independently—maintenance.
4. How it can be use in other ways—generalisation.

A FINAL EXAMPLE

To sum up this chapter we have produced a plan for teaching feeding with a spoon.

Behaviour : Feeding self with spoon at table.

Steps :
1. Grasps the spoon appropriately by handle from the table.
2. Takes spoon to dish.
3. Scoops food from dish—(i) Dish fixed.
                          (ii) Control dish with other hand.
4. Brings food to mouth.
5. Gets food from spoon using lips.

Prompts :
(*a*) Hand held.
(*b*) Wrist held.

(c) Forearm held.

(d) Elbow held.

(e) Occasional touch/reshaping.

For steps 2 and 4, prompt can be faded by 'letting go' of baby at longer and longer distances from mouth or dish, e.g. take spoon to within one inch of mouth, then let baby complete the task.

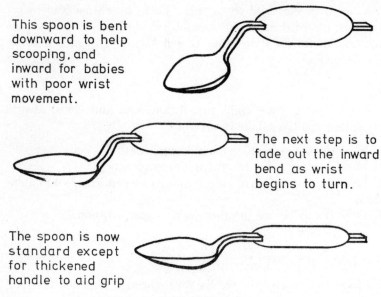

This spoon is bent downward to help scooping, and inward for babies with poor wrist movement.

The next step is to fade out the inward bend as wrist begins to turn.

The spoon is now standard except for thickened handle to aid grip

Figure 1. Adaptation of spoons

Aids :

1. Use gooey/sticky food at first.

2. Use plenty of food in dish.

3. Use dish with a raised edge so that spoon can be pushed against it to get food on to spoon.

4. If baby has poor grasp, build up spoon handle with tape, rubber hose, bicycle handle or modelling clay to make it easier to grip.

5. If he has poor wrist action, or rigidity in elbow and wrist joints, which prevent him from turning spoon into mouth, bend the spoon accordingly.

Note : Aids 4 and 5 can be faded by reducing the size of handle and bend in spoon.

6. Make sure plate is firm on table. Use non-slip surface or rubber disc on bottom of plate : a rubber soap holder is very useful for this.

Note : When step 3 (i) is learnt, teach the baby to control the dish with other hand and fade out rubber disc.

Teaching points

1. It is best to stand behind and to one side of the baby when prompting. When prompts (*a*)–(*d*) are faded out, come round to sit at side of table to increase 'socialisation' of feeding.

2. It may be best to teach feeding when the rest of the family are *not* present, to reduce distraction. When the skill has been acquired, you can generalise the training to new situations and introduce the rest of the family.

3. The child should be reasonably hungry when you start teaching, *but*

(*a*) if he is very hungry he may not be willing to put up with the 'slowness' of teaching, so give him a few mouthfuls to take the edge off his appetite;

(*b*) near the end of the task he may not be hungry enough to keep up his interest in the food. Do not go on too long and so put him off. Tell him he is very good, then pick up the spoon and dish after a little pause. Give him the last two or three spoonfuls if you think he needs them.

Rewards : His interest will depend upon the reward for him, so :

(*a*) At first use foods that the baby likes. Later you can gradually change them into more lumpy and more adult foods.

(*b*) Reward him after each correct act—with smiles and 'good boys'. Fade this out as he acquires the behaviour.

Readiness Behaviours : Before starting the training check :

(*a*) Is baby taking and chewing strained solids?
(*b*) Is baby finger feeding?
(*c*) Can he grasp a rod or spoon?
(*d*) Can he bang, pat the table (i.e. where the dish will be)?
(*e*) For step 3(ii), is he using two hands when playing with objects at the table?

Order of training : The order of training is related to the fading out of the prompts. It is in reverse of the step sequence. You start to release the hand prompt when the child has the food in the mouth. He should then bring it up against his lips to get the food off. You can fade the prompt by moving your hand down the arm and letting go sooner. The way this is done is entirely up to you and your child. The last step to fade the prompt on is scooping from the dish.

This sounds well ordered but the baby will probably be able to pick up the spoon by himself—so let him do this. Then take hold of the hand and start the prompt.

Record Chart: You can use a record chart which *shows the prompts.*

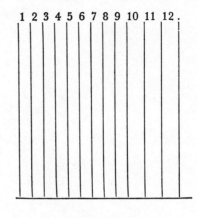

DAY/DATE   1 2 3 4 5 6 7 8 9 10 11 12 .

1. Picks up spoon apropriately

   (i) hand prompt

   (ii) wrist prompt

   (iii) forearm prompt

   (iv) elbow prompt

   (v) occasional prompt (e.g.
        attracting attention to spoon)

   (vi) No prompts

or a list of the steps in order
e.g.

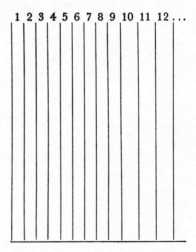

DAY/DATE   1 2 3 4 5 6 7 8 9 10 11 12 ...

1. Moves hand to mouth and gets
   food—hand prompt

2. Moves hand to mouth and gets
   food—wrist prompt

3. Hand released two inches from
   mouth—wrist prompt

4. Hand released four inches from
   mouth—wrist prompt

5. Hand released four inches from
   mouth—forearm prompt
   and so until the final step

Final Step: Baby scoops food and
takes to mouth—no prompts

The number of steps you work out in this list will depend upon the degree of handicap of the baby.

Note: No parent really has the time to work out such detailed plans as this for every behaviour. You always need to have a good idea of exactly what it is you are going to teach; but, provided you think you are making reasonable progress, you do not need to worry too much about details of prompting, rewarding and recording. It is when you find you are making little or no progress that you need to analyse in detail. Check the plan again. Check the readiness behaviours, the rewards, the prompts, and begin to record.

PRACTICAL GUIDELINES

Introduction

In this section we have attempted to provide details of exercises and games which you can use to stimulate your baby's development. We start with the newly born baby who is highly dependent upon mother for his needs and has little ability to act upon his world, and end with the independent, self-willed toddler who is constantly asserting his desires and exploring all the facets of his immediate world.

To watch this dramatic change occur, to see the unique individual child begin to emerge, and to share with him the excitement of new skills and discoveries, can be a remarkable experience. For the parent of the handicapped baby this journey can be just as exciting as it is for the parent of a normal baby—indeed, many parents have told us that in spite of their added hardships and their doubts about the future, they have gained even more from the experience of the child who needed them so much and with whose development they have had to be so involved. Of course, there are always exceptions. But we hope that you will find it deeply rewarding to observe and stimulate your child's development, and we are sure that if you do, the child will benefit.

The dramatic changes that occur in the first year of life seem to fall into three-monthly periods of normal development—each period having its own distinct characteristics. Because of this, and to make the organisation of this section of the book easier to follow, we have broken the first year's development down into three-monthly periods. However, you must always remember that behaviours build upon each other and so you should follow their progression across these periods.

By the time the baby has reached the second year his development has become so complex and so individual that it is no longer reasonable to break it up into small periods. Instead we have dealt with this year of development under the different areas.

Before you begin with practical help we would like to emphasise some points.

1. These are guidelines to suggest what you might try, not recipes to be followed exactly.

2. To make the ideas as clear as possible we have often simplified them. You may find that they sound too easy: 'Do this and results will follow!' This is not so. You will need to try them out and observe what happens. If you see little progress you will need to adapt them, to plan smaller steps and simpler behaviours.

3. The guidelines are not complete by themselves. You will need to think up other stimulation and, of course, do all the things one does with any baby. After all, your child is a baby first and handicapped second.

4. We have written the guidelines with mum and dad in mind, but of course brothers and sisters, grandmas and grandads can be of enormous help. If you have other children in the family they will teach the baby a great deal. You can sometimes make this teaching more effective if you know your objective and indicate it to them. You must be careful, however, of overdoing this and interfering too much with the children's natural interaction and play.

5. Our approach is to try to predict the baby's next step forward and to encourage it. To do this we use the developmental checklist and, of course, observations of the baby. However, there are two possible dangers in this 'looking ahead' approach.

First, it can give you the impression that the baby's development should be faster. This can cause anxiety in you, which can be transmitted to the baby.

Second, it can also cause you to 'push ahead' too quickly.

You need to give the baby time to consolidate, practice, and explore his new skills before pushing on. Try to lead the baby gently forward. If he has just acquired a new skill, give him the time and opportunity to explore it. Observe closely what he does —keeping in mind the next step forward—and let him indicate when he is ready to move on. Of course, this does not mean you cannot 'probe' his development with little games to test if he is ready to move on.

6. Throughout the guidelines, we have referred to the items in the developmental checklist so that you can use your list to see where your baby's development fits in.

7. We would remind you that ages in the checklist are averages for normal children. They tend to indicate when the behaviour can first be found in babies rather than when they are well established *and easily observed. Again, this may cause you unnecessary anxiety if you keep comparing your baby with them.*

8. *For the same reason we will repeat that all babies differ greatly in the age they show these behaviours. Handicapped babies will vary even more than normal babies. Please use the average ages as indicators of the developmental sequence, not as absolutes.*

9. *As the baby gets older he will show his individuality more and more. One way in which this happens is that he develops faster in some areas than others. For example, some babies develop quickly in the gross motor activities, such as sitting and walking, but are slower to use their hands or in communicating. Because of this, and because of special problems the handicapped baby often has, you may find that he is progressing in some areas at the three-six month stage, but at six-to-nine months in others.*

10. *Because handicapped babies develop more slowly than normal babies, you will also find that you may be working on the under-three-month section when he is many months older. This can be very discouraging, but it is the reality of the handicap and it is this that one needs to come to terms with. However, do not assume that this is always due to the handicap. It can also be due to the variability we mentioned above. It can be due to slowness in one area temporarily holding up another. No baby develops at a constant rate—all have their fast times and their slow times. If the baby is unwell or unsettled for any reason, or if other problems in the family reduce the amount of attention the baby gets for a while, this too will temporarily effect progress.* What really matters is that your baby is progressing at his best possible speed.

11. *On a similar point, the items in the checklist do not follow a constant rate. The time it takes the baby to get from one behaviour to the next varies greatly between different behaviours. It is useful to look at the average ages given between similar items to get an idea of the time scale. You may also find that, by noting the dates on which items are achieved, you can begin to get an idea of your baby's rate of development. This is useful in judging when new behaviours can be expected. But again, always remember these are estimations and will vary.*

12. *The baby is not a set of separate activities—he is a whole*

person. There is a danger of concentrating on one area of his development and so losing sight of how different areas fit together, and how the baby uses them in everyday activities. To help you keep the whole baby in mind, we have started each chapter with a description of the baby's all-round development during this time. Keep this in mind when using the separate games and when thinking up your plans for stimulation.

If you read the introductions to all the chapters in this section first, they will give you an overview of what to expect.

13. The guidelines have many ideas and exercises. It is likely that you will find that to try to do all the activities each day is impossible. It is also probably unnecessary. Remember what we said at the beginning of the book: give the baby as much attention as you can but keep the family as normal and as balanced as possible.

14. Finally, we have written these guidelines not only so that your handicapped baby will develop but also so that you can feel more able to help. We feel that this will help you enjoy the baby and he you. Do try to make all the exercises and games good fun for both you and all the family. Do not create a tiresome regime out of them which gets in the way of what is, after all, the best stimulation—the natural, happy play of parent and child.

7: The first three months

The newborn baby shows a number of behaviours which we call 'reflexes'. In response to a particular stimuli, he produces certain actions involuntarily—in the same way that your leg jerks forward when your knee is tapped just below the knee-cap.

In the first weeks of life, when you hold him in a standing position with his feet against a firm surface, he will make stepping movements (the 'walking reflex'). (See Figure 5.)

When you put your finger in the palm of his hand he will grasp it (the 'grasp reflex').

He usually lies with his head towards one side and his arm straight out on the same side ('the tonic-neck reflex'); and if you stroke his cheek he will start mouthing for food and turn towards the touch ('the rooting reflex').

Most of these behaviours disappear, sometimes reappearing in a different way at a later stage. For instance, the tonic-neck reflex gradually disappears so that by three months the baby usually lies with his head in the middle position and not turned to the side. Often the walking reflex also disappears and then, much later, the baby starts stepping out again.

One of the main characteristics of the very young baby is his lack of coordination and muscle strength. If you place him on his stomach he does not lift his chin off the mat; if you hold him in a sitting position his back is very rounded and his head falls forward—he has not got the strength in his muscles to keep his back straight and his head up. Also his hands are usually closed and he cannot move his eyes around to look at things in any controlled way. If you move an object across his line of vision, he is not able to follow it if it is moving quickly, and even if it is moving slowly he will jerk his eyes bit by bit rather than follow it smoothly.

However, during the first three months all these behaviours change.

If you look back to the development profile, you will see the main areas in which development takes place during the first three months. These are :

1. Gross Motor.
2. Fine Motor.
3. Visual.
4. Feeding.
5. Social.
6. Vocalisation.
7. Hearing and listening.

(Use any suitable items in the checklist as ideas for stimulation.)

GROSS MOTOR

During this period the baby develops more strength in his neck, shoulders and back muscles. He begins to hold his head up for longer and gains more central balance, so that eventually he can hold his head steady when he is swayed from side to side. When he is held in a sitting position his back becomes straight and he can hold his head up, at first for a moment or two then for longer and longer. When placed on his stomach he begins to lift his head, and then to push his shoulders and chest up as well. You may also find that he likes to push his feet against you, and will even take some of his weight when you hold him up on your lap.

FINE MOTOR

Although the baby cannot yet pick up an object, he will hold a rattle if it is placed in his hand. At first he drops the rattle almost immediately, but by the end of this period he will hold it for a few seconds. His hands will begin to remain open for longer periods—he is getting ready to grasp objects.

VISUAL

This is the area which you will see develop most in this period. The baby begins to watch you intently as you talk to him, and by three months he has already learnt to make *eye contact*. He is beginning to look round him, and he can soon follow moving people and objects with his eyes. His vision extends so that he can look at things that are further away 4–6 feet (1–2 metres).

This means his world has been considerably extended from that of a newborn baby who can focus only on close objects straight in front of him.

FEEDING

Some mentally handicapped babies present problems with feeding.

(*a*) The sucking and rooting reflexes may not be present or may be very weak.

(*b*) The baby may seem to take very little at feeds, or may feed extremely slowly. These are problems that can usually be resolved during the first three months, but you must seek the advice of your doctor, health visitor, or baby clinic if you feel you have any feeding problems. Fortunately, feeding problems are not inevitable with mentally handicapped babies and a number have good reflexes and strong sucking actions and can be breastfed.

However, mentally handicapped babies (particularly Down's Syndrome) *often grow more slowly* than normal babies. For this reason it is not possible to work out from the baby's age how much food he needs. It is also difficult to work out the amount of food needed on the basis of the baby's weight, as his weight can be expected to increase more slowly than normal. One of the main guidelines is that the baby should be gaining and not losing weight, and be generally healthy. Again your doctor, health visitor or clinic will be able to advise you on your own baby's weight gain and the amount of food he needs.

Often the baby *will not demand food* himself, so you will need to make the decision about how often he needs to be fed. This will depend partly on the amount of food he takes at each feed, and as you begin to get to know your own baby's pattern and needs you can establish a suitable feeding routine.

As the baby gets older he shows signs of his developing maturity in the way he feeds. By the end of this first period, he falls asleep less easily during a feed and he may remain wide awake and show pleasure when he has finished a feed. He can take more food at each feed and so the intervals between feeds become longer. By three to six months babies usually sleep through the night without waking for a feed.

SOCIAL

The first three months show great steps forward in social development. By three months the baby is beginning to make eye contact, to smile and to vocalise to you. His personality is beginning to emerge and he shows his pleasure by smiling and cooing when you talk to him. By this time parents tend to find themselves using the baby's name and noticing his individual behaviours: he or she is no longer 'the baby,' but Mark or Mandy, a little person.

VOCALISATION

During this period considerable development takes place in the baby's vocalisation. He moves from making noises, such as crying, coughing or sneezing, which are mainly related to hunger or discomfort. The beginning of simple vowel sounds and a range of vocalisations that include coos, chuckles, crows, laughs and squeals appear.

HEARING AND LISTENING

At birth babies can hear. They will quiet at the sound of a bell ringing, or startle to a loud noise. During the first three months this response develops so that the baby begins to search with his eyes for the source of the sound. He is therefore beginning to make the big step of associating sight with sound : already he has begun to learn about his world and cause and effect. He is beginning to listen for particular sounds which he can associate with some event, e.g. mother's voice, sound of food being prepared.

Imitation

Imitation works two ways—you can imitate the baby. Most parents do this naturally during play with very young babies. The baby hiccups—you copy it. Babies delight in this sort of game— they enjoy being imitated. At three or four months they will often start repeating the sound, burp, crow etc. after you have imitated it. This is the beginning of learning cause and effect. It is also the baby learning to communicate, and learning that his actions and communications have a pay-off.

There is also another very important point to make at this time. If you have had other babies you will probably remember how difficult it was to get them to do something—smile or chuckle, for instance—for a photograph, or to show off to granny. The harder you try the worse it becomes. It is as though by trying too hard to get the baby's attention, by talking more, smiling more, you overwhelm the baby and he just stares at you with a slightly stunned look on his face *or* he looks away. Mentally handicapped babies in any case take longer to respond; they develop more slowly and so build up the range of behaviour they can show more slowly; often their muscles are 'floppier' (hypotonic), and do not react as sharply or firmly as those of normal babies—this includes the muscles controlling the eyes, face, lips, tongue etc. Therefore, they often do not have the same range of facial expressions or vocalisations as normal babies at the same age, *nor* can they use what they have so quickly. We think, from our observations, that this causes parents to try harder to get the baby to respond—to smile, laugh etc. But 'trying harder' may not in fact be the best way to help. Instead, one would do better to wait for the baby to *do* something, then copy it and wait again. In this way you are (i) sure the behaviour you are copying is not too difficult or too advanced for the baby, and (ii) letting the baby indicate to you how much stimulation he can cope with and how quickly he can respond.

You will need to be on the alert for any opportunity, and for any behaviour : a sneeze, cough, hiccup, burp. Then copy it as closely as possible.

But since mentally handicapped babies do not initiate or start off behaviours well, you may also need to get something started yourself. In this case you copy afterwards. For example, you can often start a smile off with a tickle, then you copy the smile.

Vocalisations are not so easy to initiate. You will need to observe closely when the baby vocalises; what starts him off, whether he does it more in one place than another. (For example, young children often make most sounds in the bathroom—the 'echoes' seem to interest and excite them.) You can often teach a 'starting-off prompt'. For example, when the baby is making gentle 'crying noises,' you can tap his lip with your finger and so make the noise, alter or punctuate it—forming a little rhythm. Babies often like this and will learn to start making the noise when you tap their lips. You then try to get in with some imitation.

By the way, try this tapping of the lip even when the baby is crying quite hard—*sometimes*, it helps to stop the crying.

You can also, *sometimes*, stop crying by imitating the cry. The baby takes a breath, winds up and cries, winds down, takes another breath, etc. If, just before he winds up for the next yell, you imitate it he will often pause. Provided he is not too upset, you can often slowly 'wind him down' and get him into a happier mood with this game.

There is another trick which sometimes stops crying. Try, when he is crying, starting a high pitched singing noise and gradually come down to a low one. At some point the baby will usually stop crying and look at you. Then you can try to get him interested in something, i.e. walk around the room showing him things. It doesn't work, of course, if he is hungry or in discomfort.

We would like to draw out some general points from this.

1. Babies tend to imitate behaviours that are within their level of ability, or that they have already done. Imitation helps to strengthen behaviours, and increases the opportunities to use them.

2. By imitating the baby's behaviours you are letting the baby indicate to you what he is ready to do. Therefore, you are less likely to bombard the baby with too much at too high a level.

3. It is a more indirect than a direct way of stimulating the baby. That is, instead of pushing directly to get the baby to do something so that you can then reward and encourage him, you are trying to let the behaviour come spontaneously from the baby, and then developing upon it. This is explained fully in Chapter 11 in the play and language sections.

Sleeping

Many people think that sleep is the great healer and it is good for a baby to be sleeping as much as possible. However, this is not necessarily so. All children are different, some need a lot of sleep and some little sleep. In our experience mentally handicapped babies do not appear to need more sleep than other babies, but they may be particularly quiet and not cry for food or attention so that you think they are sleeping and leave them. It is best to check on whether or not the baby is asleep as often as you can, for if he is not and is left to lie on his back in his cot he is getting little stimulation and having little opportunity to learn.

Dummies and pacifiers

Many parents ask about the use of dummies or pacifiers. There are all sorts of widely differing ideas about these, but briefly we will state what we see as the advantages and disadvantages.

The disadvantages are :

(i) Hygiene—dummies easily get dirty and it is difficult to keep them free of germs.

(ii) Habit—once the baby has got used to having a dummy it is difficult to teach him to do without it when you decide that he is too old to have it any longer.

(iii) Sucking—a dummy can produce faulty tongue patterns which do not help the baby to produce sounds. In order to pronounce different sounds the baby needs to move his tongue in certain patterns—these movements are encouraged by actions such as chewing, but not by the sucking action that is used with the dummy.

(iv) A dummy can prevent stimulation for the baby—he becomes pacified easily with it and so does not seek stimulation. A dummy should never be used instead of stimulation when the baby cries for attention.

(v) When the baby has a dummy in his mouth he cannot vocalise, therefore frequent use of the dummy reduces vocalisation.

(vi) Giving him the dummy may reward unwanted behaviour. For instance, if he screams and is given the dummy, which he likes, he is rewarded for screaming and is more likely to do it again.

(vii) Never dip the dummy into sugar, honey or juice : this will cause the teeth to decay. For the same reason you should avoid dummies with small bottles attached to them for juice etc. Of course many of the disadvantages of dummies also apply to thumb sucking and this is often a harder habit to break as the thumb is easily accessible to the child !

The advantages are :

(i) They can give considerable satisfaction and comfort to the baby.

(ii) The use of a dummy in the early months can strengthen the muscles involved in sucking.

(iii) The dummy is often one of the first toys a baby plays with.

You can play popping it in his mouth and pulling it out. Once the baby manages to get his hands to it he likes to pull at it, and this is good practice for reaching and grasping.

In the end of course you must decide on your own feelings whether to give your baby a dummy. If you decide to give him one, you may find he won't take it—not all babies will. If he does have one, we feel that by six to seven months it should be used only when he is going to sleep, so that you can avoid many of the disadvantages.

GETTING STARTED

As you can see, in the first three months of life the baby makes great steps forward—he becomes stronger and can begin to control some of his muscles; he becomes sociable and begins to interact with you; and he begins to learn about the world. In the next part of this chapter we hope to give you some practical ideas about how you can help your baby to achieve these steps as soon as he is ready. But the first and most important is to *get to know your baby*. You will learn your own baby's needs gradually—how much sleep and food he needs and when he sleeps and feeds—and as you do, you can establish your routine organisation. As we explained in Chapter 5, this is very important in beginning to teach your baby. Also you need to get used to handling the baby, particularly if this is your first child. You may feel a little apprehensive about handling such a small being, and you need time to gain confidence with him. If the baby is physically handicapped, or very rigid or very floppy, you may feel even more apprehensive about handling him. Don't. Except in very rare conditions, which your doctors will have explained to you, these babies are no more or less delicate than any other babies. *Handle him with confidence*—then he will be confident when

Aspects of Early Development

All these babies have Down's syndrome and were photographed at home during everyday play.

Photographs by Steven Swirkowski

The Relax Chair 4

The Bottom Wedge 5

The Bouncing Cradle 1

Using The Bottom Wedge 2

The High Chair- note cushion to keep 3
correct level

Sitting Unsupported 6

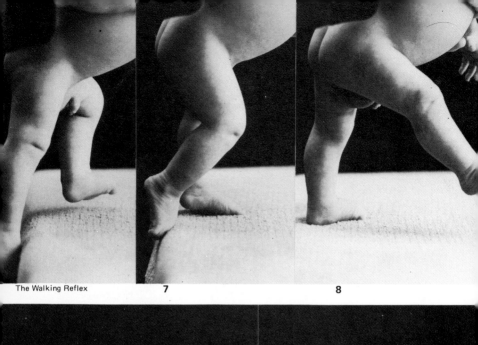

The Walking Reflex 7 8

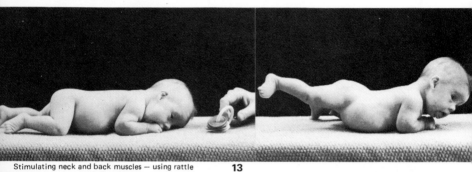

Stimulating neck and back muscles — using rattle 13

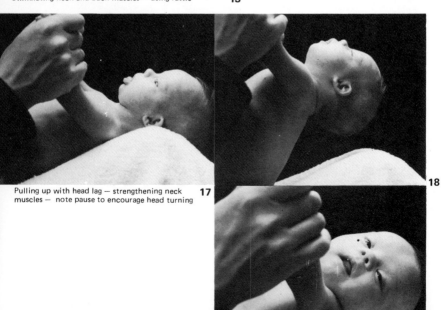

Pulling up with head lag — strengthening neck 17
muscles — note pause to encourage head turning

18

19

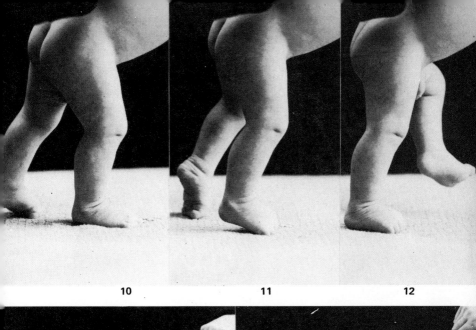

10   11   12

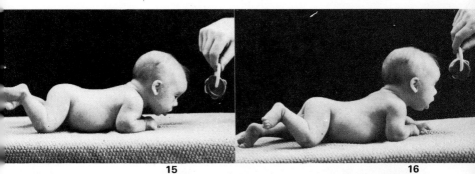

15   16

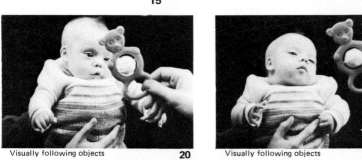

Visually following objects   20

Visually following objects   21

Visually following objects   22

Visually following objects   23

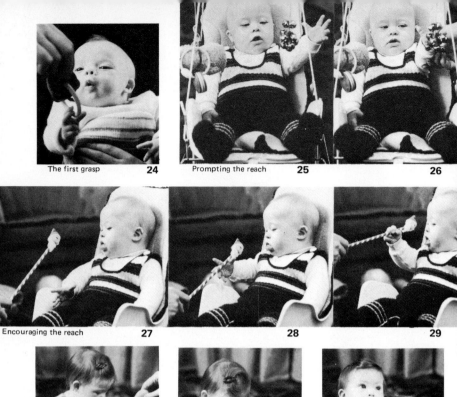

The first grasp   **24**

Prompting the reach   **25**   **26**

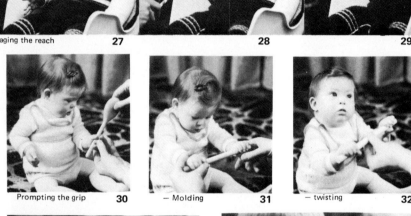

Encouraging the reach   **27**   **28**   **29**

Prompting the grip   **30**   — Molding   **31**   — twisting   **32**

Prompting both hands   **33**   Picking up cube off table   **34**

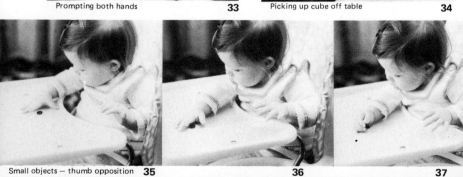

Small objects — thumb opposition   **35**   **36**   **37**

'Ready' 38 'Missed' 39 'Got it' 40

Mouthing 41

Banging 42

Pushing 43

Inspecting 44

Stroking 45

Using two objects 46

Interest in small objects 47

48

49

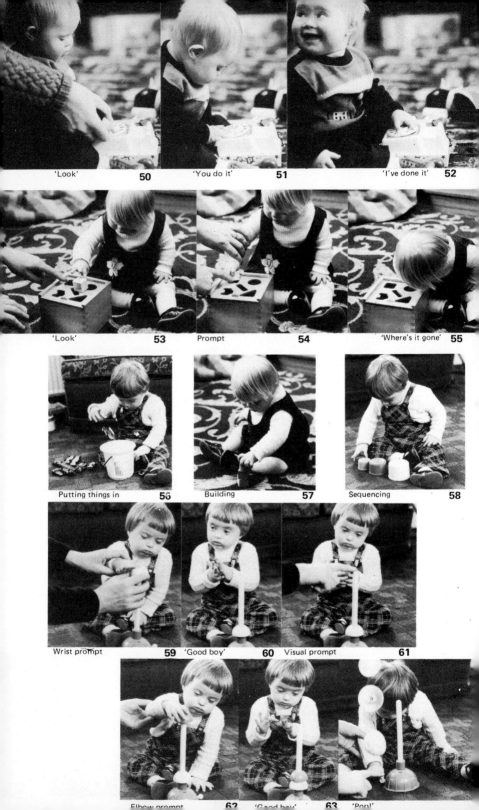

'Look' **50**

'You do it' **51**

'I've done it' **52**

'Look' **53**

Prompt **54**

'Where's it gone' **55**

Putting things in **56**

Building **57**

Sequencing **58**

Wrist prompt **59**

'Good boy' **60**

Visual prompt **61**

Elbow prompt **62**

'Good boy' **63**

'Pop!'

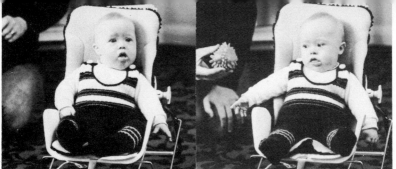
Looking at mum **65**

'What's that noise' **66**

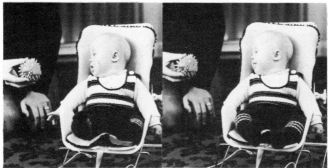
'It's over there' **67**

'I like that' **68**

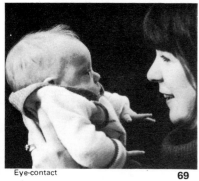
Eye-contact **69**

First smiles — using tickle **70**

Looking at mum's mouth **71**

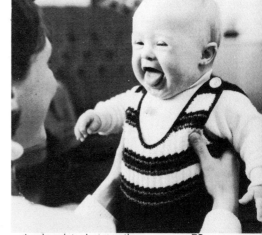
Laughs and stands at same time **72**

Feet against knees **73**	'Up' **74**	Hands lowered— takes **75** weight on feet

Using the furniture to stand **76** — note prompt and toys	**77**	**78**

Prompting walking using a trolley **79**	**80**	**81**

First steps — 'come on' **82**	'Good boy' **83**	'Oops!' **84**

Rocking off the knee to **85** help strength and balance

86

87

88

89

90

Walking with help **91**

Holding hand **92**

Standing **93**

'I'm off' **94**

'Here I go' **95**

'But I can't turn yet' **96**

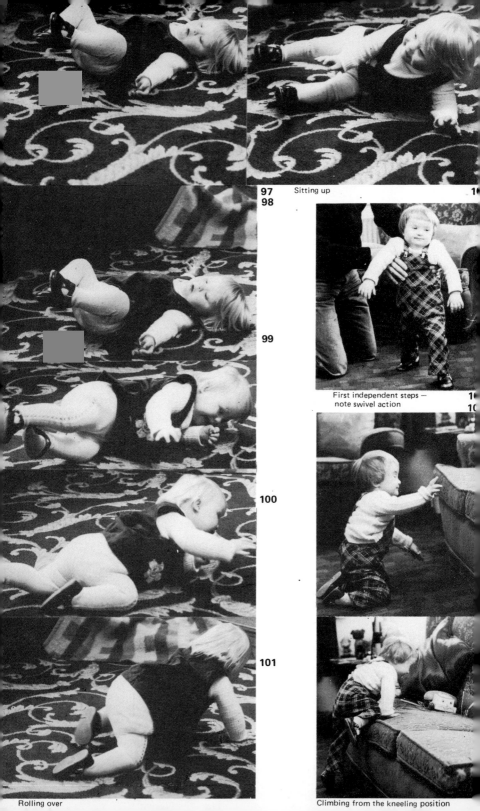

97
98

Sitting up

99

First independent steps —
note swivel action

100

101

Rolling over

Climbing from the kneeling position

103   104

106   110   107   111   108

113   114   115

'Peep oh!' **116**

Cloth over hand-held noisy toy **117**

Half-hidden object **118**

Looking for dropped object **119**

120

121

Finding large object under cloth

123

124

Hiding object under cups **125**

Transparent cup **126**

Ordinary cup **127**

Playing hide-and-seek, **128**

'Peep oh!' **129**

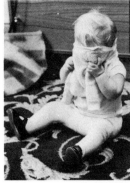

Nicola at 22 months: Self help **130**　　**131**　　**132**

Anticipation **133** 'Here I come' **134** 'Got you' **135**

'So high' **136**

'So big' **137**

'Up there' **138**

'No more!' **139**

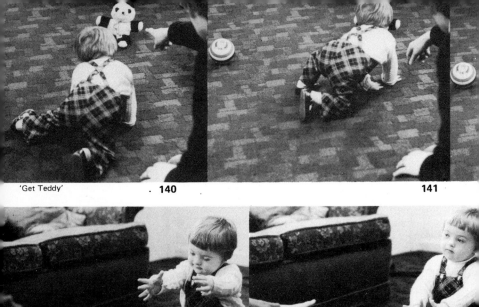

'Get Teddy'   140   141

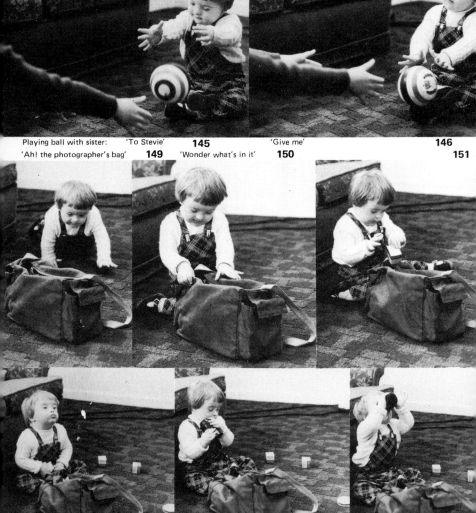

Playing ball with sister: 'To Stevie'   145   'Give me'   146
'Ah! the photographer's bag'   149   'Wonder what's in it'   150   151

'Is it still alright, mum?'   155   156   'Looks like a cup

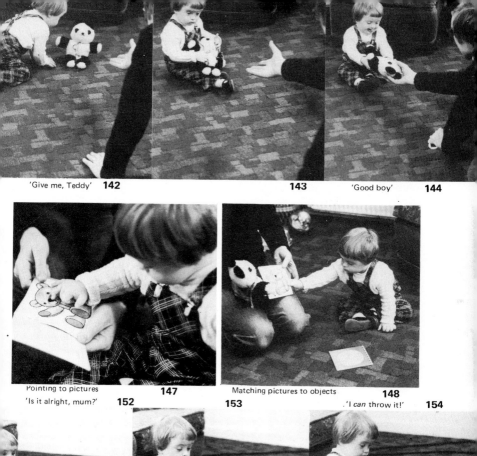

'Give me, Teddy' **142**   **143**   'Good boy' **144**

Pointing to pictures   **147**   Matching pictures to objects   **148**

'Is it alright, mum?' **152**   **153**   'I *can* throw it!' **154**

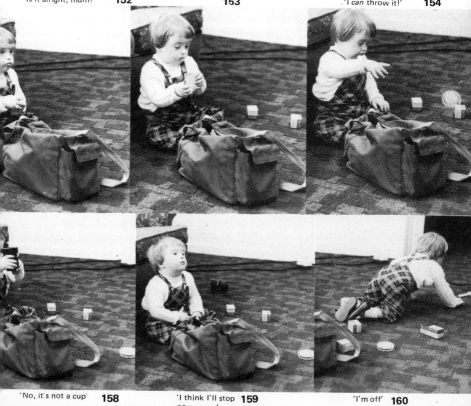

'No, it's not a cup' **158**   'I think I'll stop **159**   'I'm off' **160**

'Show me, shoe' **161**

162

'Nicola drink' **163**

'Teddy drink' **165**

'Blow your nose' **164**

'Teddy's nose' **166**

'Comb your hair' **167**

'Teddy's hair' **168**

handled. At first it may seem as if there is no time to do anything with the baby, other than feed and change him. Do not start to worry that you are not stimulating him enough. Give yourself time to establish a routine, and play with him when he is awake and alert. You will soon learn to know the best times to do this.

WHAT YOU CAN DO

In this section we will suggest some of the ways you can help your baby to develop. These are ideas for you to build upon, and we hope you will be able to use your ingenuity and your special knowledge of your own baby to devise many further ways of helping him or her.

General stimulation

If a young baby is lying in his cot looking up at a plain ceiling, he is gaining little stimulation. He is not using his eyes to watch moving objects, and there is nothing for him to focus on. Hang a brightly coloured mobile over the cot and remember to change it or its position every few weeks.

Remember that very young babies cannot focus on objects that are far away, so do not hang the mobile up too high—about 14 inches (35 cm) away is the right distance. Also work out which side the baby holds his head, and hang the mobile on that side, gradually bringing it into the centre as he learns to control his head. You can also try two mobiles—one each side of the cot. In the first weeks of life babies are attracted by sharp contrasts of shape or colour, and look at the edges of the contours of the pattern not at the whole pattern. You will need simple strong designs at first, and will have to make your own. (See page 326 for some ideas.) Later, you can use some of the many good mobiles, including some with sound, that can be purchased. When the baby is in his pram you can attach pram toys to the sides of the pram and string a pram rattle across it. Vary the position of these so that, as the baby waves his arms and legs, they contact the rattles. At first this will happen accidentally, but eventually he will learn to reach out to strike the rattle so that it moves and makes a noise—he is beginning to learn about cause and effect and to *make things happen*.

When the baby is awake, try to plan your routine so that he

F

Figure 2. Carrying with the baby facing outwards

can be in a room with you or other members of the family as much as possible—so that he can see you moving about and hear you talking. You may be able to put his pram or carrycot in the kitchen, and sometimes carry him about with you from room to room.

Carrying
When you carry him try to make sure that his head is not buried against your body—that he can see more than your shirt button. Carry him against your shoulder so that he can see over it, or carry him facing outwards away from your body draped across your arm. By draping him across your arm you are not only giving him a chance to look at things, but also the opportunity to bring his head up and move his arms, which will help to strengthen the muscles of the back and neck. Rock and swing the baby sometimes when you pick him up, so that he can feel his body in different positions and begin to develop his sense of

balance. Handle him as much as possible when you change him
—play with his feet and hands and, of course, cuddle him.

Chairs

If a baby is placed in a semi-upright position he can see much
more around him than when he is lying down.

You should therefore try to make sure that the baby can be
seated in this position for some time every day, as soon as possible. In the early stages, from about four weeks old a 'bouncing
cradle', a canvas chair strung between metal supports, which can
be obtained from most baby shops, accomplishes this very well,
and gives the baby all the necessary support. It has the added
advantage that as the baby kicks his legs, it rocks up and down so

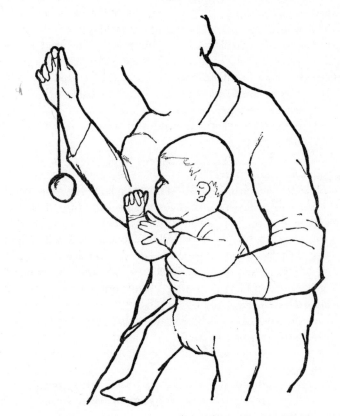

Figure 3. Encouraging baby to lift his head

giving him further stimulation. If you cannot obtain one of these, prop the baby in a slightly inclined position using pram or a foam wedge. It is, of course, important to make sure that the baby is absolutely secure when propped.

GAMES AND EXERCISES

Constantly encourage the baby with smiles and words. Especially, praise him immediately he does things.

Gross motor development

The main aim of this stage is to help your baby to strengthen his muscles and develop his head balance.

By handling the baby, rocking him, etc., you will be starting this process. The baby needs to feel his body in different positions, and gradually to learn to adjust it for balance, so developing control of his muscles. In all the games, sing and speak to him. Even from this early age you can begin to get into the habit of saying the words that go with the action: 'sit up', 'lie down', 'pull' and so on. Some parents have told us that they feel silly talking to a baby because babies don't understand. But the baby will listen to the tone of your voice and begin to understand that words go with actions.

1. Sitting and head control

Hold the baby in a sitting position on your knee for *short* periods. At first you will need to support his head all the time, but gradually as he begins to gain strength in his neck muscles he will be able to hold it up for short periods. Also his back will begin to straighten, but for this to happen he needs practice in the sitting position. When he is sitting on your knee, try and encourage him to bring his head up by attracting his attention slightly upwards, to an attractive rattle or toy or by talking and smiling at him. Do this once or twice on each occasion—but on many occasions during the day. (See Figure 3.)

2. Pulling up

You can also begin pulling the baby up to a sitting position.
(*a*) (i) Lie him on his back on your knees with his feet against your body.

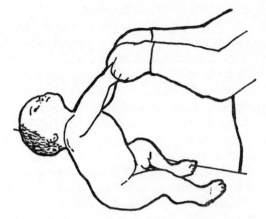

Figure 4. Pulling up with head-lag

Figure 5. Early walking reflex

(ii) Take hold of *his upper arms* and gently pull him up until you can just feel the weight of his head.

(iii) At first his neck muscles are weak and his head will hang back, so you must lift him only a little, but soon he will begin to tense his neck muscles and lift his head.

(iv) As the neck muscles gain strength you can pull him up higher, and *when he makes a noticeable effort to lift his head*, pull him up to a sitting position. Do this exercise two or three times on several occasions each day. As the baby's strength increases you *can move your support down his arms* to *his elbows* and then *his hands*.

(*b*) With the baby in a sitting position on your knee, facing you, hold him by his arms then raise them up above his head and slightly away from his body. This will encourage him to lift his head.

(*c*) In the same position, hold his arms and bring them together in the middle directly in front of him. You can make this into a game by clapping his hands, singing pat-a-cake or any appropriate nursery rhyme.

3. Standing

(i) Hold the baby in a standing position on your knee with your hands under his arms.

(ii) Bounce him very gently up and down.

(iii) When he pushes against your knees with his feet, let him take a little weight and *tell him how clever he is*.

4. Walking

(*a*) (i) Hold the baby in a standing position on a firm surface, supporting him under the arms.

(ii) Note whether you see the walking reflex.

(iii) If you do, encourage this by regular practice.

(*b*) (i) Hold the baby in a standing position next to a table so that his ankles are against the edge of the table.

(ii) Note whether he takes a step on to the table, and if so practise this a few times a day.

5. Arm and Leg Exercises

Try to give the baby some time each day when he can lie without a nappy. This is probably easiest when you are changing him.

Figure 6. Blanket roll to help develop head control

6. *Lying on his stomach*
(*a*) Place the baby on a firm surface on his stomach several times every day.

(*b*) Encourage him to lift his head off the surface by using toys to attract his attention, and by lying down with him and talking to him. This exercise is particularly good for strengthening his neck and shoulder muscles.

Note:

Some babies do not like lying on their stomachs, particularly if they have not been used to this position from an early age. If your baby cries when you lie him in this position, do not pick him up too soon, get down and talk to him. Persevere for a minute or two each time so that he gradually gets used to the position. In fact, when the baby cries in this position, it usually stimulates him to movements which in the end are beneficial—as he cries he tenses his muscles, moves and exercises them.

7. *Lifting his head up*
When baby is lying on his stomach

(*a*) (i) Kneel down on the floor behind the baby and take hold of his head.

(ii) Lift it so that he can look at an object or face about 14 inches (30 cm) from his eyes (this is a physical prompt).

(iii) Hold his head for 15–30 seconds, then let him rest before you raise it again.

(iv) Do this about three times each day, a few times on each occasion, gradually increasing the number of times as his neck strength increases.

(v) When the baby can lift his head and hold it up for one minute, he can then go on to :

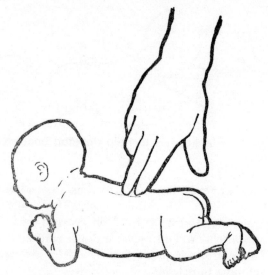

Figure 7. Stimulating head-raising

(*b*) *Supporting his weight on his elbows*
  (i) Place a rolled up blanket or towel under his chest so that his elbows and lower arms rest on the floor, and he is supporting some of his weight on them.
  (ii) Now use a toy, or play with him, to attract his attention and make him lift his head up.
  (iii) Once the baby is doing this easily, place him on the floor without the blanket roll. Press down slightly (or rub) on the bottom of his back. This may stimulate him to extend his spine and raise his head.
(*c*) You can also play these games by lying the baby across your thigh or waist instead of the rolled up blanket. Babies often prefer this because of the close contact with mum or dad.

8. Exercising his legs
(*a*) If he kicks his legs place your hands against his feet so that he kicks and pushes against them.
(*b*) Lift one foot about 2 inches (5 cm) from the mat then let it drop gently. Do the same with the other foot. After a while he will make efforts to stop them falling, or will kick a little.
(*c*) Hold the baby's foot in your hand and stroke the outside of

the sole from the big toe down to the heel. The foot will pull back (this is a reflex action), and as it does, resist this movement gently with your other hand. Do this until you can feel any attempt by the baby to push against your hand (in doing this you are using the reflex to encourage a voluntary movement of resistance to you).

(d) Again with the baby lying on his back, place one hand on his knee and push gently against his foot with the other hand, pushing in the direction of the knee. The other leg will bend and then push downwards in a reflex action. Do this with the other leg and do it several times on each occasion.

(e) If the baby does not wave his arms and kick his legs voluntarily, you can begin to exercise these for him. When baby is lying on his back, take hold of his hand or foot and gently toss it up and down until the baby begins to tighten his muscles to resist the movement. Always be careful to do this very gently and not to stretch the arm or leg too far, as the baby's joints are not very firm at this stage.

(f) When the baby is lying on his back, push alternately with both hands against the soles of his feet, until you feel *the point at which he moves his legs himself*. Continue these back and forth movements so that he begins to move his legs himself and you produce a 'bicycling' movement. Use this exercise regularly as it produces the sort of alternate pressure on the soles of the feet which is felt in walking, and appears to strengthen the legs and their co-ordination.

(g) Raise both the baby's legs slowly until they are in his line of vision, then bring first one foot down to touch his nose and then do the same with the other foot. At this stage the baby may not move his hands but he will probably open his mouth. Later he will move his hands up, and you should encourage him to play with his feet. Your aim here is both to strengthen his muscles and to help him become more aware of his feet.

(h) Another exercise which will develop this awareness is to turn the feet with the soles towards each other, and clap them together gently in the same way as you clap his hands when singing or playing games. It is a good idea to sing whilst doing this. Then hold the feet together and the toes will probably meet and move against one another. Again do this so that the baby can see his feet.

F*

Social

The social development that takes place at this stage tends to be 'close-up' rather than distant. It begins with face-to-face contact between the baby and another person. The three main things to look for are eye-gaze, smiles and facial expressions, and sometimes little reaches up to your face.

(i) Always make sure the baby is looking at you when you talk to him.

(ii) Use exaggerated facial expressions.

(iii) Give the baby time to respond.

(iv) If the baby smiles, looks into your eyes or vocalises, always respond to him by smiling and talking back, or giving him a tickle or imitating his behaviour.

1. Looking

Smiling and gazing into your eyes appears very early in most babies (see developmental checklist). At first they gaze into your eyes for long periods whenever you look at them. Gradually they learn to look away, to look at your mouth, and back to your eyes and generally explore your face. This helps them to learn about faces.

If you do not see your baby looking from your eyes to your mouth and back, you can try to exaggerate the cues (eyes and mouth) by making big movements.

(i) Turn the baby's face to you so that you are face to face.

(ii) Keep your mouth steady and make big eye movements— blinks, flicking your eye-lashes.

(iii) Watch the baby's eyes, and when you see him look into your eyes stop the movements.

(iv) Let him look into your eyes for a second or two, then talk and make big mouth movements and smiles.

(v) Given time and practice he will look down at your mouth. Carry on talking and then stop, and make big eye movements again.

After a while you will find the baby stops gazing into your eyes for long periods. He will look at you if you are talking, and will often look away from you to other parts of the room. He is beginning to *direct* his gaze (visual attention) and explore his world; to choose whether to look or not and what to look at.

2. Smiling

Once babies smile, they smile at first at almost anything. But, in the beginning you often need to tickle the baby to get a smile.

(i) Look at the baby face-to-face and talk and smile. If the baby does not smile back—and do give him time to respond —then gently tickle and touch him.

(ii) When the baby smiles, always follow this up with a big smile yourself.

Gradually the baby will smile without being tickled, and will also begin to direct his smile more appropriately (items 11, 17 of Adaptive Scale).

You may find that when the baby starts to direct his smile, he smiles less often and it becomes more difficult to get a smile. Sometimes this is because we have forgotten to give him time to respond; sometimes because he is still learning when to smile appropriately and is sizing up the situation.

Visual development

1. Visual following

(*a*) (i) Dangle a brightly coloured object about the size of a tennis ball in line with the baby's vision, about 6–8 inches (15–20 cm) from his eyes. Get his attention to it.

(ii) When he looks at it move it *very slowly* to the side of his face and back again into the middle.

(iii) Check that he is trying to follow it. His eye movements will be very jerky at first.

(iv) Do this several times, observing how far his eyes will follow the object. You can also move your head from side to side when the baby is looking at your face, and observe whether he follows it.

(*b*) When the baby is beginning to follow the object from side to side, repeat the exercise but move it slowly up and down between his chest and his forehead (item 7—Adaptive).

Note : With both these exercises you will find that, at first, you need to keep bringing the object back to the middle to attract the baby's attention to it again after he has 'lost it'. Eventually he will be able to follow it smoothly in both directions.

(c) Repeat the same exercise, but move the object in a circle about 12 inches (30 cm) in diameter. The baby will move his eyes up, sideways and down in jerky movements, as he follows. (item 8—Adaptive). Continue this until he is following quite smoothly.

2. Visual attention

Begin this when the baby is following objects fairly easily.

(a) When he is looking in front of him, bring a toy in from the side of his face towards the middle. Use an attractive rattle and shake it to gain his attention so that he will turn his eyes to look at it.

(b) Do this on both sides of his face so that he gains practice in using the full range of his vision.

(c) Eventually you can use a toy that does not make a noise, and he will be able to catch sight of it and turn his eyes to it before it is directly over his eyes.

3. Distance

Help the baby to extend the range of his vision.

(i) Bend over him and look at him, and talk to him with your face about 18 inches (45 cm) from his face.

(ii) Slowly move your face closer until your noses touch, then move away slowly until he looks away. (If the baby reaches out to your face, hold his hand gently on your face and withdraw slowly to his arm's length).

(iii) Repeat this exercise using a small toy.

4. Looking at small objects

(a) Hold a pencil above the baby's eyes, about 8 inches (20 cm) from his face, and attract his attention to it. Very slowly move it from side to side.

(b) Use other small objects. This helps him to focus his eyes *together* on small objects (item 12—Adaptive).

5. Fast following

As the baby becomes more efficient at following moving objects, you can increase the speed of movement *gradually*.

(i) When he is in a sitting position, pull a toy across the table in front of him (attract his attention to it first).

(ii) Gradually—over several days—pull faster and faster.

(iii) Roll a ball across the table (item 13—Adaptive).

6. *Looking at hands* (item 19—Adaptive)

Towards the end of this stage of development, babies begin to watch their hands—and then to watch things held in their hands (item 20—Adaptive). This is the first stage of eye-hand co-ordination. You can begin to prepare by :

(i) Holding his arm at the elbow (so that he does not watch your hand), bring his hand up into his vision and gently move it about. You can also bring both hands up and touch them together.

(ii) When he will hold an object for a few seconds or more, bring this up in the same way.

Hearing, listening and vision

Hearing is difficult to test in the young baby. This is because you test it indirectly. You have to watch the baby's responses to sounds, and so with handicapped babies, it may be that they are hearing the sound but not responding. Items 4, 5, 6, 10, 13 and 15 of the Communication Checklist will help you to observe any responses to sound. However, *if you do not get them—do not think that this necessarily means there are hearing difficulties.* It is worth trying the games even if you are not sure of some of the responses.

However, if at the end of this stage of development, the baby is not passing any of the hearing items, do consult your doctor or health visitor or clinic. Hearing loss, from slight to severe, is common in mental handicap and so it is very important to keep a close watch on it. When the child suffers from catarrh and congestion, as happens frequently in Down's Syndrome, this can cause some temporary hearing loss, and even a temporary hearing loss can result in the loss of valuable learning experiences. Therefore regular checks are important. They are also important because even if the child can pass the hearing items on the checklist his hearing is not necessarily perfect. He may still have some loss of certain sounds.

Because of this we would recommend that you always talk clearly and distinctly to the baby. Do not be afraid to talk close to his ear, varying the level of your voice.

The main games for the first stage involve providing a range of sounds, and teaching him to put sight and sound together, and to begin to distinguish between sounds.

(*a*) Collect a range of noise objects (clicks, bells, rattles, taps, crinkly paper, whistles and so on). When the baby is lying on his back, make the noises with the objects just out of vision, level with the ears. Start quietly and work up to the louder noises.

(i) Watch to see if the baby responds. If he does:

(ii) Wait to see whether he turns his eyes toward the sound. If he does:

(iii) Wait to see whether he turns his head to look at the object. Then shake it and laugh and smile. This does not usually happen until three or four months.

In each case, if he does not, move on to the next step. Slowly bring the object—keeping up the noise—into his vision and get him to look at it. Then laugh and smile.

After a few trials you will have a good idea whether or not the baby will move on to the next step. If not, do not wait too long before bringing the object into vision.

Also do this on both sides of the head. You may find that one side is better than the other. This does not necessarily mean he is deaf in one ear. You will need to wait for him to develop much more before this can be tested by the doctor.

Also, remember that babies can get used to sounds and so stop responding. Therefore, do a little at a time but frequently, and use a range of sounds.

Grasping and reaching

Most babies are born with the ability to grasp objects. When you put your finger into their hands they will grasp so tightly that you can lift them up. Often this reaction disappears, and then reappears as a controlled grasp. Handicapped babies do not show such a strong grasp and some show no grasp at all. It is important to start training the grasp and the reach as soon as possible for two reasons: Strength and Coordination.

Try these two tests:

(*a*) Stroke the outside edge of the hand from wrist to little finger. Does the baby bring his arm and hand up and around, and grasp the object or your finger?

If yes—keep practising.

If no—repeat several times on different occasions to make sure. If still no response, then either the baby has grown out of the reflex action or it was not present.

(*b*) Place an object or finger across the baby's palm pressing against the palm and twisting. Does the baby grip the object or finger?

If yes—keep practising and go on to (*c*) below.

If no—repeat as before. If still no then :

(i) Place an object (e.g. piece of dowel or a large ring) across the palm and mould the fingers around it, making sure the thumb is opposite the fingers. This is a prompt.

(ii) Gradually let go of the baby's hand and twist the rod up against his fingers, or pull the ring gently up against the fingers.

(iii) When you think the baby has a firm grip, let go.

(iv) Repeat with the opposite hand.

Gradually fade out the moulding prompt and get the baby to grab as soon as the object touches the palm.

(*c*) When the baby can grasp an object placed in the palm, begin to train the grasp when the object just touches the finger-tips. This means the baby has to move his hand forward a little and grasp.

(*d*) When he will hold objects for a second or two,

(i) Practise holding on to objects for a few seconds longer each time.

(ii) Start to use different objects—different thickness, textures etc.

(iii) Practise moving the objects about—at first this will just be gently waving.

(iv) Play little tug-of-wars with the baby—laughing and smiling and making it a fun game.

By this time the baby will pass item 16 on the Adaptive checklist, and item 3 on the Fine Motor checklist.

(*e*) In item 15 on the Adaptive checklist, the baby fingers one hand with the other.

To start this game the baby must already be opening his hands for some of the time, *or*, if you pull his arm up, his hands should open and the fingers extend. Now bring them across and stroke the fingers of one hand with his other hand. Make sure he is looking at his hands.

(*f*) Reaching: Sometimes in the early weeks of life a baby will raise his arms as though reaching for an object he is looking at. This is often mum's face when she is talking to him. If this happens, try to keep it going and use prompts by raising the arm from the elbow. (This does not mean that you should always be doing this when playing with the baby.)

AN EXAMPLE OF A GAME TO HELP EYE-HAND CO-ORDINATION

We shall end this chapter with a programme worked out and written by a mother of a 12-week-old Down's Syndrome baby girl. This is the sort of game you should be on the look out for, or invent for yourself.

'The game was devised after baby accidentally knocked her toy cat out of sight and appeared pleased with the result.

'The baby was lying on her back and a cat (or any four-legged animal—more stable) was sat on the side of the changing mat so that when pushed by baby, it fell on to the floor. The changing mat had slightly raised edges.

'Rules

'1. When cat knocked off, I exclaim "Oo, gone!"

'2. Cat always reappears as though climbing back.

'3. If cat is pushed into position where it is not possible for baby to knock it off, I put it back to accessible position, in the process making sure cat moves at baby and says "Miaaow" so baby knows she is responsible for any other movement of cat.

'4. Cat is first put in very easy position for baby to reach with right arm, then moved gradually so baby has to stretch more.

'Game started when H. was three months old and it was played for a little every day. At first H. obviously found it very difficult. Improved considerably so she could hit cat most times by three weeks later. But then, if she did not hit cat first time, she would "deliberately" look away and aim where she thought the cat ought to be, then have a sideways glance to see if she had hit cat.

'Occasionally when she had tried really hard and could not hit cat, she would start "frustration" crying.

'More usually, would take a swipe at the cat, and if she missed it she would start finger sucking or other types of "displacement activity" before having another try.

'At first, if H. had several tries and did not hit cat, I would hold her arm and move it so it did knock cat off. Then I immediately replaced the cat and encouraged baby to try again.

'H. has rather lost interest in this game now, but used to really enjoy it and looked for "Pushka" as soon as she was put on the changing mat. If she did not hit him she would get cross and start shouting at him, and then when she did knock him off would look at me for approval, and gurgle and wave her arm as though waiting for his next appearance.

'Now ($4\frac{1}{2}$ months) she prefers to play with her rattle.'

Points

1. Notice in this example how the game was invented as a result of mother's observation when the baby 'accidentally knocked the toy' and 'appeared pleased'.

2. Mother devises a game with a set of rules to provide consistency.

3. Uses reward—'Oo gone'—when baby acts.

4. Slowly increases the difficulty by making baby stretch further and further to knock off the toy.

5. Notice how long—three weeks—the mother persevered before the baby became proficient.

6. And how mother interpreted the thumb-sucking not as losing interest but as meaningful behaviour.

7. Think about how this young Down's Syndrome baby, even at the age of three to four months, was 'deliberately' trying to act upon her world—and showed 'frustration' when she failed.

8. Notice how mother used a physical prompt—at first—to help the baby, but only after the baby had had a chance to do it herself.

9. Notice how the baby began to anticipate the cat when placed on the changing mat.

10. Take note of how the mother was sensitive to the changes occurring in the developing baby, and moved on to more advanced games as the baby indicated the need.

11. Finally, this game occurred naturally and happily during the everyday activities of caring for the baby.

8 : Three to six months

Remember to check the exercises and games against the developmental checklist to get an idea of the timing and sequences of the behaviours.

The main characteristic of this period is that the baby becomes more active, starts initiating a lot of behaviours and is more and more involved with things about him. He becomes considerably stronger. He holds his head up steadily for long periods when he is in a sitting position and he begins to turn his head to look around him. By the end of this period he is able to sit on his own for a very short time and to sit well with support. He also learns to roll over, and he may begin to move around by rolling—he is becoming 'mobile' and can start to explore the world beyond his reach.

Now he begins to use his arms and hands to reach out and grasp objects. By six months he can reach out and pick up an object off the table in front of him, and he has learnt to use his eyes to guide his arms and hands. This is a very important step and, combined with his ability to sit up, it means that his world has greatly extended. He can now pick up and play with all sorts of different toys.

He has also developed considerably in his social behaviour. He smiles and laughs and is much more vocal, cooing for long periods when you talk to him, and beginning to babble. In fact, a baby is often more 'talkative' at this stage than at six to nine months.

GAMES AND EXERCISES

Mirror
If you have a large mirror you can begin to let the baby see his body moving. He will first have to get used to seeing himself in the mirror, however, which may take some time.

Sitting
1. Carry on pulling the baby up to a sitting position *until* he is

able *to pull himself up completely* without any head lag (items 32, 44—Gross Motor), just holding on to your thumbs.

2. When the baby can sit with support (item 29—Gross Motor) and is beginning to move his arms out and reach for objects, you will find that the bouncing cradle becomes too restrictive. Now is the time to move him to a Relax chair (see Plate 00). At first you can set it on the lowest position and then gradually move it to a more upright one.

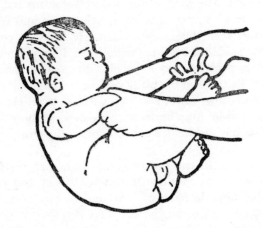

Figure 8. Pulling up to a sitting position—no head-lag

You will need to make sure that the baby is well supported in the chair, as at first he will probably slide down and end up in a slouched position with his head on one side and his arms *stuck* at his sides. This is bad for his posture and *is not going to help him to reach out*! It may help to use a foam pad or a small blanket behind the baby to give him more support. Also the straps provided on the chair may not support him enough, so you can adapt a pram harness, or use a 4-inch (10 cm) wide band of corset elastic fastened with velcro round his middle.

When you are able to adjust the chair into a semi-upright position, you can fasten the table on to it and place objects on the table for the baby to reach out to.

At this stage it is important that his arms are free and that he can reach the table easily with his hands. If your baby is fairly small, you will find that he is too low down in the chair and you will need to raise him by placing a folded blanket or a small cushion behind and underneath him.

When you first move the baby into the Relax chair, he will probably put up with it only for short periods at a time. Gradually you can increase the length of time he sits in it, making sure that you lie him down before he becomes overtired.

3. When the baby is able to sit with slight support (item 30, 31—Gross Motor), you need to encourage him towards sitting on his own, and to do this you must help his strength and balance. We have found that one of the best ways to do this is to sit the baby on the floor supprted by a foam block. The block should be about 4–6 inches (10–15 cm) deep and 24 inches (60–70 cm) square. Place the baby on the block and draw around his bottom. Cut out this area so that you can wedge the baby's bottom into it. It should be a firm fit. The baby can then sit in this, with the lower part of his back supported, though he has to control the

THE 'BOTTOM WEDGE'

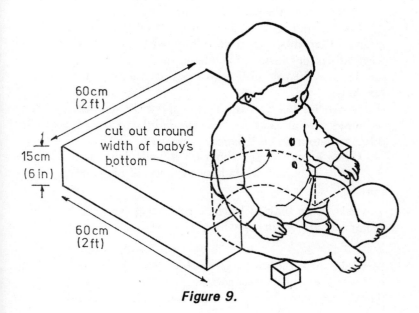

Figure 9.

upper part of his back and his head himself. You can place objects on the sides of the block and on the floor, and his arms are free to reach out to them. If he should slide down he is, of course, cushioned by the foam. Remember to use this for short periods, *not* all the time. And of course, put some toys around him to play with.

4. Balance is necessary for sitting unsupported (items 39, 45— Gross Motor).

(*a*) Sit him on the floor and rock him gently from side to side. Watch whether he reaches out with his arms to catch himself. If he does, let him put his hand on the floor to steady himself, then rock him over to the other side.

(*b*) Place the baby in a sitting position on the floor with his legs apart, his knees slightly bent and his hands on his feet. Support him in this position for a few minutes. Then attract his attention to the front of him, by placing a toy or your face directly in his line of vision. Make sure that his head is held straight and his eyes are looking straight in front. Do not move your face or the toy, as this will cause him to wobble. Then :

(i) Gradually reduce the amount of support you are giving (this is fading out the physical prompt).

(ii) Encourage him to sit for longer periods—a few seconds at a time. Remember to reward him with smiles and cuddles when he sits for the period you have set.

(iii) He may be using his arms to steady himself—if not, show him how.

(iv) When he can sit like this for about 30 seconds, you can try moving your head or the toy slightly to one side or the other, to help train his balance.

(v) When he can sit for about 60 seconds, hand him a toy to play with. This helps to fade out the use of his hands for support.

It can take some time to learn to get sitting balance. You may feel that you are getting nowhere. If so, try using a record chart to plot the progress.

(i) Make sure you have a clear objective, e.g. the baby will sit without support for 60 seconds.

(ii) Sit the baby on the floor, arrange his legs at about 45°

angle and get his attention. Let go and time how long before
he topples over.

(iii) Do this three times, for three days, twice a day, morning
and afternoon. Record how many seconds he sits before
toppling each time. Work out the daily average by dividing the
total number of seconds for the three trials by three, and mark
it on a record sheet. (See example below.) This three days *without
training* will give you a *baseline*.

(iv) Now train him to sit, using prompts, as noted above, and
once a day (or every other day) repeat the test, e.g. three trials
without help. Record your scores on the chart and look for
progress.

If you do not have a watch or clock with a second hand, you may
need to count. But remember to keep your counting even. If you
have a clock with a loud click you can count one for every click
and then work out the time afterwards.

Here is an example of a chart kept by a mother of a six-month-

Figure 10.

old Down's Syndrome girl. Her objective was to get the baby to sit without support.

Note : (i) How many days mum had to work at before getting a change. (4–12 days.)

(ii) The ups and downs—especially as the baby got to the 55–60 sec. level.

Standing (items 46 and 20, Gross Motor)

1. When the baby can pull himself up to sit, you can begin to help him to get used to pulling up to stand. Place him on his back on the floor, and kneel down in front of him so that *his feet are against your knees.* Hold his hands and get him to pull himself up to a sitting position; then carry on talking and smiling to him, and pull him up further into a standing position. You will need to give him quite a lot of help at this stage, but gradually he will begin to pull a little himself. At first you may need to hold his upper arms, then the elbows and finally the hands.

Figure 11. Pulling to a stand with baby sitting on a stool

Do not make the mistake of holding his hands and lifting him straight up because :

he is not learning to pull up on to his feet using his legs;
he may learn the game of lifting his legs up and having a swing—great fun but not helping the training.

2. You can also try sitting him on a ledge, box or small stool so that his feet are *flat on the floor*. Then bring him forward to a stand as in 1 above.
3. We have found that the baby's favourite game for helping him to find his feet is usually rocking off the knees.
(*a*) Kneel down and sit on your heels.
(*b*) Sit the baby on the end of your knees so that

(i) he is facing sideways;
(ii) his feet are flat on the floor at the side of your knee.

(*c*) Put one hand on his chest and the other on his back and then rock him forward on to his feet and back on to your knees.

The idea is to make him feel his feet on the floor, and also to take some weight on them. You can play this game for quite a long time before the baby gets tired. You can also use the game until the baby is walking.

We have found this game to be a great favourite of fathers, because you can rock the baby (which keeps him happy), train him to find his feet and strengthen his legs and balance (which keeps up the stimulation), and watch the football on TV at the same time (which keeps dad happy!)

Baby bouncers
Many parents find these very useful to help the baby feel his feet and to hold him in a position where he can move and look around. We would like to make three points :

(i) The baby must be able to control his head well before he can use a bouncer.
(ii) The bouncer should be adjusted so that the baby's feet touch the floor, with his knees very slightly bent. He can then push against the floor to bounce himself.
(iii) Use the bouncer for short periods at a time, as the baby easily becomes tired in it.

Note : If the baby has a physical disability—for example, if he is spastic or athetoid—do not put him in a baby bouncer without consulting a physiotherapist or doctor.

Lying on his stomach (items 22, 37—Gross Motor)

When the baby can lift his head and chest off the floor and support his weight on his elbows, the next stage is for him to support his weight on his hands. In order to do this his hands must first be *open*, so that he can place his palms flat on the floor.

1. If the baby does not open his hands himself, lie him on his front on a firm surface, then stroke the back of his hand from his knuckles to his wrist until the hand begins to open. As it opens place it palm down on the floor or table for a few seconds. If, and only *if*, the baby does not open his hand when you stroke it, you will have to open it for him.

2. Once the baby is opening his hands, his upper arms and back still need to be strengthened before he can support his weight on his hands.
(*a*) The exercises you have already been doing, pulling him up to sit, moving his arms and clapping his hands, will help this, so continue to do them.
(*b*) Use a large, inflatable ball and blow it up until it is partially inflated but still fairly soft.

    (i) Lie the baby on top of the ball and kneel in front of him.
    (ii) Hold his arms out from his sides and gently roll the baby and the ball backwards and forwards and from side to side. At first the baby may be frightened and cry a little. Talk to him gently to help him get over this, and then make it a game by using singing etc.

(*c*) Swing the baby in a blanket and do plenty of 'rough and tumble' activities with him (item 30—Social).

3. Teach the baby to support his weight on his hands when lying on his front (item 47—Gross Motor).

(*a*) (i) Place a rolled blanket under his chest (Now the roll should be fairly big, so that he cannot rest his elbows on the floor.)

(ii) Place the baby's hands with his palms flat on the floor in front of him.

(iii) Place toys on the floor in front of the baby, or lie on the floor in front of him, and encourage him to support his weight on his hands by gently rolling him forward.

(iv) Move the toy or your own face up and slightly behind his head, so that he needs to lift his head and push up on his hands to look at you or the toy.

(*b*) (i) Lie the baby on his front with a nappy or scarf under his chest.

(ii) Grasp the ends of the scarf and lift his chest off the floor until his arms are straight and his hands are resting on the floor.

(iii) Gradually release the scarf so that he takes a little weight on his hands. Allow him to take more weight as he becomes stronger.

(*c*) Hold the baby in the air and 'zoom' him towards a flat surface (the floor or a table), face down. Do not let him hit the surface but note whether he extends his arms as if to stop himself (this is called the 'parachute response'). When he begins to do this, let his hands touch the surface and then gradually let him take some weight on his hands. (N.B. It may take some weeks for the parachute response to develop.)

Remember this is a fun game so let yourself go and make some good 'whizzing' noises.

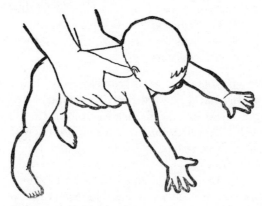

Figure 12. Baby extends his arms—'the parachute response'

Rolling

At the same time that the baby is raising his head and chest up off the mattress when lying on his front (item 22—Gross Motor), he is ready to begin the first step towards becoming mobile—rolling over (item 21—Gross Motor).

Note : It is easier to do these exercises without a nappy.

The first stage is for him to roll from his side to his front and from his side to his back. Start by showing him what you want him to do. Place him on his side and roll him over, back and over again a few times. If he cannot do it himself, teach him by :

1. (a) (i) Lie the baby on the floor on his right side.

   (ii) Attract his attention to a toy on the floor at his side. If he does not bring his left arm over to reach for it, prompt by bringing the arm over yourself.

   (iii) If he does not bring his left leg over his right leg on to the floor, prompt by bringing the leg over.

   (iv) Shake the toy and encourage him to roll over on to his stomach. If he does not roll over, prompt by giving him a slight push against his back.

   (v) Repeat with the baby lying on his left side. *Remember to fade out the prompt.*

   You may find he has a preferred side and does it best on this side. If so, start with this side but also give him practice on the other. You may also find you need four hands!

2. When the baby can roll from his side to his front and from his side to his back, he is ready to begin to roll from back to front (items 28, 36, 42—Gross Motor). Remember always to give him a few roll overs before you start.

(a) (i) Place the baby on his back with your hand against the small of his back, and attract his attention to the side by shaking a rattle so that his head is turned the way you want him to roll. (You may find it easier to do this with two people —one to attract the baby's attention and the other to push against his back).

   (ii) If the baby does not roll over to reach the toy—prompt by gently pushing up against his back. (N.B. You may need to use the arm and leg prompts described in (1a)).

(iii) Repeat this procedure encouraging the baby to roll over towards the other side.

(iv) Fade out the prompts.

(*b*) At the same time he can begin rolling from front to back.

(i) Place the child on his stomach on the floor. Kneel beside him and attract his attention so that he turns his head towards you.

(ii) Lift the arm nearest to you and bend it. Place the hand flat on the floor, about 2–3 inches (5–8 cm) from his shoulders. Try to make sure he is looking at what you are doing when you place his hand on the floor (this is a model).

(iii) Make sure the other arm does not restrict rolling over —either :

tuck it straight along close into the body,

or

bend it up with the hand to the shoulder underneath the body.

(iv) Place your hand underneath the baby's chest and gently push up and over (the physical prompt). You may need to hold his hand flat down on the floor for the first part of the push over. Say 'push up' or 'push over', emphasising the push —this is the verbal prompt.

(v) An alternative prompt to try is to push his elbow in slightly as you push the chest, so that he can feel the pressure on his hand as he goes over.

Remember to fade out the physical prompt. Also try lying down and rolling over yourself before you do this with your baby.

3. Play games in which you roll the baby on different surfaces— carpet, table, mattress, towel, paper, etc. You may find the baby is particularly stimulated when lying on crinkly paper—he likes the noise. So use this. Sometimes babies are interested in patterns or pictures on the sheet or mattress. If so, use them. In other words, if you observe anything that interests the baby try to use it.

Of course, this is only the way to start trying to help—the baby actually 'tells' us what to do, as Owen's mother found :

'When Owen was trying to roll but we were getting nowhere,

he gave us the cue how to help him. He would lie on his back and stick his legs up in the air, as though trying to roll over. If we then raised his legs a little and turned them a little, he got the message and rolled over on to his stomach. We had to prompt him for about three days before he mastered it. I mentioned this to a friend whose 'normal' baby could not roll and he learnt quickly in the same way!'

Creeping and crawling

When the baby creeps, he moves forward on his stomach. He crawls when he lifts his middle off the ground and moves forward on hands and knees. Not all babies creep or crawl, some hitch around on their bottoms. Some roll over and over and some move hardly at all before they walk.

At this stage, you can try the activities we describe to help your baby creep, but you will not yet know which method he is going to favour. Creeping usually precedes crawling, and both are coordinated activities which do seem to help towards walking.

But, if your baby shows later that he is determined to be a bottom hitcher do not worry : you can still help him to walk.

Creeping
When the baby can lie on his front and support his weight on his hands, you can begin to exercise to develop creeping.
(*a*) This requires two people.

> (i) Lie the baby on his front on the floor with a favourite toy *just* out of reach.
> (ii) One person should kneel behind the baby and place a hand against the baby's foot, encouraging him to push with each foot in turn. You can do this by exerting gentle pressure against the foot until the baby bends his knee up and then pushes against your hand.
> (iii) At the same time the other person kneels in front of the baby and attracts his attention to the toy, so that he pushes his head and chest up taking the weight on his hands.
> (iv) The person in front then takes one arm and moves it forward, placing the hand flat on the floor in front of the baby—the arm is outstretched but still slightly bent. If this

is the *right arm* the person at the back should be pushing against the *left foot*, and the baby should move slightly forward. Let him get the toy. You then move the left arm and right leg. When the baby moves forward, again let him get the toy. Do this a few times, on each occasion gradually increasing the distance he has to move to get the toy. This can be quite a difficult exercise to do, but it is worth trying.

Reaching and grasping

It is very important to be able to reach out and grasp things. Once you can reach out and touch objects you can begin to explore them, to feel their texture and size. When you can grasp you can pick things up, feel their weight, shake them, suck them, tap them, drop them. When you can use both hands you can twist them apart. In this way you can learn about the objects which make up your world and you can begin to do it *by yourself*.

The first thing to learn is to look at an object and guide your hand to it using your vision. (In the case of blind babies, they need to do this by sound, and they learn about the space around them, within their arms' reach, through their hands).

Always make sure that the baby is looking at the object, and try to make sure that he sees his hand and the object come together when reaching.

Reaching develops like this :

1. Babies reach first with one hand, to an object at the *side* of the body and at *eye level*.
2. They then learn to reach objects placed in the middle, at eye level.
3. Then they begin to reach for objects above and below eye level (e.g. on the table).
4. For (2) and (3) above they often use two hands, then gradually the hands can be used separately.

Grasping also has a pattern of development.

1. At first the baby reaches with his hand either fisted or wide open. When he contacts the object he often taps it or strokes it or pokes it with one finger.
2. Gradually he learns to shape his hand during the reach so that he can grasp the object—if it is small enough to grasp.
3. At first the object is grasped between all fingers and the palm.

4. Gradually, the thumb comes around and opposes the fingers (3 and 4 will not appear until much later than 1.)

Try to keep this picture of the development in mind when training the reaching, and remember always to watch the baby's eyes and make sure he is watching his hands and the object. (At this stage he will often watch his hands until he has grasped the object, then he will look away and may drop it. It is not until later that he begins to turn objects over and over and look at them.)

1. You can stimulate and train reaching either when the baby is lying on his back *or* propped up in a sitting position. If he is sitting remember to make sure his arms are free to move and he feels secure.

(*a*) (i) Bring a small object in from the side of the baby at *eye-level* and *within the reach of his arms*.

(ii) Make sure he looks at it and bring it *very slowly* toward the middle.

(iii) Give him *time* to reach—if he does not, take the object slowly down toward his hand, trying to keep him looking at it, and also bring his arm up (by taking his elbow and lifting.) If he does not touch the object, then touch the back of his hand or finger tips to encourage him to pat or grasp the object.

(iv) If he grasps the object let him play with it—do not take it from him immediately to try the reach again. To get the object to play with is the whole reason for the exercise, and this is his reward. You can also play a 'give it to me' game by gently pulling at the object, *or* a 'shake it up and down game', etc. This should help him to learn to play with the object, look at it for longer and grasp it for longer.

Remember to work on both arms, and also to fade out the prompts.

2. When the baby is lying on his back, suspend objects above him. A broom handle across two chairs (tied at each end) will work. From this, hang 'interesting' objects (that is—ones that catch the eye or make a noise).

(*a*) (i) Always check that the objects are within reach.

(ii) Use two objects at first, one on either side of his head, just above each shoulder. This will help him to learn to look from one to the other.

(iii) Gradually bring them into the middle—not too many objects.

(iv) Change them often.

(*b*) String objects between chair or table legs so that the baby can reach and grab.

(*c*) Later, when he is grabbing objects, you will find that dangling ones are difficult to grasp—also if tied on string they cannot be pulled down to the mouth etc. You will need to experiment with elastic and different shapes and weights (see 3 below).

(*d*) Observe if the baby is using two hands—one to grasp and one to steady the swinging object. If not, prompt the second hand.

3. When the baby will *reach* for *the ring or object without a physical prompt* (item 27—Adaptive) but does not grasp and control it :

(i) As he reaches, bring the object to touch the palm of his hand. If he does not grasp, then you will need to go back to Chapter 6 and use those plans for grasping.

(ii) When he will grasp after touching the palm, begin to touch only the finger tips.

(iii) Take the object towards his hand but do not touch the fingers.

(iv) Keep the object steady in the middle and make him bring his hand to it.

Remember to tell him how clever he is *after* he has achieved the objective you have set for him.

4. When the baby can reach out and grasp the object at chin level (item 28—Adaptive), hold it slightly higher than eye level, then slightly lower. If he does not reach, gradually bring it to the middle and level with his chin. Play these games until he can reach and grab anywhere within his arms' length.

5. When he can (i) *sit with support in a chair* and (ii) *reach out and touch objects*, place him in the chair with a table in front.

Remember that he has to learn to reach down for objects

before he will be able to pick small ones off the table. Try these three games :

(*a*) Get a toy with a rubber sucker at one end and a rattle or bright object at the other, and stick it on the table within his reach. You may need to model and prompt to show him how to use it—*but before you do, give him a few minutes to discover what to do for himself.*

(*b*) Place large objects on the table which are high enough for him to reach, but which are also graspable or good fun to bang or feel. When he can reach and contact these—gradually try smaller objects.

(*c*) Place a smallish object like a rattle on the table and get his attention. If he does not reach, gradually bring it a little higher, pausing every inch (2 cm) or so until he does reach.

If you find the table top is very smooth and the objects slide around too much when he is grasping, cover it with a non-slip surface. Later, when he can pick up an object on a surface where it does not slide, he will need to learn to use two hands to control the object on other surfaces.

6. When the baby can pick up a small object, such as a cube, from the table in front of him (item 33—Adaptive):

(*a*) Alter the position of the cube, placing it to one side then the other, then gradually further away to give him more practice at reaching.

(*b*) Also sometimes place it just out of reach. When he has tried to reach for it *once or twice* move it towards him so that he can get it.

7. Place a smaller object, the size of a currant, on the table. Attract the baby's attention to it and try to get him to reach for it and touch it—he will probably not be able to pick it up at this stage. (Item 12—Fine Motor.) If he tries to reach for it but does not succeed, push it toward his hand and prompt him to pick it up.

Grasping (items 4, 5, 6, 7, 8, 10—Fine Motor)
1. Observe the baby's grasp on the ring and cube. At first he will use his fingers against the palm of his hand, but gradually he should begin to use his thumb. If he does not begin to do this during this stage, use the ring or a wooden spoon handle for him

to grasp. Mould his grasp so that his thumb goes round one side of the rod, and his fingers round the other. Whenever he grasps, try to make sure his thumb is coming around opposite his fingers.

2. (a) Holding objects in both hands at the same time (item 34—Adaptive): place a cube or small toy in each of the baby's hands. If he immediately drops one or both, place them in his hands and hold his hands around them for a few seconds. Gradually fade out this prompt until he can hold them on his own.

(b) Also, get two short rods about half an inch (1 cm) thick. Whilst you are holding on to one end of each, get him to grasp the other so that he has one in each hand. Twist the rods to encourage a grasp and play a pulling-the-rod game.

3. When he can hold an object in each hand for 30 seconds or more, place one object in his hand and a second object, that he likes, on the table (item 39—Adaptive). Encourage him to reach for it, using prompts if necessary, so that he picks it up and holds both objects in his hands for short periods. You can then bring the two objects together and bang them in a 'clapping' game.

Learning to manipulate objects (items 24, 25, 32—Adaptive)
1. Give the baby lots of different materials to feel and play with.
(a) Stroke his hands on velvet or fur.
(b) Crumple paper and silver foil with him.
(c) (i) Put a piece of string in his hands and twist it and pull it against his fingers.
(ii) When he is holding objects in both hands, put one end of the string in each hand so that he is pulling it tight (item 37—Adaptive).
(d) Give him hard and soft things, warm and cold things, rough and smooth things. You can use anything you can think of, even ice cubes or sandpaper.
(e) Try surprising him by giving him objects which are unexpectedly different from the ones he is used to, e.g. a small heavy object, a big light one, rattles that *do not* rattle!

2. When he holds objects, make him look at them as he feels them. If he does not look when he has something in his hand, bring his hand up towards his eye level and gently shake and move it about in his vision.

3. Learning to use both hands (item 38—Adaptive): when he will hold objects in both hands for a few seconds or more:

(*a*) (i) Take a rod or wooden spoon about 9–12 inches (20–30 cm) long and hold it up for him to grasp.

(ii) When he has grasped it, bring his other hand up and get him to grasp the other end. If he will not grasp, then mould his hand around the rod. Then let go. This is a great game for teaching coordination of the two hands. At first babies let go quite quickly. Later they are not sure what to do, and pull with each hand—one lets go and the rod jumps up. This often attracts the visual attention, and they look at it.

The advantage of the long rod is that it can be grabbed by two hands, transferred from hand to hand, used to knock things, brought into the visual field or used to touch the body.

Make it more interesting by winding strips of coloured tape around it and tie little bells at one end.

(*b*) You can also play this game with a ring. Get the baby to grip it in both hands first, then let him hold it and move it.

(*c*) Also get him to grasp the ring or rod in one hand, then bring it up so that he is looking at the other end or side. Now bring his other hand (prompting from the elbow) up so that he grasps it and changes hands.

(d) When he will transfer the rod or ring from hand to hand, start using different shaped objects and smaller objects. Remember to think about the objective of the exercise—changing hand to hand. Many rattles on the market fit neatly into one hand and have a round end which is too big to grasp—this means it is difficult to transfer from one hand to the other.

4. (*a*) When the baby will hold on to the rod or spoon for a few minutes, give him plenty of opportunity to use it as a 'tool': to bang it on the table, a drum or tambourine and so on. You may need to show him how to do this *but remember always to give him time to try to discover it for himself before you demonstrate.*

(*b*) When he is lying on his back, suspend objects above him but a little too far away to reach. Then give him the rod or spoon so that he can reach them and bang them with it. This is quite difficult as it involves understanding what the rod can do—that it extends the range of the arm—and solving a problem. Try it out every few days (a probe) for a few seconds. But don't leave the baby with the objects suspended over him while he cannot do anything to them.

5. Turning the wrist (item 11—Fine Motor): It is important to be able to turn the wrist—rotate it from side to side—if you are going to turn objects around and look at them. When the baby is up to this level of development on the checklist, start to show him how to turn the wrist. Play a 'pull the object' game and gently turn his wrist from side to side by twisting the toy.

Hearing and listening
By now the baby shows interest in sounds, searching with his eyes for them.

1. When the baby can (i) hold his head steady when he is supported in a sitting position, and (ii) turn his head from side to side, you can try shaking a rattle or bell just out of his sight. The rattle or bell should be held on a level with his ear, and slightly behind so that he cannot see it. *Do not* make the sound immediately above his head or behind the baby, as he cannot locate the sound in these positions at this stage.
When he begins to turn to the sound in this position, gradually bring the sound lower so that he turns then looks down.
Note : Do not make the sounds too loud at first. Start quietly and gradually make them louder. If the baby does not respond, try two or three times then wait before trying again. If the baby does respond by turning his head and searching with his eyes, but does not locate the sound source, bring it up into his vision.

2. Give the baby objects which make different noises to play with—rattles, bells, a drum, squeaky toy etc. When he is holding the object show him how to make a noise with it—take his hand and do it with him if he does not do it himself. Eventually he should try to produce the sound himself (item 28—Communication).
Note: Some squeaky toys are quite hard to squeeze—you need to search for soft rubber ones.

3. At this stage the baby develops his interest in the noises of the world around him—his feed being prepared, the telephone ringing etc. Look for his responses to this sort of noise and show him where the sound comes from. Draw his attention to different

sounds like the fridge motor switching on and off, clock ticking, ice cream van chimes and so on.

Vision

Follow instructions in item 26—Adaptive. Move the spoon *very slowly* and observe the baby's eyes. When he stops following the spoon, bring it back a bit, attract his attention and then move it again. Gradually increase the distance you move it.

Permanence of objects

During this period the baby begins to understand the permanence of objects: when an object disappears from view he does not immediately forget about it. You can tell this because he looks at the place it disappeared from as though for it to reappear, or later, looks to see where it has gone. In peep-bo games he keeps looking in anticipation to see when your face or an object will reappear. This is a very important stage in development and well worth stimulating.

You can start this when the baby has begun to recognise his mother (or father). This is the beginning of memory, but mere recognition does not mean that his memory of her is still active when she is not there—only that he recognises her when she appears.

(*a*) You can begin to teach the baby to anticipate that you will reappear by calling to him before you come into the room, If he is beginning to look for sounds and to respond to his name, he will look round and see you as you enter the room.

(*b*) You can play hide and seek games with the baby, once he can follow your movements with his eyes. Attract his attention then move behind a chair.

> (i) Quickly reappear at the same point that you disappeared.
>
> (ii) Later, let him see the top of your head move across behind the chair (visual prompt), then show him your whole face as you come out at the other side and laugh and smile and say 'Peep'.
>
> (iii) Remember that the longer the time when he cannot see you the more likely he is to forget, so at first make the time very short, then gradually extend it and also fade out the visual prompt.

(*c*) You can play the same game hiding your face behind a screen or cloth or even your hands. When the baby is looking for noises you can use noise prompts to attract his attention to the screen by making noises behind the screen before you reappear. Remember to fade out these prompts.

(*d*) Take a rattle and move it *slowly* across the baby's line of vision shaking it, then move it down towards the floor shaking it to keep the baby's attention. When he stops following it bring it up, attract his attention to it, then move it again.

(*e*) (i) When he can follow it down past the edge of his chair *gradually* increase the speed until eventually you can move it across and then drop it. Make sure it makes a noise when you drop it. It may help to drop it on to a tin tray.

(ii) If he does not look for it, bang it on the floor saying : 'Look, here it is'. Give him a physical prompt—push him over to have a look !

Then bring it up—big surprise—and drop it again. By this time the baby is ready to look for things when he drops them himself (items 44 and 45—Adaptive).

(iii) Put a tin by the side of the chair so that the dropped objects make a good bang.

(*f*) When the baby can track moving objects well, you can build upon this by playing a game where the object disappears behind a screen.

(i) Take a toy cat or dog and attract the baby's attention to it.
(ii) 'Walk' it across in front of him and behind a small screen, keep it moving so that it reappears at the other side. Saying things like : 'pussy walk,' or 'where's pussy gone, here she is.' (Again remember that the longer it is hidden the more likely the baby is to lose it).
(iii) Gradually build up the time it is hidden, starting with a *very short time*. You can also use noise prompts at first—for instance use a toy that makes a noise—then gradually fade them out.

When you play this game, watch the baby's eyes to see if he looks to the other side of the screen before the object reappears, and so shows that he is beginning to *anticipate* its reappearance. Be very pleased when he does because this is a big step forward.

Problem solving

(*a*) (i) Attach a favourite toy to a piece of coloured wool or string that will show up against the table.

(ii) Place the toy out of the baby's reach and extend the string to him.

(iii) Put the string in his hand and at first wind it around once or twice so that it will not slip. Attract his attention to the toy.

(iv) Give him time to play and to discover that he can pull the toy to him. If he loses interest in the toy, get his attention and, holding his hand with the string in it, pull it back so that the toy moves (physical prompt). Say 'Look, get the . . . ' (verbal prompt) and pull the toy up until the baby can reach it. Repeat this a few times.

(v) Gradually fade out the prompt by pulling his hand back less each time until he pulls the string himself (item 51—Adaptive). Eventually he will pull the string to get the toy (item 55—Adaptive).

(*b*) Also tie noisy toys on to short lengths of string and then fix the strings to the table. If he drops them off the side he can then pull the string to get them back. If you use a rubber sucker fixed to the centre of the table and tie the strings to this he can discover for himself that if he pulls them the toys make a noise—even if he can't see them. If he pulls more the toy reappears (object permanence).

Social

At this stage the baby is becoming more socially aware. He probably smiles more readily, and is beginning to recognise familiar people and reach out for them.

1. If the baby does not reach up to you when you approach and lean over him talking and smiling, exaggerate the movements that you make before you pick him up. Stretch your arms out to him, pause just before you touch him, place your hands around him under his arms and pause again.

As soon as he makes a movement, e.g. lifting his arms up or

head up as though *anticipating* your picking him up, lift and cuddle him (items 27, 47, Gross Motor).

2. (*a*) Hold a mirror in front of the baby so that he can see himself. Take his hands and pat them against his reflection in the mirror, then against his face. Move the mirror up and down so that his face appears and disappears.
(*b*) Let him see your reflection appearing and disappearing in the mirror.

3. As we noted in Chapter 6, if you imitate the baby's noises and expressions he will find it an enjoyable game. This is the best way to build up his social development at this time.

Feeding (items 13, 24, 25, 26, Personal—Social)

Sucking, chewing and swallowing
1. Babies usually start on solids at about three to four months, and your health visitor or doctor will probably advise you on the right time to start introducing solids to your baby. At first the food is given strained and fairly runny, but it is advisable gradually to thicken the consistency and begin to introduce a somewhat lumpier consistency when the baby begins to make chewing movements.

2. Remember that the baby has learnt to suck by pushing his tongue forward and backward. When you come to solids he will do the same and will push some food out of his mouth. He will then *learn* to use his tongue differently—pushing the food between the gums to chew, and back to swallow. Handicapped babies take longer to learn this and will continue pushing the tongue forward for some time. Do not mistake this as meaning he does not like the food.
You may find that the baby is very hungry at the beginning of a feed and gets frustrated with the spoon feeding. In this case give him some milk first to take the edge of his appetite.

3. The tongue and lip movements needed to chew food are also needed to produce different sounds ready for speech.

G*

(a) Tongue

To 'exercise' the tongue and to help the baby to learn to chew and swallow instead of sucking :

(i) Place food on the centre of the tongue rather than the tip.
(ii) Encourage the baby to chew and swallow with the mouth closed. This behaviour may take a long time to develop but it is worth encouraging as soon as possible. You can try to help by gently pushing the chin up to close the lips as the baby chews. *But* some babies will not like this, so do not make the task of teaching him to feed from a spoon more difficult by doing this if he does not like it. Do one thing at a time—teach him to feed from a spoon first, then when this is well established start teaching him to keep his mouth closed.
(ii) As soon as you can, start to teach the baby to lick—use ice creams, lollipops, food on spoons.

(b) Lips

(i) You can now start to encourage the baby to use his lips to take the food off the spoon. Try taking the spoon up against the top gum and lip so that the food is dragged off, and then gently push the chin up to get the lips to close.
(ii) Any games or imitations that get the baby to close his lips tightly as in kissing, blowing, humming will help.

Note: For the baby to keep his mouth closed he needs to be able to breathe through his nose. If your baby has a lot of 'snuffles' or nasal congestion you should consult your doctor for advice.

Self-feeding skills

1. When the baby can suck well and begins to hold objects and to take them to his mouth, give him rusks, fingers of toast or biscuits to feed himself with. At first you will need to hand the rusk to him, and when he drops it he will probably not pick it up again unless you draw his attention to it. But the main aim is for him to get it to his mouth and discover that he can eat it. It is best to start finger feeding at this age, when babies start taking things to their mouths, as if you leave it later you may find that the baby shows more resistance. Of course, you must always be with the baby when he first starts to feed himself and watch him carefully in case he bites off too large a piece and chokes. Experi-

ment with different tastes of foods—put different flavoured jam or spreads on the toast, for instance.

2. When the baby can pick up a rusk and chew on it eating, some of it, give him smaller pieces of food to pick up. This is good practice for his grasping and picking up. Small chocolate buttons are often extremely successful in persuading a baby to pick up small objects, and to use his thumb and fingers against each other in grasping. (Remember to place the buttons round side down— so they are easy to pick up.)

3. Towards the end of this stage he can also start drinking from a cup. Many people find that the feeding cups with special spouts are most useful at this stage, and they do ensure that the baby does not pour the drink all over himself, although a fair amount will end up all over him even with one of these! However, some babies object to the spout. In this case use a small, ordinary cup.

(i) If possible obtain a cup (with or without a spout) with two handles, that is not too heavy.

(ii) Half fill the cup and place the baby's hands on the handles (prompt).

(iii) Guide the cup to his mouth and tip it so that he gets a small amount of the drink (prompt). When he swallows this tip it slightly again.

The amount of liquid in the cup is important— if there is too much it will spill out too quickly, if there is too little you will have to tip the cup up too far before it comes out, and it will be more difficult for the baby to learn to do this himself. Experiment until you find the right amount.

(iv) Gradually fade out the prompts until the baby can pick up the cup off the table and drink from it. (Do not be too worried if he spills a lot down his front.) At first he will probably just drop the cup when he has finished or wave it about —be ready to catch it before it falls!

Note: *At this stage he will not be able* to put it down himself as he has not yet learnt *to release objects at will*, so you will need to guide it down for him.

Vocalisation

The baby considerably extends the range of sounds he makes during this period—he will be more 'talkative', and coo and laugh and begin to pronounce different syllables (items 16, 19, 23, 24, 25 and 26—Communication).

However, one of the most important things for him to learn is that the noises he makes have some 'pay-off' (reward). React to his vocalisations as though they have meaning. In face to face situations, when he makes little sounds, reward him immediately with a big smile and talk back to him.

Imitating the sounds he makes it particularly useful at this stage, and remember, having imitated his sound, *give him time to respond* before you talk again. When you talk and imitate remember to exaggerate your mouth movements.

If he is in his chair or lying down and making sounds, look at him and go to him as much as possible.

Comprehension (items 29, 30—Communication)

The baby is not only learning that his vocalisations have a pay-off, but also that your vocalisations have a meaning for him. This is the beginning of comprehension.

(*a*) At first it will not be the words themselves but the expression in your voice, the inflections and intonations, that have meaning for the baby. Exaggerate these to help the baby.

(*b*) When you approach the baby to feed him or pick him up, greet him by his name—putting lots of emphasis on it. For instance, when you go to him when he wakes up in the morning, always say 'Hello *Johnny*' with emphasis on the Johnny. In this way he can begin to associate the sound of his name with your approach to him, being picked up and other pleasant things— he will begin to respond to the name.

(*c*) When you do things with him tell him what you are doing, using the same words each time, e.g. 'roll-over', 'up you come', 'pull' etc.

Similarly, when you go to pick him up say 'come on'—holding out your arms in a clear gesture—'Up you come'.

Point to things with a big gesture and say 'look'. Take him to things and say 'look'.

(*d*) Simple nursery rhymes and rhythms can also be very useful at this stage. They help with intonation, and they are fun.

9 : Six to nine months

The main characteristic of this period is that we see the beginnings of understanding and independence.

The baby increasingly explores his world and the objects in it, and begins to control them, act upon and understand their use.

By the end of this period the baby can sit steadily on the floor for long periods. When sitting he can lean forward, pick up objects and then sit up again. He may also begin to pull himself up to a standing position on the rails of his cot or on the furniture and so open up new visions of his world.

He may begin to creep on his stomach or sit and hitch himself around, finding new places of interest and excitement.

His reaching and picking up should now be quite efficient and he begins to learn more about the objects he plays with. He learns that if he drops them and cannot instantly see them he can find them if he looks down—they still exist. He begins to imitate and to develop some understanding of the familiar words that he hears every day—'no', 'bye-bye', 'clap hands' etc. In short he is really beginning to make sense of his world.

Sitting
1. When the baby can sit without any support for a minute or two (item 45—Gross Motor) :

(i) Sit him on the floor and kneel in front of him.
(ii) Make sure that he is steady and balanced, then hold a toy for him to reach out to. First hold it straight in front of him at chest level. When he can reach and grab it easily—
(iii) Move it to one side, then the other, giving the baby time to reach and grasp it each time. When this is achieved—
(iv) Move it down to the floor in front of him, and finally to the floor at his side.

You will need to be ready to support the baby at first, but gradually decrease the support so that he is learning to bend, turn, and readjust his balance (item 52, 59—Gross Motor).

2. When the baby can sit with a little support he does not need all the support provided by the Relax chair, which may also restrict his movement, particularly the movement of his arms. You should now move him into a high chair. At first you may need to pad his back and raise him up so that his navel is in line with the table. Make sure the pads are secure and do not slip. It is a good idea to use foam pads, as cushions tend to slide. You may also need to slip some pads either side of his thighs at first, and to rig up a harness or elastic holder as described in the last chapter. If possible use a high chair that has an adjustable foot rest. If it has not, pad the foot-rest so that the baby's feet can rest flat on it when he is sitting in a straight position in the chair. This helps sitting and posture enormously. It is a good idea now to put the baby in the chair when you are playing with objects, and, of course, when you are feeding him, so that he is sitting with a straight back for as much of the time as possible. He will, of course, also need to sit on the floor to play, to give him opportunities for movement and adjustment of posture; but babies often tend to sit with rounded backs when they sit on the floor, so you should ensure that he is able to sit up straight for some of the time each day.

Sitting up by himself

This develops at the end of this stage (items 60, 68—Gross Motor), but you can begin training when his back is strong and he can sit unsupported for 10 minutes or more, and when he is happily rolling over or twisting around.

1. You will have been doing the exercises of pulling up to a sitting position with the baby for some time now, and when he can pull himself up easily holding on to your thumbs, he is ready to learn how to sit up by himself. This requires a slightly different action from the one you have been doing up to now.

First try it yourself—lie down flat on your back on the floor, then sit up. You probably pushed up with your elbows, then hands *or* you rolled to the side and pushed yourself up with one arm. If you try to sit up without turning and without using your arms to push yourself up it is quite different—try it!

When the baby needs to learn how to sit up, we can help him by building upon his ability to roll over (items 36, 42—Gross Motor).

(*a*) (i) Lie him on his back on the floor and kneel by the side of his head.

(ii) Take hold of his arm nearest to you, and bend it, placing it against his side so that his elbow, forearm and the palm of his hand are flat on the floor. Put your hand on top of his hand to hold it down against the floor.

(iii) Take hold of his other hand and pull his arm across his body towards you, then upwards until the baby is in a sitting position, holding the other hand down on the floor as you do this. Don't just pull him up. Make sure he helps himself by pushing up with his hand and pulling on your hand.

Gradually fade out the prompts so that the baby does more of the pulling himself and also pushes against the floor.

(iv) Remember to alternate the sides you use.

(*b*) When the baby can pull himself up in this way holding on to your hand, lie him in his cot and place him in the same position, but instead of taking his hand in yours place it on the bar of the cot. Attract his attention upwards and encourage him to sit up by saying 'sit up' (verbal prompt) and if necessary pulling a little on his arm (physical prompt). You will need to experiment to find out which bar of the cot is best for him.

Fade out the physical prompt.

Figure 13. Balance in sitting position—attention attracted to a toy in front of him

Figure 14. Balance in sitting position—attracting baby's attention to the side to encourage him to turn

Standing

By now the baby should be able to take most of his weight when standing (item 35, 46—Gross Motor). The objective now is to teach him to stand for longer and longer, and also to pull to a stand (item 50, 53—Gross Motor).

1. (*a*) You can use the exercises described in the last chapter for standing.

(*b*) (i) Also place toys on a table and stand him at it so that he supports himself with his arms.

(ii) Make the toys do things to keep him interested, and try to keep him standing for a few seconds longer each time.

2. When the baby can pull himself up to a standing position holding on to your thumbs :

(a) Attract and maintain his attention by talking to him. Try to keep him in a standing position for a few seconds at a time, so that he is bearing his weight on his feet and your hands are only helping him to balance.

(b) Teach him to pull himself up to stand using the furniture.

(i) Sit him on the edge of your knee in front of a low table or the sofa. Make sure that it is low enough for him to rest his hands easily on it, so that he can pull himself up. (Often you can do this by taking the cushions off the sofa.)

(ii) Place a favourite toy on the table or sofa just out of reach. Attract the baby's attention to the toy.

(iii) When he attempts to get it and his hands are resting on the edge of the table or sofa, raise your knee very slightly so that his weight goes on to his feet (this is the prompt). Continue raising him until he pushes with his feet against the floor and brings himself to a standing position.

Gradually fade out the prompt.

(iv) When the baby can raise himself to a standing position against the furniture when sitting on your knee, gradually lower the level of your knees—as far as possible! Also move him further away from the edge of the table/sofa, until eventually he is sitting on the floor and pulling himself up to stand (item 56—Gross Motor).

(c) Another way to pull up to stand is from a kneeling position. Therefore it is useful for the baby to learn to take his weight and balance on his knees. Place the baby on his hands and knees on the floor and kneel behind him so that his feet are against your knees. Place a nappy round his stomach and pull gently on it until he comes up into a kneeling position. Remember to make the baby participate so that he pushes up on to his knees. You can link this exercise with 1 (a) of crawling.

3. *At the same time* as pulling to stand the baby needs to develop his balance in a standing position. To help him do this try these exercises.

(a) Sit in a chair and sit the baby on the floor, so that his back is against your legs. Put a nappy, towel or scarf round his chest and under his arms. Pull slightly on the nappy to bring him into a standing position. This helps him balance, as his arms are free. Once he is standing, gradually release the pressure of the towel so that he has to balance for himself.

(b) When he has pulled to a stand holding on to your fingers, gradually slacken your hold so that he has to balance himself.

Once he is standing for a second or two, you just work at making it longer and longer. Remember to keep his attention on you. Also remember you can make record charts of his standing, to look for progress and to check whether the exercises are working.

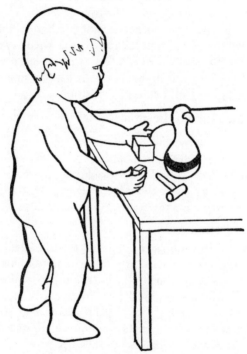

Figure 15. Standing at a table

(c) One of our mothers who had been strongly directed to match toys to the baby's developmental level, went to the TOY LIBRARY to find something that would help the baby to develop sitting balance and standing—and be good fun as well. She found a rocking horse with a chair in place of a saddle. The baby sat in it happily and soon rocked—helping his balance. Also she found that he could hold on to the cross-bar and pull himself up into a standing position—his feet being on the floor or support bar. Within a few weeks he was also rocking in a standing position. This is excellent practice, and had a noticeable effect in reducing mum's backache.

Choose toys carefully and try to select those that allow the baby to learn by himself.

Baby walkers

When he can sit unsupported, baby walkers are very useful. You will need to introduce the baby to the walker very gently. Start by just having it around for him to see. Then let him hold on to the rail from the outside and just look at it. When you sit him in it the first few times, make sure you are kneeling beside the walker at eye-level with baby, and maintain plenty of physical contact. Just let him sit in it for a while before you start to move it around. Then do it very slowly.

You will need to make sure that the height is correct so that the baby can get his feet on the floor.

Once he is using the walker, make sure that he has opportunities to find and play with toys after he has 'walked' to them, e.g. place toys on low tables etc.

At first babies often simply stand in the walker and it may be some weeks before they actually walk it. Don't rush them into using it—you may put them off. When they are making stepping movements (item 47—Gross Motor), then teach them how to use the walker—if they have not started.

Note : In certain cases it is possible to obtain specially constructed baby walkers through the National Health Service. You can ask your Health Visitor or Physiotherapist about this if your baby has any additional physical handicaps.

Crawling (items 48, 49, 51, 58—Gross Motor)

When the baby can push himself up on to his elbows and hand, begin to teach him to support himself on his hands and knees.

(*a*) Lie him on his front on the floor with a nappy under his chest. Kneel behind him and gently pull him up with the nappy until he is on his hands and knees. Hold him like this for a short time, then begin to rock him back and forward. Gradually reduce the help you give, until the baby can push himself on to his hands and knees and rock.

(*b*) Use a very firmly rolled up blanket or a roll of foam under the baby's middle so that his hands and knees are on the floor in a crawling position, and his middle is supported. Gently roll him forward and backward to take weight on hands and knees. (N.B. This roll must be very firm now—it may help to use a large cardboard tube or two large tins taped together in the middle of the blanket or foam roll).

(*c*) You will need two people, one at the front and one at the back of the baby.

(i) If the baby can support himself on his hands and knees, place him in this position. (If not, use the roll or a towel around the waist to maintain this position, but keep trying him without and practising exercise one.)

(ii) Place a favourite toy just out of reach of the baby and attract his attention to it.

(iii) Move the baby's arms and legs as you did in the creeping

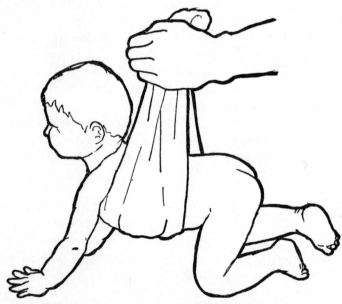

Figure 16. Pulling onto hands and knees

exercise, i.e. right arm and left leg, left arm and right leg. To move his legs, push slightly against the foot so that he moves the leg himself.

(iv) Gradually decrease the help you give with moving the arms—first moving the arm for him, then pushing it slightly, until the baby can move his arms forward himself.

(v) At the same time decrease the pressure on the foot, until the baby can move both arms and legs himself.

(vi) Always make sure that the baby obtains the toy and is therefore rewarded for the movement he makes. Praise him and talk to him.

Grasping (items 12, 13, 14, 16—Fine Motor)
1. Continue with the exercises described in the last section, giving the baby a variety of objects to pick up, and encouraging him to reach and pick up smaller objects, particularly very small objects using his thumb and fingers against each other.

Manipulation

1. Letting go
At the end of this stage the baby should be able to release an object. First he will be able to release it against a firm surface (item 15—Fine Motor), then eventually to drop it when he wants to.

(*a*) (i) Sit the baby in his high chair and place a small toy or object on the table for him to pick up.

(ii) When he has picked it up, let him play with it and examine it for a few seconds, then, taking hold of his hand with the toy in it, say 'put it down' (verbal prompt). Place the hand with the toy down against the top of the table, and stroke the back of his hand so that he opens his hand (physical prompt).

(iii) When he releases the object, pick it up and say 'Good boy,' *showing him* you have got the toy.

Gradually fade out the physical prompts.

(*b*) You can also do this exercise by saying 'Give it to mummy' and placing the baby's hand against yours.

2. Two objects together (items 55, 58, 61—Adaptive)

Learning to relate two objects to each other, like banging a drum with a stick, or banging two cubes together, is an important first step in learning about objects and how to use them. This builds up into more complicated play, such as putting things into tins, pegs into holes, cups on saucers or reaching into a bag to take out a sweet or crisp. If you offer a young baby a bag with sweets or biscuits in it he will often grab the bag, as he has not learnt the use of the bag and the relationship of the sweets to the bag— that is, that they are inside the bag.

The following games will begin to develop these activities.

(*a*) (i) Take 2 small toys yourself and bang them together, say- 'bang bang' or something similar.

(ii) Give him the toys. If the baby does not imitate you, hold his hands and bang them together in a clapping movement (physical prompt), saying 'bang . . . bang' (verbal prompt). Gradually fade out the physical prompt.

Or, both of you hold toys and bang them together at the same time

(*b*) Take a drum or tin, and a spoon. Give the baby a spoon as well, then bang your spoon on the drum saying 'bang the drum' (verbal prompt). If the baby does not imitate you, take his hand and bang the drum with him (physical prompt).

Fade out the physical prompt.

You will have noticed that these items are beginning to use Imitation, and we will go into this further in the next section.

3. Attention span (items 39, 46, 48, 52, 62—Adaptive)

When the baby is able to hold two objects, he can begin to extend his *span of attention* to include three objects. By span of attention we mean the number of things he will take note of at one time.

(i) Give the baby a cube in each hand, then place a third cube on the table in front of him. Bang the cube on the table to draw his attention to it. At first he may drop the other cubes and reach for the third.

Continue practising the game for short periods each day, until he will look at the third cube without dropping the other two.

(ii) Try it with other objects. Note that some will attract him more than others, and if these are on the table he will be more likely to drop one of those he is holding.

(iii) When he will hold two objects and look at the third without dropping one, offer him the third. Note if he reaches for it whilst still holding the other two. He may try to bang it or even try to get hold of it between two hands. When he attempts to get the third object you offer, place it on the table.

If he does not reach, prompt a reach by moving his arm forward. Always end by getting him to do something to the third object—tap it, push, etc. without letting go of the ones in his hand (item 62—Gross Motor).

Fade out the reaching prompt.

Imitation (items 54, 61, 65—Adaptive)
The baby will soon begin to imitate actions, and this is an important aid in learning.

There are all sorts of actions you can use when you begin to teach imitation. Those used with rhymes are useful—clap hands, so tall etc., and everyday actions like waving. You can also use the actions the baby performs himself, like banging objects on the table, to get him to do this after you.

We shall take the example of beating a hand on the table (item 54—Adaptive) to show you the sequence to follow.

(i) First show him a model : do the action yourself, using the appropriate verbal prompt, like 'pat the table'.

(ii) Say 'baby (or name) pat the table'.

(iii) If the baby does not imitate your action, take his hand and do it with him (physical prompt), again using the verbal prompt. You also pat the table with the other hand.

(iv) Fade out the physical prompt, e.g. let go of his hand but keep patting the table yourself.

(v) When he has learnt this and will copy your action, go on to other actions. This is generalising the learning. (see Chapter 5).

When the baby imitates quickly and easily you can begin to use imitation whenever possible.

Permanence of Objects

At this stage the baby begins to :

Look for things he has dropped (item 53—Adaptive), and

Find things that are hidden (items 57, 64—Adaptive).

The baby should be looking for dropped objects quite consistently by now—that is four out of five times—providing he is interested in the game.

If he is not, you will need to continue with the games discussed in the last chapter.

You can also play the following games.

1. (a) Give the baby a rattle and, when he is holding it in his hand, cover it with a cloth. Now he can feel the rattle, and when he moves his hand he can hear it but he cannot see it.

If he does not pull the cloth off to look at the rattle then :

(i) Lift the cover saying 'find the rattle' so that he can see the rattle, then replace it.

(ii) Say 'find the rattle' again : encourage him to lift the cover himself. If he does not make any move to do this, prompt by placing one end of the cover in his other hand. When he moves his hand and pulls the cover off attract his attention to the rattle.

(iii) Fade out the prompt so that the baby will take the cover off the rattle himself.

Note : If he drops the rattle and plays with the cloth, or pays attention to the cloth and ignores the rattle, let him explore and get used to the cloth first.

At this stage you can also :

(b) (i) Place a large attractive noisy toy on the table in front of the baby. Half cover it with a cloth so that he can see part of it.

(ii) Lift the cloth and show him the toy, then replace the cloth so that it is half covered again.

(iii) Say 'find the . . .' and if the baby does not lift the cloth, then either

shake the toy to attract his attention, or

slide the cloth slowly back, or

prompt the reach, or

do all three—until he obtains the toy.

This is also a good game to teach him to *listen* for sounds. When the baby can remove the cloth himself, use non-noisy toys and go on to :

2. (i) Using a large toy again, cover it completely with a cloth so that the baby can see the shape underneath the cloth but not the toy itself.
(ii) Go through the same stages as before, until the baby will find the toy by removing the cloth.
(iii) When he can do this you can move on to using a smaller toy, until eventually he will find something very small that does not show as a lump under the cloth (item 64—Adoptive).

Note : When you are playing this game you may again find that, as soon as the baby grasps the cloth, his attention is transferred to the cloth itself. If you have given him plenty of experience with bits of cloth then you will need to attract his attention back to the toy by banging it on the table, etc.

3. Toys under see-through containers (e.g. plastic glass or small jar) :

(i) Attract baby's attention to the toy.
(ii) *Just as he is about* to reach and grasp it pop the cup over the top. You can also play with see-through bags etc. and see how he gets on.

A short story
One of our mothers was finding it difficult to get the baby interested in looking for the hidden object under the cloth. As soon as the object was hidden the baby would just look away or look at mum and laugh.

Mum was determined. She needed an object or something which really interested the baby. She asked herself, what does she look at most. After observing the baby's looking behaviour for some time she found the answer. It was their pet Alsatian dog. So, she covered the dog with a table cloth !

The baby laughed and got excited and was delighted when mum whipped off the cloth and there was the dog.

Off went mum covering the television, the chairs, dad. . . .

Within a few days the baby had got the idea and was finding objects under cloths.

Moral

Don't give up. Be determined. Be inventive. In fact when you are stuck try to think of the most bizarre thing you can do to make your point. It often works.

Feeding (items 35, 36, 37, 38, 41, 43, 46, 47—Social)

Self feeding

The baby will now be making progress both with drinking from a cup and with finger feeding. You may find that as you are feeding him he will try to grasp the spoon. When he does this, you should use the opportunity to begin teaching him to feed himself. This will of course be a very messy business, so be prepared before you begin.

When the baby grasps the spoon, you can put your hand over his and guide the spoon to his mouth whilst he is still holding it, then help him remove the food (see below), then guide the spoon down to the plate to scoop up more food and up to his mouth again. It is often easier and more successful if you stand slightly behind the baby when you are doing this, so that your action is the same as his. (See Chapter 5 p. 141 for details).

Sometimes, however, you will find that the baby strongly resists. He does not want your hand over his—he wants to have the spoon himself. In this case give him a spoon and have one yourself as well. In this way he can make some attempts to put his spoon in his mouth etc. but you can also give him some food and he may learn to do it himself by imitation. If not, you will need to be insistent and train him.

The two difficult stages are scooping from the dish, and getting the food off the spoon when it is in the mouth.

Scooping is helped by correct physical prompts, and also by having a reasonable amount of food—sticky and gooey, at first— in the dish.

Try getting the food off the spoon yourself. You will find that you place the spoon in your mouth, close your lips over it to drag the food off, at the same time lifting the spoon out and up against the upper lip. When you are prompting the feeding this is what you do. You may also need to push under the baby's chin to get the mouth closed (see previous chapter).

Chewing

By this time the baby will usually have been taking strained foods for some time, and you can begin to thicken the food and encourage chewing. You can gradually make this strained food thicker by adding things, such as mashed potato or mincemeat. Try to get him used to slightly different textures of food so that he does not become so used to one texture that he will not take any other.

To encourage him to chew, give him rusks and biscuits, and when you are doing this model the chewing movements yourself for him to imitate.

Note : If the baby is teething and his gums are painful he will not chew well.

Dressing (item 54, 55, 56—Social)

It seems very early to think of dressing at this age, but you can begin to train some of the skills needed. The main one at this time is pushing the arm up through the sleeves. You do this by placing the hand in the sleeve or arm-hole of the vest, saying 'push' and if necessary prompting from the elbow.

You can also teach pulling down over the head. First games are :

(*a*) Pulling cloth or paper off the face.

(*b*) Pulling hats or cloths off the head.

(*c*) Place the vest or jumper over the head so that it is covering the face, but the hair and top of the head are poking out of the neck hole. Then leave the child to pull it down, saying 'peep-oo' when he does. If he does not pull it down, then use a physical prompt.

Communication

1. Listening

(*a*) Draw the baby's attention to all the different noises around him, to help him to become more aware of sounds and distinguish between them. If possible, show him the object that is making the noise and tell him its name. If it is an object which vibrates when it makes a noise, e.g. sometimes the fridge will vibrate when the motor switches on—take him up to it and let him feel the difference between the vibration when the motor is on, and therefore making a noise, and the stillness when it is off and silent.

(b) Play a game using a few different noises. Collect suitable objects such as a clock that ticks, a bell, a toy car that makes a noise. Make the noise with the object just behind the baby, then bring it into his sight, giving it to him and naming it. Gradually he will begin to link the different sounds with the different objects.

(c) Continue the game described in the last chapter, where the baby has to turn to a sound. When he can turn to a sound at ear level, and then slightly below ear level, bring the sound down further until he turns smoothly to find it.

The development of turning to sounds is :

    (i) looks for a sound at ear level;
    (ii) looks down in a curve for sound;
    (iii) looks straight down to sound.

Follow this progression in your games.

2. *Vocalisation* (items 31, 32, 33, 35, 38, 39, 40, 41, 42—Communication)

All babies and adults for that matter, make noises, such as sneezing, crying, squeaking, gurgling, which are not found in actual speech. In the first months of life most babies begin to make noises that are like later speech sound, e.g., b, g and k. At about 5–6 months these speechlike sounds become predominant, and the baby begins to link them together, e.g. b- b- b-, then ba-ba-ba-, etc.

This is what we call 'babbling', and it is extremely important in the development of language. You should try to encourage it so that it does not stop before words come. If it does fade out, the baby may have particular difficulty in learning to speak. You can encourage 'babbling' by imitating the baby's sounds. This does two things : (i) it draws the baby's attention to the sound he makes; (ii) it rewards the baby for making the sound.

You may have to continue the 'babbling' for a considerable length of time, and this takes patience and persistence. If your child is two or three, you may feel a bit silly in babbling to him, but it is very important for his later speech that you try to do this. A useful way of doing it sometimes is to imitate familiar noises with him, e.g. animal noises—baa-baa, moo-moo; an engine—brrm, brrm; a clock, t- t- t-, blowing raspberries, etc.

When the baby's range of sound has increased and he begins to joint sounds together, ba-ba, da-da, ga-ga, he is ready to begin to imitate sounds. Often he first imitates sounds such as blowing raspberries. You can help him to learn to imitate sounds by always making sure that he can see your face when you are teaching him, and by exaggerating the movements of your face. You may notice that at first he imitates the movement of your mouth but does not make any sound. Always reward him for this by praise, smiles, etc., and then repeat the sound until eventually he can imitate it.

3. Comprehension

(a) Many parents say that the baby understands what they say all the time. But when you observe the parent they are often *using a gesture* as well as the words. When you then test the baby with *words only* he does not do what you ask. The comprehension of gesture and words *together* develops first, followed by words without gestures. Make sure that you use good clear gestures (prompts) when teaching comprehension *but* also make sure that you fade them out (item 43 Communication).

(i) Try one of the actions the baby knows well, such as clap hands or bye-bye, but do not provide a model (gesture), just use the verbal cue.

(ii) Give the baby time to respond, and then repeat the verbal cue. If he does not respond, provide the model for imitation and repeat the instruction.

(iii) Fade out the model until the baby will respond to the verbal instructions alone.

(iv) Do this using different gestures.

(b) The baby should now begin to understand the word and tone of 'no' (item 34—Communication). Say 'no' whenever you stop him from doing something that he is not allowed to do. Eventually he will make the link between the word 'no' and you stopping him. However, you should not expect him to stop altogether at this stage. When you say 'no' he will probably stop what he is doing and look at you for a few seconds, then go back to it. In this case you may have to remove him from temptation and distract him.

Therefore : say 'No'.

(i) If he looks at you, say 'no' again and gesture by shaking your head and perhaps waving a finger. Then distract him.

(ii) If he does not look at you, repeat 'no' and if again no response go over to him, stop him doing whatever it was and at the same time look at him. When you have his attention (you may need to pull his chin around to look at you) say 'no', again using gestures. Then get him interested in something else.

(c) As we said in the last chapter, at this stage baby responds to and understands the intonation in what you say when he does not understand the actual words. Remember to make the intonation clear, and exaggerate it.

Eye level

Imagine you are the same height as your child. Think what it is like when people talk to you from a great height—not very good for interaction. People are far more friendly when they are on the same eye-level with you.

As your child gets older and begins to stand and walk, get into the habit of squatting down so that you have face to face contact and are on the same eye-level. It really does make a great deal of difference to communication.

10 : Nine to twelve months

During this period the baby becomes really mobile. He rolls, crawls or hitches around and he can easily explore. He begins to move sideways when he is holding on to the furniture, and he can walk with his hands held or pushing his baby walker. By the end of this stage he is beginning to take one or two steps on his own. He is now much more skilful with his hands and he can release things when he wishes, so he begins to take things out of and put things in containers. His memory is developing, he can look for things that have disappeared, and also get to them when they are out of reach or out of sight.

He shows his growing understanding of the world by the way in which he uses objects. For instance he recognises the use of a cup—he may pick it up and put it to his mouth, even though it has no liquid in it; and if given a cup and saucer he may put the cup on the saucer in the appropriate way. He recognises familiar situations and anticipates happenings. For instance, he may hold out his foot for his shoe when he sees you pick up the shoe.

He begins to use gesture to communicate—pointing to things he wants and shaking his head to mean 'no'. Once he can imitate sound he begins to imitate words and by the end of this stage, he can say two or three meaningful words and understand many more.

GAMES AND EXERCISES

Sitting
Try to use a small chair for the baby to sit in so that he can sit with his feet on the floor. This encourages straight posture. You may find that you can take the long legs off his highchair and use it as a low chair with a small table.

Standing (items 61, 65, 66—Gross Motor)
At this stage you can begin to teach the baby to stand *without support*. You need to help him to develop his balance and his confidence.

(*a*) (i) Stand up yourself and stand the baby in front of you, with his back supported against your legs.

(ii) When he is in this position place a folded towel around his chest. Hold the towel behind him and move slightly away, so that he is standing supported by the towel. As he becomes steadier, gradually give less support with the towel until he is standing without support.

(*b*) Stand the baby facing you and hold him around his waist. Let go momentarily, being ready to catch him if he wobbles.

(*c*) When the baby is standing holding on to a table or the sofa, place a favourite toy to his side and *just* out of reach. Encourage him to lift one foot and move to the side to get it, making sure that he does get the toy after each effort. Gradually increase the distance he has to move to get the toy. If the baby makes no move at all at first, you may need to prompt.

(i) Take hold of him and move his body very slightly to one side away from the toy, so that his weight is on one leg.

(ii) Lift the free leg and move it to the side towards the toy.

(iii) Move his body to this side so that his weight is balanced over both feet again.

(iv) Let him get the toy.

Remember to fade out this prompt.

Walking (items 64, 69, 71—Gross Motor)
Once the baby will take weight on his legs and step out, you can 'walk' him around holding his hands. Don't forget to use the words to match *the actions*, e.g. 'hold on', 'walk', 'around we go'.

However, you may find that if you hold his hands up above him, the baby lifts his legs to swing them—if you allow him to do this and swing him you are rewarding him for doing it and he will learn to do it every time. There are two ways of avoiding this :

(i) Kneel behind the baby and hold him around the hips. Swivel him from side to side so that his weight transfers from one foot to the other, and move him forward at the same time so that he moves with a walking movement. Or

(ii) Kneel in front of the baby and hold his hands in front of him at shoulder level, then walk him towards you.

You should also play other games to help him balance his weight as he walks, without having his hands held :

(*a*) Bring him into a standing position holding a towel around his chest, as we described earlier. Have another person kneel in front of him holding a favourite toy and encouraging him to get it; or place it on a chair or table. Hold the toy just far enough away for him to have to take one or two steps to get it. Support him well with the towel to begin with. As he gets better at this, increase the distance he has to go and gradually relax the support of the towel.

(*b*) When the baby can stand quite well holding on to something, and is beginning to take one or two steps, you may find the trundle trolley useful. Place a couple of house bricks wrapped in cloth in one end so that it does not tip. Help the baby up and get him to hold the handle. At the same time make sure the trolley will not suddenly shoot forward. Kneel at the side of the baby and, holding the trolley, take it forward a few inches. If the baby does not step forward use your other hand to prompt the feet.

This is a useful game, as it only needs one adult, and the baby will usually enjoy pushing the trolley.

As he becomes steadier and can push the trolley quite well, take out one brick and a little later both bricks.

(*c*) When the baby can walk with little support from the towel, give him a rope to hold in both hands. Stand behind him, holding the ends of the rope, and if possible get another person to stand in front and encourage him to walk forward. If the baby can balance well the rope should be fairly slack so that he has to use his balance, but if he starts to fall you can tighten the rope.

(*d*) Stand the baby with his back against a chair, and kneel in front of him. Encourage him to take one or two steps on his own to reach you.

If he makes no attempt to step forward :

(i) Take his strongest leg and bring it forward so that he is in a stepping position.

(ii) Bring both your hands up and get him to reach out for them. But keep the distance such that he has to put some weight on the front foot and pivot forward.

(iii) Remember to start from the point where he will grab your

H

hands and step forward, and then gradually increase the distance.

(iv) Always reward him for taking a step—two steps—then
three steps, etc.

(e) When he begins to take steps on his own, encourage him to
walk from one piece of furniture to another by placing a favourite toy on the next piece of furniture and by bringing the pieces
of furniture closer together. This is a good variation on encouraging him to walk to you, as he may tend to throw himself towards
your arms.

Grasp (item 17—Fine Motor)
Continue to practise picking up small objects with him, to
encourage him to use his thumb and forefinger together to grasp.

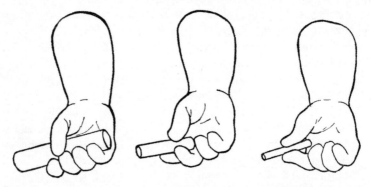

Figure 17. Stages in the development of a neat 'pincer' grasp

Rolling and throwing (items 18 and 19—Fine Motor)
(a) Play a game with him where he has to roll a ball to you and
you roll it back.

This teaches him both to roll a ball and *to take turns.*

When you first start this game, you will need two people to
play it. One sits facing the baby about a yard (1 metre) away
from him, and the other sits behind the baby. Roll the ball to the
baby, then say 'roll it to me'. The person behind him can then
take his arm and roll the ball with him. Gradually fade out this
prompt, until the baby plays the game independently with you.

(*b*) Repeat this game using throwing instead of rolling.

(*c*) At a *later stage* you can have three people, and use the same game to teach turn-taking and names, e.g. 'roll the ball to daddy, daddy to mummy, mummy to . . . ' etc. At first he will not understand the words, so do cue by pointing gestures to show what you mean, then fade these out over time.

Permanence of objects (items 73, 82, 83 and 89—Adaptive)

(*a*) *Objects under tins and cups*
Continue with games where objects are hidden and put under things and the baby looks for them, in order to maintain this behaviour.

If the baby can do items 64–73, then go on to the following games :

(*b*) *Removing Lids* (item 81—Adaptive)

(i) Find a box with a lid
(ii) Show the baby the box and place a toy in it, then put the lid on.
(iii) Demonstrate how to lift the lid to see the toy (model), then give the box to the baby saying 'find the toy'.
(iv) If the baby does not respond by lifting the lid, prompt— put his hand on the lid and lift it with him so that he can see the toy.
(v) Fade out this prompt first, then fade out the model, so that eventually he will lift the lid to find the toy on his own without demonstration.

(*c*) When the baby can move around he can go after things that disappear.

Play a game where you roll a ball behind a chair and the baby has to get it. Make sure he is looking at the ball when you roll it, and that he follows its path with his eyes, then encourage him to get it. Always say 'get the. . . .' This is a useful general cue or instruction for later language-training. If he does not get it, prompt—bring it out from behind the chair, attract his attention to it, then put it back.

When he can get it alone, extend the time he has to wait before he goes for it—hold him for 5 then 10 seconds before you let him get it.

You can also use other toys, hiding them in different places. Teddy can hide behind the sofa (just peeping out at first).

Always make sure you have the baby's attention when you hide the toy, and use prompts if necessary at first, fading them out as soon as you can.

This game also lays the foundation for language games in the next section, when we hide two toys and he has to find them when they are named.

(d) Play hide and seek—this is a favourite game with many children and you can start playing it with the baby now. At first it is best if you have someone to be with the baby when he is hiding or seeking, so you need two adults to play. One person hides and the other person seeks with the baby. Then the baby can hide (with an adult or older brother or sister) and the other person seeks. When hiding, call the baby's name softly or make different noises. This will help him develop his listening and respond to his name.

When the baby gets used to the game, he can begin to play it alone with you. You will find that for a long time he will have an ostrich-like attitude to hiding—if he can't see you, you can't see him; so he hides his head behind something, leaving the rest of his body sticking out! However, if you pretend you can't find him at first this makes the game more fun.

Note : Always use the same words when playing—'find mummy' and/or 'mummy gone'—'find mummy'.

Use of objects
When the baby can pick up an object easily from a flat surface and release it, he can begin first to take objects out of containers and then to put them in containers.

Taking things out of containers (items 66, 77 and 89 Adaptive)
(a) You can start this by putting the toys he plays with into a box. When he wants to play with them he has to take them out of the box. If he is mobile, you can have a special place for the toy box so that he learns to *remember* where the box is and to go to it when he wants to get his toys. At first you may need to prompt by placing his hand in the box.

Note : Do not use too large a box so that the toys become very jumbled. A few toys, easily accessible, in a smaller box is much better. But even a simple matter like this can have its complications as one mum points out :

'We found that although Owen would take things out of a box nine inches square, he was totally confused by a play saucepan of four inches diameter. Over a half-hour period I put the same ratio of toys one by one into saucepans of different sizes, starting with a big kitchen one. Owen took them out one by one, until he could pick out one-inch square bricks from the four-inch diameter play saucepan. All this in half-an-hour!

Next day he played taking out of the little saucepans and other small containers.

(b) When the baby can reach into a box to get a toy, you should try him with a small container, such as a cup. Put a small toy in a cup and show him the toy. If he makes no move to take it out, provide a model—take it out yourself then put it back and say 'get the. . . .' If he still does not get it, you can prompt by placing his hand in the cup. Fade out the model and the prompt, until he will take the toy out of the cup following the instruction 'get the. . . .'

Note: At first he may be more interested in the cup. You will need to give him time to play with it. Give him plenty of opportunities to play with containers and pull out objects.

(c) Later, after he has also started putting things into cups, you can go on to use even smaller containers, where the baby has to tip the container to get the object. You can use a small bottle or plastic cylinder here.

(i) Put the object (e.g. small piece of chocolate) inside the container, then show him how to tip it out yourself—model.

(ii) Put it back and give the container to the baby, saying 'get the chocolate'.

(iii) If he does not get it, prompt by taking his hand and tipping it with him.

Fade out the prompt.

Note: At first make sure you use a container that allows the baby to see the chocolate or toy. Later on you can put it in a container that cannot be seen through, and just rattle it. He then has to get it out.

Putting Things in Containers (items 75, 76, 89 and 92—Adaptive)

When the baby can release objects and take them out of containers he can learn to put them in.

(*a*) (i) Use a fairly large container that will make a noise when the object is dropped in it. A metal waste paper bin or a large tin is ideal.

(ii) Take an object such as a small building block, and drop it into the container, saying 'put it in'.

(iii) Encourage the baby to take it out—if he does not do this, give it to him.

(iv) Then say 'baby put it in' (verbal prompt). Give him time to respond and prompt him again.

(v) If he still does not respond, you can use a physical prompt take his hand with the object in it and place it over the container. You may find it works if you stroke the back of his hand, to get him to open it and drop the object, or you can put his hand down in the container so that the object touches the surface at the bottom and he can release it against the surface.

Fade out the physical prompt.

(*b*) When the baby can put one object in the tin, give him two then three objects and encourage him to put them all in.

At first you may find that after he puts an object in the cup, he does not pick up a second one—his attention goes off somewhere else. *You* need to redirect his attention to the next object. Try to build up the number of objects that will go into the tin before you need to redirect. This is his span of apprehension. Do not fall into the trap of handing him one object after another to put in, and thinking that he can do a lot.

(*c*) Use a smaller container—a cup or small box.

(*d*) Use a container with a hole in the top so that he has to drop the object through the hole.

An upside-down shoe box with a hole in the bottom is also a good idea, but make the hole fairly large at this stage—about the same size as the top of the cup. You can gradually decrease the size of the hole as the baby gets better at the game. And remember to show him how to find the object after he has posted it, by picking up the box. Later on you can use a lid and show him how to take it out.

(e) Use a container where the baby can see the object come out at the bottom. A large washing-up liquid bottle or the plastic drum that nappy powder often comes in is a good container here. You can cut off the top so there is a fairly large circular hole, then cut an opening at the side at the bottom so that the baby can see the object when it drops down.

(f) The next stage in this development is for the baby to learn about fitting things into holes—round pegs into round holes, etc. We will talk about this in the next chapter.

However, before he begins to do this the baby will need to begin to investigate holes—put his finger in small holes etc.

He can put things into bottles. A plastic see-through bottle is quite useful. Use a long stick that pokes out of the end when put into the bottle. Later, when he is getting things out of containers, you can use smaller objects.

By cutting the neck of plastic bottles at different places you can also make bigger or smaller holes.

You can also give him toys with holes in them so that he can poke his fingers in and explore (e.g. telephone dials provide interesting opportunities for this).

Putting objects on top of each other (items 77 and 93—Adaptive)
When the baby can put an object in a container he can begin to learn to build.

(a) The first stage is to learn to put one object on top of another.

(i) Turn the shoe box upside down and show the baby how to put the block on top of it : model and use verbal instruction. 'Put it on the box'.

(ii) Give the block to the baby and repeat the instruction. Prompt if necessary as before.

Fade out the prompt.

(b) When the baby can pile blocks on top of boxes, or books on books etc., start to use a smaller base for the building : a large brick, for instance. Then gradually progress to putting one brick on top of another the same size, then to using more bricks. This is all part of helping eye-hand coordination and is useful in play.

Imitation (items 74, 76, 80, 81, 85 and 86—Adaptive)
At this stage in the baby's development, his ability to imitate you becomes far more noticeable. The imitation is mostly of you doing things with objects. Then give him the object and he tries to copy what you have done. It is useful for teaching the use of objects, and actions, e.g. rolling a ball, stroking a dog, washing hands etc. However, it is still worthwhile to imitate him as well.

Learning about objects

This is probably one of the most important parts of this stage of development. By watching how the baby uses objects, you can begin to tell if he understands them. For example, does he try to roll a car, kiss a teddy, stroke a toy dog? You know whether he has learnt the functions of the object, and some of the differences between objects (this is discrimination of objects).

We have found that many handicapped babies seem to get stuck before moving on to these things, but you must persevere and think up exciting games to teach with.

The general approach is to select a few everyday objects and

(i) Model the use of each object, e.g. comb the doll's hair, push the car, draw with the pencil.
(ii) Give it to the baby and if he does not imitate the action, then prompt him.

We shall now discuss helping your baby to learn about two objects. The objects are books and crayons or pencils. (We shall discuss discrimination of real objects in the next section on communication.)

(*a*) Books (item 69—Adaptive)
At first the baby will use a book like any other object. He will bite, bang it and throw it. Your first objective is to get him to understand the use of books, which is looking at pictures, turning pages and then relating the picture of the object to the real object.

(i) Always do this when he is happy to sit on your knee, and not when he wants to be very active, walking or crawling or having a 'fight'.
(ii) Choose a book with clear pictures of familiar everyday

objects. Many books are too big, and the baby looks at one part of the picture but not at the whole shape; others are so 'fussy' that the simple shape is confused. It is best to use books which have one object per page, and the object is no bigger than about four inches (10 cm) square. (You can make up your own books with pictures cut out of catalogues or magazines. Choose pictures of objects that he uses in everyday play.)

(iii) Open up the page, and with a big smile and excited voice say 'oh look'—pointing to the picture. Make sure the baby is looking at the picture, and use the name, e.g. dog, cup, ball, etc.

(iv) Take the baby's hand and touch the picture and point to it. Pretend to stroke the dog, or eat the apple. Prompt the baby to stroke the dog.

(v) Take opportunities to show the baby the real object as well as the picture. For example, if he is looking at the picture of a shoe, draw his attention to his own shoe, show him a toy car as similar to the one in the picture as possible.

(b) *Using a pencil or crayon* (items 80, 90—Adaptive)
At this stage we can expect the baby to learn to handle a crayon.

(i) Take a fairly short thick crayon which, when grasped in the baby's hand sticks, out $1\frac{1}{2}$ inches (6 cm) or more.

(ii) Show this to the baby, and whilst he is looking at it make a mark on a white surface and say 'look' or 'look, at this'. (Remember—'look' is a useful general verbal cue).

(iii) Place the crayon in the baby's hand so that he grasps it firmly and appropriately, and say 'draw a picture'.

If he does not respond, prompt first by drawing with your finger on the paper. If you use a second crayon, you often find the baby wants to grasp that one and ignores his drawing.

(iv) If this visual prompt/model fails, take the baby's hand with the crayon in it and physically prompt him. Always make sure he is watching the point of the crayon and the mark it is making.

At first he will make a few marks and lose interest quickly. Later—discussed in next chapter—he will learn to scribble and draw with some purpose.

H*

(*c*) You can also do similar games with finger paints. The idea is to get the baby using his hands to do new things.

(i) Paint the palm of the baby's hand with non-toxic paint, then press the hand on to a white surface, making sure that he is watching so that he sees the mark left.

(ii) Put a blob of paint on the surface of the paper, and take his finger and spread the paint about with it. Try to get him to do this himself.

(iii) Use a short broad brush and teach him to use it in the same way as you teach him to use the the crayon.

Social—Dressing (items 54, 55, 56—Social)

When the baby's memory and comprehension are developing, he can begin to cooperate a little in tasks like dressing and undressing. You can help this by giving him time to do a small amount himself when you are dressing him.

For instance, when you put on his coat, hold out his sleeve and wait a little to see if he puts his arm towards it. If not, prompt by moving the arm up to the sleeve from the elbow, and gradually reduce the prompt until he will hold his arm out himself.

You can use the same procedure with shoes. Hold out his shoe to him, saying 'shoe'—'put it on'. If he does not lift his foot, again prompt by lifting his leg a little from under the calf.

When you are undressing him, encourage him to perform simple tasks like taking off his hat—many babies will happily do this when you do not want them to, so see if he will do it when you ask him as well. You can say 'hat—give it to mummy' and hold out your hand for it. Prompt by placing his hand on his hat (make sure it is easy for him to pull off).

Similarly he can pull off his shoes when they are unfastened.

Play (Look at the play section in Chapter 11)

Continue with playing games and nursery rhymes, using gestures as you have been doing previously, and work towards the baby doing the gestures on his own when you say the rhyme (use models and prompts as necessary, then fade out until the baby can do it).

Feeding (items 59, 62, 63—Social)
Continue with progress towards the baby learning to feed himself (see Chapter 6 for ideas on how to do this) and introduce different textures and tastes of food.

Encourage finger feeding and give him smaller pieces of food (e.g. chocolate buttons broken into small pieces) for him to pick up, so that he is practising using his thumb and forefinger to grasp.

Communication
During this stage the baby becomes far more communicative. At the end of it, he not only receives signals (e.g. words and gestures) from you, but has started to send out his own, and he expects you to do something in response. To receive and comprehend the words he will need to *hear* and to listen. To send out signals he will need to make more precise noises and gestures. It is not only different noises like ba, ma, da, ga, that he will need, but also groups of noises together, e.g. ma-ma-ma-ba, and of course these should begin to sound more like everyday talking. This learning of the intonation or speech patterns requires hearing and listening.

Therefore, at this stage you should continue to develop listening, and also exercises for tongue and lips to help vocalisations.

Listening and hearing
You can continue the games from the previous stage, but adding more sounds and noises and, of course, making the difference between the noises smaller.

1. For example, when you know he can hold an object in each hand and shake one hand at a time, you can give him two bells, or rattles with different sounds. If you have some bells, you can play taking turns in ringing them in sequences (this may come near the end of this stage).

2. If you have a xylophone, you can try imitation games, playing the highest note and then the lowest note. You both have a stick, and, at first, you copy the notes the baby hits, then see if he will begin to copy the one you hit. Once he is imitating, play the highest and the lowest note, singing it as well. Again, this will not just happen but will take many weeks. However, all the time you are playing you are creating different sounds. If you find the

baby just bangs all the notes, or scrapes along the top of the xylophone, you will need to make it easier. He may be 'overcome' by the eight notes all so close together. You can take two bottles or saucepans and place them six to eight inches apart. Then take turns in banging them. When you can get the baby to copy a pattern of banging one then the other, you bring a third saucepan with a different sound and play all three—high, middle, low, etc.

These sorts of games can be developed right through the second year stage. You will be teaching sequences—high, middle, low—and also rhythms. Two bangs on each, and, much later, patterns such as two bangs on the highest, one on the middle, two on the lowest etc.

3. You should also find that the baby will begin to pick out sounds from the street or other rooms. If you hear a new noise from outside, like a road drill or a band, take him to the window and show him.

4. Keep a close watch on his *hearing*. Notice not only whether he reacts to sudden loud noises, but if he is turning or paying attention to a range of noises, high pitched ones, low pitched ones, loud ones, soft ones. If he has a cold or is snuffly, his hearing may be less acute because of congestion. At these times you may need to talk louder and more clearly to him.

Comprehension and language are beginning to develop at this stage, and so it is important to observe his hearing. Even temporary problems, caused by colds, may slow down his development : we do not know this for certain, but it is worth keeping on the safe side. So, do not be afraid to ask the doctor or clinic for regular checks if you have any doubts.

Tongue and lips

You will still need to encourage the development of tongue and lips, especially if the child has 'floppy' muscles, as do many Down's Syndrome babies. As we noted in earlier chapters, you should try to keep the child breathing through his nose, and eventually (probably well into the second year stage) teach him to blow his nose.

During eating, you should try to encourage him to keep his mouth shut and to chew food. You may still be gradually increasing the lumpiness and chewiness of his food. It is well worth persevering with this : the longer he remains on strained foods, the more difficult it will be to get him to move on to ordinary ones. Unless the doctor has given you some reason why he should not have more solid foods, there is no physical reason why he should not be chewing by this nine to twelve month stage. Of course, if he is cutting teeth you may find he will not chew, although some babies chew more at this time.

If he does not keep his mouth shut whilst eating it may be because of poor muscle tone in the lips. You can remedy this by using blowing toys like whistles and trumpets, and by copying 'funny faces', forcing the lips together and blowing. Blowing out candles or matches is good fun at this time. Later he can try blowing through straws, and later still drinking through straws (this may not be achieved until well into the second year stage). Using mirrors which you both look into while you make 'faces', kiss, blow, etc. can be useful.

You will also need to think about the *tongue*. The position of the tongue in the mouth, against the teeth, is very important for making precise sounds. Try saying 's', 'th', and 'c'. These particular sounds usually appear quite late in development, and many three- and four-year-old children are still practising them. However, you can strengthen the tongue in readiness by certain games and exercises.

Most of the games are to do with licking. Give him opportunities to lick ice-cream, lollies, things off spoons. You can also place sticky substances, either sweet like jam or honey or savoury like Marmite or beef extracts, on his lips—the top, bottom and sides of the lips and just behind the teeth.

When the baby will imitate your mouth and tongue movements, you can play games where he has to wave his tongue around like you—up, down, side to side etc. *But always keep the tongue inside the mouth.*

You will need to keep many of these games going into the second year stage, and certainly until the child can make a wide range of sounds and words.

Vocalisation
The baby will begin to increase his range of sounds and will link more together during this stage.

The main way to help this, apart from talking to him, is to imitate the sounds he makes. Then give him time to make them again. You can also try to *expand* the sounds by not just imitating the 'babble' he produces, but adding a little bit more and emphasising the sing-song pattern and the intonation (i.e. the rise and fall of the sound pattern). Babies often enjoy this game when you 'babble' back at them and most parents do it. But the secret is to do it regularly, to copy the sound he makes, and to expand it by small steps.

By the end of this stage and the beginning of the second year stage, the baby will be having long 'jabbering conversations' that sound very like speech but have few recognisable words. You may find that he does this most in certain situations or at certain times of the day. The bathroom often seems to produce more noises—probably because of the 'echo' effects. For the same reason babies often like to 'babble' into largish tins. Be on the look out for this, as you can use it to help. Also watch for your baby's best time of day. Many babies seem to 'babble' a lot in the morning just after they wake up. Certainly they are less likely to 'babble' when the room is full of noise, from the radio or television or lots of people talking. Again look for this, and use it to plan your stimulation.

Comprehension
The baby's understanding of the sound and gesture signals sent to him should increase at this stage. Of course, you will know if he understands them only by observing his responses or actions closely. The general guidelines are :

(i) Use words and gestures in all the activities you do with him. If you are pulling him to stand, say 'stand up'.
(ii) Always use the same words in each specific activity, and try to make sure he is attending to them.
(iii) Use plenty of large gestures : a big open hand with 'give me, a good point with 'look' or 'there it is'. These prompts can be slowly faded out as he learns the word.
(iv) Try to keep to a few words in each situation, especially when you are giving him an instruction such as 'hold on', 'sit up', 'look', or asking a question.
(v) He should begin to imitate your actions with *objects* a lot

more at this stage: for example, having a drink from a cup, pushing a car, rolling a ball. In each case use the words 'push car', 'roll ball', 'drink'. At first you will model the action by doing it, but gradually try to get him to do it when you say the words. If he does not, then model, repeating the words.

Towards the end of this stage he will begin to imitate gestures more. Again you can model these, using a mirror so that he can see himself; and, of course, nursery rhymes with *simple* actions are very useful.

(vi) You will need to build his comprehension and language on these early abilities, so *start to keep a list of the words and phrases he understands.* This is very useful indeed.

(*a*) When the baby is showing some comprehension of words in this way, you can begin to teach him to respond to the question 'where is . . . ' by pointing to the appropriate object or person. Start with very familiar words that you are fairly sure he knows the meaning of. For instance, say 'where is daddy' or some other member of the family. Observe whether the baby looks towards daddy. If he does, you should both react by smiling, saying 'yes, daddy's there'. If he does not look, then dad can attract the baby's attention to himself (stand up, move into the baby's vision etc.), and then, when he does look, reward him with smiles and praise. Once the baby is looking in the right direction when you say 'where's daddy', you can teach him to point. Prompt by taking his finger and pointing it towards dad.

When the baby has mastered this himself (item 50), you can go on to using other people and objects.

(*b*) When you are dressing or undressing the baby, name his clothing and the parts of his body to him.

You can begin to teach the baby parts of the body by naming parts of your own, and putting the baby's hand on the appropriate part. Hair is usually the first thing to be learnt, as babies love to pull at your hair! When bathing and washing the baby name each part as you wash it, e.g. hands, nose, ears, eyes, belly etc.

The baby will usually learn to identify parts of your body first, then of his own body and eventually the same parts on a doll and finally on a picture. When he begins to understand that the word 'hair' relates to your hair, you can put his hand on his own hair as well to show him the link between the word and his own body. It is useful here to use a mirror to show him his hair, eyes, nose etc., as he cannot see these parts on himself otherwise.

Speech words

The 'first' word is something all parents eagerly await. They see it as a notable milestone in development. We hope that by now you will have seen the amount of development that takes place before the first word. Also we would point out that, whilst the appearance of the first word is exciting, it will be many months after that before the child is 'talking' and using sentences. And there is a danger here for parents, if in their desire to get a word they, in fact, 'put the child off'.

At this stage it is more important to create situations where the child can babble, shout and gesture, and then respond to him, than to try too hard to get a word. When he does try to communicate (see items 44 and 49—Communication), respond to him in such a way that he understands he *has* communicated. If he does say a sound that is like a word, then expand on it and show him the object.

For example, from your list of the sounds he makes and your knowledge of objects he 'understands', you may find some possible links : 'b' and ball, or baby, 'b' and brum-brum for car, 'd' and daddy etc. When playing with him, say the word and if he makes the sound or any sound that seems the same, react by showing him the object. Also expand the communication if he says 'br' and you think it means car, then say 'yes, the brum-brum', and show it to him and push it towards him.

On no account try to force him to say the word clearly at this stage, or correct his pronunciation. Merely repeat it and encourage plenty of sounds, gestures and communications.

See the language section in Chapter 11 for more details.

11 : Into the Second year

By the time the baby reaches this stage he is mobile, he is capable of using his hands to manipulate, he is beginning to build up memories of events and objects; he is also beginning to anticipate certain actions and events, and to communicate his wants and his dislikes. In short, he is quite a skilled person with a mind of his own and a great desire to explore his world.

His emerging individuality, strengths and interests become more and more noticeable. He may be one of those children who are very mobile—walking, running and climbing—but whose fine motor skills are less advanced, or he may prefer to sit for long periods playing and manipulating some objects or construction toys. Or he may be very sociable and outward going—constantly trying to get someone to talk to him, yet not beginning to show much interest in walking. Or, of course, he may be equally competent in all these areas.

This individuality raises a problem for describing the child's 'normal' development. The time-gap between the child who attains a particular behaviour very early and the one who attains it very late becomes greater the older children get. If you look at Chapter 13, on average ages and ranges for Down's Syndrome children, you will see this problem.

Because of this increased individuality, we have not attempted to break down the second year into smaller stages—indeed it is no longer possible. Further, the baby will soon be a child—a determined, self-willed, toddler and will move beyond the scope of this book.

Therefore, in this chapter we have described briefly the main areas of development : play, language, social-emotional development, motor, memory and self-help. In doing this we have tried to put forward what we think are the essential points of the development, and discuss their implications for the mentally handicapped child. We have noted some examples of games and activities, but have left much to you. By this time we hope that you will have become far more skilled in your planning and teaching, and once you have been given the idea of what needs to be encouraged, will be able to devise your own activities. Indeed, because the mentally handicapped child will often be more 'individual' than the 'normal' child, we could not specify exact games to play.

The checklist continues up to the end of the second year, so you will be able to pinpoint the child's present level of progress and get some idea of the next step. However, remember that the average ages given are less and less useful as the child shows his increasing individuality. Also, you will find that the order of development from item to item may not be so accurate. Again, some children will do things in a different way from others.

Finally, we have described these second year developments as they occur with 'normal' children. This is because our aim is to keep the 'mentally handicapped' child as normal as possible. But the mentally handicapped child does have learning difficulties, and often does not initiate play or communication activities as much as the 'normal' child. You will have to continue to be the planner, the initiator and the originator for the child, whilst at the same time trying to teach him to plan and initiate activities for himself.

PLAY

In this section we have tried to explain why we think play is important and how you can use it to help your children. To do this we have had to be analytical. But we certainly don't want to take the fun out of play for you. So let us repeat again that *the most important thing is the happy relationship between you and your child*. This is what you must build on when applying the ideas.

Let's start by looking at the main characteristics of play, and their implications.

First, there is always *pleasure* in the play for the child. He enjoys it. He finds it satisfying. He finds it rewarding. It is important to realise that the pleasure or reward he gets from his play does not come from outside—from you rewarding him for playing—but from the actual play itself. (In Chapter 5 we discussed the importance of this.) Therefore, when we say that play is important for learning, one of the things we mean is that it is the motivation of playing that keeps the child interested and active. This then provides more opportunities for practising skills and trying out ideas.

This pleasure in play arises from the fact that the child is doing *what he wants to do*.

There are some important implications in this which will affect the way we use play to help the child.

(i) If by definition, play must be pleasure, then as soon as it stops being a pleasure it stops being play. Therefore, only the child can let you know when it stops being fun. The decision to stop the play then, must come largely from the child. You can tell when this happens because you will begin to use more coaxing and more rewards to get the activity or he will just refuse to carry on. (We would again refer to Chapter 5.)

(ii) In using play to help the child's development, you will need to be more *indirect* in your approach, and not try to force him to do *what you want*. Once you begin to force or cajole, you are beginning to move away from play into work or training.

Of course, there are many occasions during the day when you will need to insist that he does things the way you want him to—like tidying up, feeding, keeping still in dressing, etc. *But do keep the distinction between these occasions and play in your mind*.

Also, you will often have to be part of the child's play—modelling, prompting, reassuring, and, of course, letting the child see you are enjoying it!

(iii) The fact that the child is doing what he wants, leads to three important aspects of play.

First

(a) He will repeat and practise many skills happily which would become boring in repetitive exercises. This will improve his proficiency, yet he will not become bored with the practice.

(b) He will often want to do something that is beyond his present level of skill. Thus the drive to play will stretch and develop the skill.

(c) He will often use his present skills and knowledge to explore and discover in new ways. This is helping to maintain and generalise his skills (Chapter 5) as well as building up his confidence and reasoning ability.

These are all important functions of play.

Second, there is always some *activity* going on in the play. It may be rather quiet, as when the child is examining an object— tapping it, taking it apart; *or* it may be boisterous, as when he is running around pretending to be a train.

The activities in the play reflect the child's developmental level —his skills, memories etc. By observing these closely we can find out his present level of development and then compare this with the checklist. From this we can plan the next activities that we want to include in his play.

Third, the young child often initiates his play *spontaneously*. He seems just to start playing, moving from one thing to another. This 'sparking-off' of the play can occur for many reasons, but we would emphasise two :

(i) He is *attracted by a new toy, object or situation*. Of course, the newness alone does not necessarily attract the child. As we said in Chapter 5, it can be overwhelming and he will need reassurance from you to approach it. This in turn will depend upon :

How much the new object or situation fits into his past experience and what he can remember about it; and the 'temperament' of the child. Some children are more cautious than others; some are less confident. Caution is a way of approaching and examining things—it is a style of exploration. Confidence is more an emotional state resulting from past success and failure and belief in oneself.

(ii) Spontaneous play can also be sparked off by *imitation*. This can be immediate—imitating what someone is doing at the same time—*or* it can be an imitation of an act associated with an object or situation previously observed.

We can 'spark-off' the child's play by using *objects, situations*, and/or *actions to be imitated*. For example, if a child has access to pots and pans in the kitchen, and sees mum using pots and pans, he is likely to play with them and explore their properties.

Therefore, it is not enough just to observe, think and plan the *toys* which might help the child. You must observe in which *situations* he is interested, give him *space* to play, *let him see* you doing things, and encourage him *to imitate*.

Since we have mentioned space to play, we would like to digress a little here and relate a story.

Some years ago when we were involved in a television programme on mentally handicapped children, one of our stars— a little Down's Syndrome girl—began to set out toy pots and pans on the floor to play with. Suddenly she jumped up and started to push the interviewer and crew away. The interviewer asked if all these children were aggressive? This was a telling example of jumping to conclusions. The child, who had very little language, was creating a play-space, a bit of territory in which to play. To the watching adults she had plenty of space, but to her we were imposing.

Children need to have their own little territory, so when considering the play situations keep this in mind. Our observations of children playing are leading us to believe that many of the 'squabbles' that flare up for no apparent reason at this early age of 'solo-play' are due to others imposing on personal play-space.

When selecting the *toys and objects* for the child's play :

(i) Do not have too few or too many. You want enough to allow the child to choose between them, to spark different interests, but not so many that he becomes confused and cannot concentrate his attention.

(ii) Remember that everyday household objects such as cardboard boxes, tins, plastic bottles, combs and brushes are as stimulating, if not more so, than expensive, attractive (often only to the adult buying them) toys.

(iii) As we said in Chapter 5—always have a few new objects and some old familiar ones. The new ones excite curiosity but the old ones give reassurance.

(iv) Make sure the child has easy access to the objects.

(v) Select the objects to match the child's level of development.

With mentally handicapped children, *you cannot assume that merely giving them lots of things to play with is enough.* You may need to plan their play as carefully as you plan how to teach them to put on their pants. It may even be more important to teach them at this stage to play than to put on their pants. This is because :

1. All human beings from birth to death need stimulation. Play prevents boredom and relieves distress. Children who do not play frequently find stimulation in other ways : they start rocking or tapping or may even damage themselves by scratching, biting and hitting their bodies. (Before you become too anxious, you will see many of these behaviours in all children on some occasions. It is only when they dominate the child's behaviour that they become worrying.)

Teaching the child to play, teaching the skills to play with, and maintaining and encouraging the play will mean that there is far less possibility of these types of unwanted behaviours developing and taking hold.

2. Many mentally handicapped children easily get into stereotyped play. That is, they keep repeating the same simple play pattern for long periods. They may sit tap, tap, tapping with a rattle or rocking a doll. Obviously this will reduce the quality of the stimulation considerably and not help their development.

Because of this lack of initiative and originality, these children often need another person—child or adult—to be involved in their play far more than 'normal' children do.

The way this person is involved in the play is important. They are not there merely to entertain the child. For example, many adults play with the toys, building towers or rolling the car, whilst the baby just watches. This is good modelling but unless the baby then *does something* other than sit and watch, it is really only entertainment. The objective is to teach the baby to entertain himself—not to be dependent on others.

This person should aim at initiating *actions* by the baby, using modelling and prompts.

This person should not be too 'heavy-handed' in initiating and directing the play. In Chapter 5 we emphasise the importance of not interrupting too much, and in this section we have pointed out the need to encourage the play 'indirectly', rather than make it too much of a training exercise.

Much of this can be done from *a distance*. You need to place the child in a play-space where he can see you and you him. Get his play started and then carry on with your own work or activity. Keep looking at him, checking the level of the play. If he has stopped or has got into too fixed a pattern, redirect him to other toys or activities.

It is when 'monitoring' his play from a distance that referent looking (p. 109) and vocalisations or language became important.

If he is truly discovering new things in his play, he will want you constantly to note them and to reassure him that everything is all right. This can be done by eye-contact. He may also begin to use sounds or words which mean 'look at me' or indicate excitement. You will need to listen for these and react appropriately.

Young children at this level of development are beginning to explore their world, to move out into it. This needs confidence and a feeling of safety. Thus they need to know where their safe base is—i.e. mum—and to maintain contact with it to keep up their reassurance that all is well. This is one reason why they are always 'around your feet'. The other is that mum is their main playmate at this time and they like and need to play with other human beings.

The person involved in the play has another job. As we said earlier, in play the child does something he wants to do. This is his motivation. He then uses his skills to try to do it. Many mentally handicapped children will often know what they want to do, either because you have modelled it or because they suddenly get an idea. But when they try to do it their skills are not yet advanced enough to complete the task. For example, they want to put the little peg men into the holes in a lorry truck, but their eye-hand coordination is not good enough yet. They persist for a few tries then give up. The giving up may be shown by :

(i) Frustration—they push or throw the toy away.

(ii) Regression—they go back to an earlier play skill such as sucking the men or banging the truck.

(iii) They turn their attention to another object.

(iii) is a useful solution and we can leave it alone, but in (i) and (ii) there may be problems. Regression does not really help their development and too much frustration and failure might cause them to stop playing.

Now all children meet frustration like this in their play but in the case of normal children :

(a) they can more easily switch to other ideas and activities; and

(b) the skills needed will develop fairly quickly anyway.

With mentally handicapped children (and we have noticed this particularly with Down's Syndrome children), motor skills may be less developed than their memory and imitation skills.

The consequence of this is that they are likely to meet with more failure in their play than normal children. This will not help their confidence and will not encourage them to play.

You will need to plan for success in their play, and also be more alert to the failures. When you see, or foresee, failure, you will need to help the child to achieve success and reassure him.

In the example of the peg-men, you could prompt the child so that he gets it in the hole. Having done this, if the child indicates he wants to do it again, you will need to stand by and help him—thus training the skill. If he does not indicate he wants to do it again, put it aside and direct him to some new activity, preferably one he can do.

Content of play
Play can encompass all areas of development and all activities. Therefore, in looking at the content of the play—at what is happening in the play—we need to look at the development of the child.

All the behaviours in the checklist can be incorporated and developed in the child's play. You should use them to decide on your objectives for the child and help plan the stimulation. We have not gone into this in detail. As we said in the introduction, by this stage in development the children have become so individual their stimulation has to be planned with a detailed knowledge of the actual child. Second, as we indicated, almost anything goes into play, in terms of the objects you use and situations you create. You will have to be an opportunist—constantly observing the child and using your initiative to interest and help him. In the booklist we have noted a number of books which contain useful ideas for play and you should also talk to other parents and use Toy Libraries, where available, to pick up ideas.

Some landmarks in the development of play
It may be helpful to note the major changes taking place in the type of play shown by the child in this second year of life.

Between 6–9 months the 'normal' baby has tended to play with one object at a time : banging it, sucking it, turning it over and so on. By doing this he was learning about the properties of the object—its size, feel, weight, colour and shape. He then began to learn about its function and use—putting things in, making noises etc.

His play with the objects was very brief. He tended to have short bursts of activity with one object, then lose interest and look around or turn to another. His span of attention and concentration was short and you would have to allow for lots of changes during play. Your aim, of course, was to extend his attention span by increasing his interest in objects through using them, imitating your child, showing him new objects and how they work.

By 9–12 months he began to relate two objects to each other. At first this was simply a case of banging them together or putting one on top of, or into, another.

Gradually he began to relate objects on the basis of their similarities : either because they looked similar, or, more often, because they were used together in similar every-day situations : for example, cups on saucers or spoons into cups. This was quite a break-through because the child showed that he had built up memories of objects and could consider both at the same time.

At the beginning of the second year stage babies begin to play with sets of objects rather than with single ones. Their play activities may still last only a few minutes, but there appears to be more 'meaning' in the play. They increasingly put objects together because they have similarities. This ability to classify objects will develop considerably during the year.

Another important development at this time is the child's increasing ability to connect actions with events—that is, cause and effect. When this happens they begin to take more interest in toys such as activity boards, jack-in-the-boxes, and toys with push-buttons, hinges and lids, switches and so on.

This development of increasing memory and concentration, of ability to consider two objects or events at the same time, and of awareness of cause and effect, produces a noticeable change in play.

1. The play becomes more constructional : examples include building towers, making patterns, placing blocks in lines, putting

things in toys on wheels that can be pushed or pulled. By 18 months one can see clear objectives in the play. *The child has a very clear idea of the end-product of a set of actions.*

2. *Between 12–14 months* the first signs of *symbolic* play appear. The child uses toys and objects as symbols to add meaning to the play. He pretends to drink from a cup, or to eat something off a plate. At first this is simply imitating the function of the object, but gradually it becomes more and more symbolic and imaginative. This ability to symbolise develops considerably *between 14 and 20 months*, and this development is very important :

(i) It indicates that memory that has built up.

(ii) It frees the child from having to have all the real objects or situations present before he can use them in his play, e.g. he does not need a piece of cake to play eating or feeding teddy.

(iii) Pictures—which symbolises the real objects—become more and more useful in stimulation, and by 15 months most children are beginning to show great interest in pictures and books.

(iv) Language—which is built of 'sound symbols' for the things and actions we see—is built on the child's ability to symbolise.

At first, the pretend play may be 'sparked-off' by an object or situation that closely relates to it. The child sees a plate and pretends to eat, or he has a cloth or tissue and pretends to wash dolly's face. He may see a cushion or pillow and play at going to bed and going to sleep. If he has a toy car he pretends to drive it, turning the wheel, hooting the horn. Later on a round disc or wheel may be picked up and off he goes driving the car. By 24 months he will do this even if he has no object. He just holds his hands out and is in *make-believe* play.

Two points are important to keep in mind :

(i) He is frequently imitating at this stage, and so we can use imitation to teach him to pretend.

(ii) He will have memories only of familiar every-day things that he comes into contact with. Therefore, we must use these as the base to help him develop his imagination. Thus toys which represent real-life things can be very useful. Dolls can be put to bed, have their hair combed, be sat on chairs, fed, washed, bathed. Dogs on wheels can be taken for walks.

Table 2

APPROXIMATE AGE AT NORMAL DEVELOPMENT	ACTIVITY	EXAMPLE USING A TOY TEA SET
6–9 months	Object oriented: simple exploration by banging, looking, mouthing etc. All objects tend to be treated in the same way.	Picks up cup, bangs it, drops it, turns it over.
7–10 months	Relates objects but with little 'meaning'. Will attend to more than one object at a time.	Bangs cup with spoon. Bangs two spoons together
9–12 months	Relating objects and *imitating* uses. (Imitation at this stage occurs only immediately after the model, so does not involve remembered events).	Puts spoon in cup and copies you stirring the tea.
10–14 months	Spontaneously relates objects with similar functions or situation-use. Using memory and knowledge of the object to direct play.	Places cup on saucer, lid on teapot, spoon in cup.
12–18 months	Starts to put objects into categories. Simple pretend play.	Puts two cups together, saucers together. Gives doll or mum a 'drink'.
18–24 months	Make believe play with role-play and situational play.	Sets up tea party. Child may pretend to be mum. Puts doll or teddy at table as part of the tea party.
22–24 months	Sequencing of activity.	Sets 2 or 3 places, pours, stirs, drinks the tea.

Note: The things that the child does with the tea set are very brief activities up to 20–24 months. Only then does one find more prolonged and structured play appearing—*unless an adult or older playmate is present.*

By about 20–24 months the child has also begun to do things in *sequence*. For example, if he uses a tea set, he will put one cup on a saucer *and then* another cup on another saucer. Or he will (*a*) put the cup on the saucer, (*b*) pretend to pour some tea into the cup from the pot, (*c*) stir in the 'sugar' with a spoon and (*d*) drink.

If you reflect for a moment on how many things in life have to be done in *sequence*, you will see why this is so important. Again one can teach this through play, using appropriate objects and imitation.

We can sum up this development of play with objects by looking at how the child's use of a tea set changes as he develops. (See Table 2.)

Social play
This is also an important part of development in this second year stage. Social play is the ability to play cooperatively with others. It has to be developed and learnt in the same way as other forms of the play. This takes many years, but it begins during the second year stage.

At the beginning of this stage the child is learning to cooperate with adults in games such as rolling a ball, hide and seek, etc. However, he is still at the stage where his world is centred on himself and he cannot share or understand another person's role. Thus he is able to play in this way only with adults or older children who can adapt themselves to him.

The development of play with other young children shows two main stages within the second year.

(i) At first each child plays as if he is on his own and takes little notice of others.

(ii) Later they start to take notice of each other, although they generally do not play together or cooperate. They may play separately but in a similar way, one child may imitate the other. At this stage children often want to play with the same toys—when one child starts to play with a toy the other child immediately wants it. However, they do not share. The other child will try to get the toy, or simply stand by waiting on an opportunity to get it. This is the beginnings of interaction and, of course, some communication may take place.

However, sharing and interacting does not usually appear until late into the second year.

The mentally handicapped child, who learns more slowly, needs help to learn to play with other children. This is important not just for the reason that he will be able to play and have friends, but also because:

(i) the child extends his ability to communicate through his need to make himself understood in play with other children;
(ii) he learns from other children;
(iii) he learns to share, to give and take, to take turns and consequently he becomes less 'me-centred'.

You can begin to help the child to learn to cooperate in your own games with him. You should plan for give and take to occur in your play, and make sure that it is not always the adult who does all the giving or the directing. Look for ways in which the child tries to communicate in play, and when he does this let him take the lead. Devise games, such as rolling a ball to each other, where the child has to take turns with others. In playing these sorts of games with adults, the child begins to learn about cooperation and turn taking.

The child also needs to get used to other young children. He needs opportunities to play in the company of other children, and there are various ways in which you can organise this. There may be a play-group or nursery class in your area where you can spend a couple of hours a week. If you have neighbours with young children you might arrange for the children to play together in each other's homes once or twice a week. Do not expect the children to cooperate—even if they appear to ignore each other or continually fight over the toys, they are still benefitting from each other's presence.

When the child is used to being with other children, you can begin to extend the games you play to include another child. For instance, in the rolling a ball game you can arrange it so that you roll it to one child, he rolls it to the other child who then rolls it back to you. At first you will need to prompt the children to achieve this, and to join in yourself. Do not just leave the children to attempt to play it together—it will be some time before they can do this.

There are many games you can devise to encourage the development of the ability to play together; for example, using a see-saw, tug-of-war, using the toddler truck for one child to sit in and the other child to push, arranging 'tea parties' where one child pours the 'tea' and the other hands it around.

The basic rule to remember when devising these games is that they should require the participation of both children to make them work.

Finally, do not feel that your child is 'different' and cannot join in with other 'normal' children—he can learn to do this, and he will benefit from it, particularly as he gets a bit older and his language and communication skills begin to develop.

LANGUAGE AND COMMUNICATION

By the time the child has reached the 'second year' stage he will be communicating quite a lot. He will be sending out information and receiving information, using signs and symbols such as gestures, expressions, voices and perhaps one or two words. These developments are closely related to developments in other areas taking place at the same time :

(a) *Memory* for objects, actions and experiences.

(b) *Anticipation* of people's actions, and setting expected end-products to his own actions—to communicate you must anticipate and expect a response.

(c) *Imagination* and the beginnings of the use of symbols in play —he will thus be able to learn that the sound symbol (the word) is associated with specific objects or actions.

(d) *Mobility, activity* and *socialising.* To develop language you have to develop the need to communicate, so you have to do things with people and to people—you have to have something to communicate and a need to get each other people to do something, e.g. 'get me a drink', 'look at my tower', 'where is my teddy?' 'come and play'.

Because all the areas of development are important to the development of language, we recommend that you think of the all round development of the child and do not concentrate on one aspect. The way in which play, motor and self-help activities affect speech development is nicely shown in an activity devised by Steve's mother :

At 4 pm I push the armchair into the window and help Steve climb up onto it. The armchair is safer than the stool, and he is still a bit wobbly. I say 'is Lisa coming yet? where is she?' and we look up and down the road. Then I point and say 'look, there's Lisa'. Lisa waves and Stevie gets very excited and we wave back.

After a few weeks of doing this, all I have to do is say 'is Lisa coming yet?' and he gets up on the chair and has a look. Now I can say to him 'is daddy coming yet?' or 'is that daddy's car?' and he goes and looks. He will say, 'brrm-brrm.' Sometimes he will come to me saying 'brrm-brrm' to tell me that daddy has arrived.

Notice that this exercise is helping Steve not only with his motor skills in climbing up on the chair, but also with anticipation (looking for sister to appear), comprehension (understanding the phrase—'is Lisa coming?') and communication (waving to Lisa). Most important of all, he has *generalised* his learning from 'is Lisa coming' to 'is daddy coming' and, having got something to communicate, comes to mum to tell her that daddy is here—'brrm-brrm.'

This example is typical of the things we all do with our children. However, if we are going to use and create opportunities for helping language, we need a framework to guide us. We will now discuss some of the main points which might help you. You will find useful books noted in the booklist for extending this.

Language can be considered in two ways—receptive (understanding) and expressive (speaking).

Receptive language
This is the ability to receive signals, interpret them and understand their meaning.

This ability will *come before* the child can say the words, or even copy the 'sing-song' patterns that sound like speech.

To do this the child needs to :

(i) Be able to *hear* a wide range of sounds and distinguish between them. It is important to make sure that his hearing is checked.
(ii) *Listen* to different sounds. This means he should direct his attention to different sounds and sort out the important ones

from the general background noise. You will need to continue with the games which involve listening to different sounds and making different sounds described in Chapter 10.

(iii) Associate the words he hears with the appropriate object, action or situation. Before he can do this he needs to have an understanding of the object or action—for example, that a ball is a ball and that it rolls. Similarly he is most likely to learn words to do with familiar situations : eating and feeding at the table, for instance, leading to play with toy spoons, cups, etc.

Expressive language
This is the ability to send out meaningful signals, e.g. words.

To express himself the child needs to be able :

(i) To recognise the object or event he is looking at, and to draw the correct word from his memory.

(ii) To listen to and interpret what is said to him and, again using his memory, to reply correctly.

(iii) To pronounce the sound or use the tones of the sounds sufficiently well for the other person to 'understand'. This skill is related to that of articulation, and the exercise and games noted in Chapter 10 for lips and tongues are still necessary.

At first these expressions are simple. They are often vocalisations, strings of sounds and then single words. Gradually single words are linked together in twos, then threes, then simple phrases and sentences.

There is also development in the use the child makes of his vocalisations and speech.

At first they are very clearly directed at other persons : he attempts to express his feelings and wants. In the early stages he is mainly concerned with getting other people to do things—to pick him up, to play with him and so on. As his command of language increases he begins to use it to find things out by asking questions, to explain things and tell you what he did or what happened, and to express his feelings.

But the child also uses expressive language with objects. At first this is rather simple : he pushes the car and says 'brrm-brrm'. As his imagination, memory and knowledge of objects increases he talks to them—telling teddy to sit down or have a drink. By the end of the second year stage, language is playing a dominant part in his play with objects. This provides lots of practice and opportunity to generalise his use of language. For this reason it is important to use language when playing with the handicapped child, in the hope that he will use it when playing by himself.

A third use of expressive language can also be observed : using it to direct oneself. The child begins to tell himself to do or not to do something. You may have seen young children tempted to do something which is not allowed, such as switching on the television, and saying to themselves, 'no, don't touch'. This use of self-directing language becomes common in the third year, but sometimes can be observed sooner.

Before discussing different ways to teach receptive and expressive language, we will make some general points.

1. A child cannot or will not communicate unless he has someone to communicate with and something to communicate about. Hence he needs to engage in plenty of activities and to go out, see people and places. Some parents however, worry about taking their handicapped child out into public places, so to reassure them here is a story written by the mother of an 18-month-old Down's Syndrome child.

> Mark was 12 months old and getting to that stage when he cried if I went into the shop and left him in his pram. I felt a bit nervous about taking him into the supermarket. I don't know why, but I thought he would pull things off shelves or that people would stare at him. They would also say tactless things that would upset me. In the end I had to take him in. I put him in the trolley seat, held my head up high and marched in.
>
> Immediately he started looking around, eyes bright and wide open. He was so excited. He even pointed to things as though to tell me to look or get them. When we got to the meat counter he gave the butcher a smile and the butcher said 'you're a nice chap, what's your name?'
>
> It has been most rewarding putting Mark in the shopping trolley, high up where he can see things and people instead of hidden away in his push-chair. He knows all the shopkeepers and where just about all the 'good-things' in the shop are.

I

He smiles and waves to all the assistants and they always wave back and talk to him.

He is even beginning to know the shop, and gets excited as we go near it. Sometimes he points to it as we go by as though to say 'take me in!'

We don't need to point out how useful this outing is; but do notice that putting Mark in the trolley raised him up to 'eye-level' so that he could see things and so that people could see and talk to him.

2. At this stage, children live mainly in the here and now. They do not think about past or future. It is important therefore to link the language you use to the things that they are doing, and the things they like to do.

In the same way, the child is more likely to learn the words about eating, washing or playing with a ball whilst he is doing these activities. It is the *use* of language or communication to *do* things that is important, not just the ability to say words.

Many parents concentrate on learning words and end up with a child who can label objects but does not use language to communicate. For example, you have a set of pictures, you name them, he points or you point and he names, but he cannot use the names in any other situation.

The functional use of language to express needs, emotions and desires can become obvious even when a child starts using single words. He may say the word 'dog' when looking at a picture or seeing the dog, and this is only labelling; but if he says 'dog' with an expression in the voice meaning 'where is the dog?' or 'the dog has come in', or to show he is frightened of the dog, or even pointing to dad meaning 'daddy should get down on hands and knees and play doggies', this is more than labelling: it is expressing a whole idea and is a far more useful form of language.

Therefore, when playing and talking to the child, one does not just want to build up a long list of words of objects that he can name or point to: he needs words that will 'work' for him, that he can use in everyday situations and which allow him to express himself.

To do this,

(i) Look for meanings in the child's gestures, vocalisations or words.

(ii) Don't just label. Build up the word in new ways or situations. If, for example, the child points to a picture of an orange or cake, pretend to eat it. If he gets teddy or a cup, when you ask him to, pretend to cuddle the teddy or drink from the cup. If he points at the door and says 'daddy' interpret and express the meaning 'yes, daddy's gone to work', 'daddy'll be home soon'.

Let us return to the differences between receptive and expressive language.

Receptive language

Remember, receptive language (comprehension) involves receiving a signal and interpreting its meaning. It comes before expressive language (production).

Unfortunately, the mentally handicapped child is not very good at receiving and interpreting language. Let's take an example and consider the difficulties. Suppose you want the child to get ready to go shopping. You might, like the mother of a Down's Syndrome boy we were observing, say something like :

'I'm ready to go shopping now, Johnny. If you're coming with me you'd better come and get your coat on. I hope your face is clean—come on and get your coat on'.

At the same time the mother was getting her bag and purse together, and she was not looking at the child. The child was playing with a toy, was sideways on to the mother and did not respond to her call.

Let us consider what might have gone wrong :

(a) Attention

The child's attention was fixed on the toy and his play. We know that many mentally handicapped children do not switch their attention from one thing to another quickly or easily. Until the child attends to the signals sent to him, he cannot begin to respond.

Therefore, the first thing to do is make sure that you have the child's attention. You know this if he is looking at you.

(b) Attention span

We have noted that as children grow they develop the ability to pay attention to more and more things at the same time. This development is slower in mentally handicapped children. Therefore, we need to build up the number of things they attend to step by step. In the putting of cubes or objects into a tin we progress gradually from one to two or three and so on. The same idea can be applied to language. Instead of giving him a long complicated instruction like 'Stop playing and come here and put your coat on' you will need to break it down into small bits or steps, e.g.

Step 1: Get his attention—'Johnny, look at me'—give him time to respond and repeat if necessary.

Step 2: 'Come here.' Then when he comes over,

Step 3: 'Put your coat on.'

(c) Sorting out the information

We need to work out what the signal means. To do this we will need to keep it in our heads whilst sorting it out. This suggests some kind of memory—a memory which keeps things in 'store' for a short time, a short-term memory. We then need to compare the signal with the knowledge we have stored in our long-term memory. Both these types of memory develop as the child grows. Therefore, at first the child can keep only one or two things in his short-term memory. If you overload it he will get confused.

Because of this you should again keep the instructions short and build them up bit by bit. Repeating the signal will also help.

There is some evidence from research with mentally handicapped children that suggests they have more difficulty 'sorting out' sound signals, such as words, than visual signals such as gestures. This appears to be particularly true of Down's Syndrome children. For example, if you are holding the coat and gesturing for the child to come and put it on, he is more likely to do it than if you merely tell him to put it on. In the first case he does not have to interpret the words—the sound symbols representing the coat: the sight of the coat is an immediate reminder, whereas the words have to be 'stored up' for a short time whilst the child works out their meaning.

This is why gestures and objects are so useful in helping to teach early receptive language. They act as a kind of prompt to help the child. But herein, on the other hand, lies a danger. Our objective is to help the child learn the language—the spoken word. If we *always* use the gesture, he may come to rely exclusively on this and not try to learn the words and interpret their meaning.

Therefore, in the above example, we might try the following approach:

Step 1: Get his attention—'Johnny' or 'look at me'. If after several attempts this did not work, we would need to use a prompt—go over to him, repeat the instruction and turn him to look at you.

Step 2:
(ii) If we were standing by the coat 'Come here'; if he did not come over after several repeats—use a gesture with the hands, repeating the instruction.
(ii) If we were standing by him—'Go and get your coat'; again if this did not work, use a gesture—pointing to the coat 'Go and get your coat'. If this did not work we could prompt him by taking him *to* the coat.

Step 3: 'Put your coat on.' Whether he can do this or not will depend upon his motor skills. However, you give him the instruction and wait to see if he makes any attempt—even just picking it up. Then, of course, you get into the training programme for putting coats on. If he does not make any attempt to follow the instruction, you will again need to prompt by picking up the coat or taking his hand and getting him to do it.

You will notice that we withhold the gesture or visual prompt until *after* we have tried the verbal instruction. This will ensure that you are giving him the oportunity to build up his receptive language and not rely on gesture. Therefore, in teaching receptive language :

(i) Do not bombard or smother the child in language.

(ii) Break it down and build it up bit by bit.

(iii) Keep your instructions or comments short, clear and simple.

(iv) Use gestures and objects to prompt. But remember to fade them out.

Expressive language

If we turn to expressive language, you will see some important differences.

1. In receptive language the child usually responds to your communication with some physical action, such as pointing or fetching. These physical actions are very closely related to your communication : 'show me the dog' means 'point to it.' *But*, if he has to respond with a word, he has to find the 'symbol' to represent the object or action. This is more complicated.

2. The main thing about expressive language is that it is often spontaneous. The child uses the words or gestures to try to communicate. He does not say the word simply because you ask him to.

When we talked about spontaneity in play, we said you should not try to force it but encourage it *indirectly*. The same is true of expressive or spontaneous communication. If you try to force the words, or try too hard to get him to imitate or say the words, you often put him off. Therefore, when a child is first learning to express himself with words, wait for them to come from him and reward him when they appear by being very pleased and repeating the word.

3. This danger of inhibiting expressive language can arise in other ways. Most parents, for example, like to get the child to 'show off' a new skill. When we visit homes to check on the child's progress, parents are often eager to let us see the new behaviours —but they are usually disappointed and the child will not 'perform'. If you analyse this situation, you can see the dangers. First, at this stage the child is aware of strangers and may be becoming a little self-conscious. Second, he is beginning to understand

what he is expected to do, and therefore, that he might fail. If he does not do as mum asks or he fails, she is disappointed. It is difficult to conceal this from the child and he may learn not to try.

Getting a child to 'show off' his new words does not really benefit him. It is the *use* of the word to communicate in the natural everyday situation that matters. Therefore, do not take the risk—do not ask him to perform. If he wants to show off his achievements he will do it for himself.

4. A similar point arises over the temptation to correct the child's pronunciation. The first words are usually mispronounced—'bup' for cup, 'gog' for dog, 'der' for there, 'wh-at' for what's that etc. This is mainly because the skill of using the tongue and lips to form the sounds is difficult, and needs a lot of practice. Also, some sounds develop later than others : the 's' sound, for example, develops quite late in the third year for most normal children. To practise the sounds you need to use them. To use them you need to be talking quite a lot. If, almost every time you get excited and want to communicate or get someone to do something, they don't respond to your communication but instead correct your speech—in other words indicate you are wrong—you will soon give up trying to talk.

Therefore, *do not directly correct the child's pronunciations at this stage*. Many people who have worked with slow-learning children have found that correcting the pronunciation and try-ing to make the child speak correctly too soon can actually slow down and inhibit language development.

When the child says a word or phrase, repeat it, where appro-priate, with good pronunciation; but do not over-emphasise the correction of the pronunciation. If, when the child is older and is using quite a lot of words and two or three words together, he still has very indistinct pronunciation, you should consult the school for advice on speech therapy.

5. One more guideline for helping language. If the child uses a gesture or a word or phrase, respond to it appropriately, repeat it if possible, but also *expand* on it. For example, suppose you have been playing games to teach him 'up'—taking a teddy and saying 'teddy up', shooting the teddy high up into the air. When the child says 'up', you can expand this by saying 'yes, teddy jumps

up, up to the ceiling'. Expanding the child's expressions is very important to the development of language. But remember to keep the expansion fairly simple, and not overload the child with too much new information.

6. You can sometimes try to draw out the expressive language more directly. In the above example, if the child has said 'up' after you said it, and teddy has gone up, and if he is still excited by the game, you can pause before the teddy jumps up hoping the child will say 'up'. If he does, he is now instructing you to do something. If he does not say anything, you might prompt by saying 'teddy-y-y——'.

7. We must turn now to the use of gestures. As in receptive language, gestures play a great part in expressive language. But this time they come from the child. When he first starts to communicate he will use a lot of gestures. You need to respond to them immediately and appropriately. However, there is a particular danger that mentally handicapped children will rely on gestures and not develop expressive language. Indeed some of them become great experts in their use of gesture.

We need to try to encourage them to fade out their gestures and use words. For example, if the child can use the word 'up' but instead persists in coming to you with his arms held upwards to be picked up, instead of picking him up you can pretend not to understand. You might ask him what he wants. If this does not work, you might try a verbal prompt by saying 'Do you want to come *up*' or just 'up' with a questioning tone. Similarly, he might bring you his cup indicating he wants a drink. If he can say 'drink', 'milk' or 'juice' you could again pretend not to notice him or not to understand until he says 'drink'.

Of course, you will have all spotted the problem. By not fulfilling his wishes he is likely to get frustrated or give up. This can cause him not to try to communicate. Hence you need to judge carefully how far you can 'push' him before you 'suddenly understand' the gesture. This timing of our responses, prompts etc. is the true art of teaching. When you feel you can do it, you know you are mastering the skill!

Therefore, build up on the child's communication with gesture, but do not allow it to replace expressive language.

To sum up
1. Use words to describe what is happening in the here and now activities.
2. Try to use words which are part of the child's everyday life and interests.
3. Try to respond to all acts of communication by the child.
4. Keep in mind the use of language to express and communicate needs, emotions, desires rather than just building up a list of word labels.
5. Remember that reception of the words comes before the expression of them.
6. Do not force expressive language : teach it indirectly, try to get the child to use it spontaneously, and do not put him off, by making him perform *or* by constantly correcting his pronunciation.
7. Expand his expressions.
8. Use gestures as prompts and aids but fade them out, and do not allow them to replace the spoken word.
9. Keep a list of words and phrases he can understand and comprehend and those that he can say or express.

Finally, and this may be very obvious, children at this stage seem to learn the names of objects (nouns) more easily than words of actions (e.g. verbs). However, both are important, so you need to think of useful words other than names of objects. For example, more, up, down, come, go, give, me, look.

Games
We will now describe some games which might help. Others can be found in the books noted in the booklist, and, of course, you will need to invent your own.

(a) *Understanding names of objects*
    (i) Take two toys which are very different (e.g. teddy and a ball) and which he knows.
    (ii) If he can move around place them on the floor about 4–6 feet (1–2 metres) away and about 3 feet (1 metre apart). If he is not mobile, place them within reach—a foot apart.
    (iii) Say 'get the ball' : if the baby does not look at the ball or respond, prompt him by pointing to it—big gesture. If this does not work, touch the ball, and move it to attract his atten-

I*

tion, repeating 'get the ball'. If he does not move towards it, prompt him, crawl with him, etc. and get the ball.

(iv) When the baby crawls to the ball and picks it up, say 'give me the ball' using a gesture.

Fade out the gestures (prompts).

When he can get both objects :

(i) Replace *one* object with another familiar toy, and

(ii) around the same time, start placing the objects closer together.

(iii) When he can get several objects, place three and later four side by side.

(iv) When he can do this, put them in a box and play 'find the. . . .'

(v) Also play putting them in the box as you name them, and, of course, if he names them spontaneously, you put them in the box.

(b) *Teaching him to point to objects in books or magazines*

(i) Point to the object yourself and name it.

(ii) Prompt him to touch it or point to it.

(ii) Use pictures of familiar objects which are not too complicated. It is useful to cut out pictures and stick them on a card with a plain background.

You can also make his own picture books, using photo-albums that have a clear sheet of cellophane under which you place the picture. These can then be changed and built up. You can include pictures of the family in this book.

(c) *Understanding instructions.*

We have already mentioned the need to teach simple instructions like 'come here', 'look', 'give me', 'get the' or 'find the', 'put', 'show me' etc.

When the baby is beginning to relate objects to each other, you can use instructions which relate the objects, e.g. 'comb your hair', 'comb dolly's hair', 'put the spoon in the cup', 'stir the tea'. Similarly, it is useful to use dolls in play with simple instructions such as 'sit dolly on chair', 'wash dolly's face', 'wipe dolly's nose', etc.

(*d*) *Part of the body.* Keep naming the parts of the body as you wash him or play games. At first the baby will point to your body parts. Use a mirror to let him see his own. Also use a doll and point to the various parts when naming them.

(*e*) *Action words.* Model action words with dolls—'dolly's walking', 'dolly's jumping', 'dolly's gone', etc.

(*f*) When the baby will hand things to you or put things into tins, try teaching the word 'more' or 'again'. Have several similar objects and when he gives you one say 'more!', 'give me some more'. When you play any game, such as bouncing or jumping, and you stop, look for an expression or indication that he wants to repeat it and say 'more' or 'again'.

(*g*) Words such as 'push' or 'go' can be taught in many ways. 'Push the car', 'push daddy', 'push the box', etc. Similarly, you can teach 'go', at first with a ball saying 'go' and pushing the ball away; or holding on to the baby when he is wanting to go and do something, and saying 'go' before letting him go.

(*h*) *Putting words together.* This is an important step in language development and begins near the end of the second year stage.

It will begin when the child uses a number of words frequently. He should have several names of objects (nouns) and some action words. You may already feel he is putting words together. He may say 'bye-bye', 'give me' or even 'all gone'. However, though these are very useful, they are not really two-word utterances.

In the first two-word utterances the child will bring together two 'ideas'—an action and an object. For example, 'gimme teddy' or 'gimme sweet' or 'want car', 'want daddy'. The action word, e.g. gimme, want, sit, gone, more, can act as a central point on to which we can attach many other words, e.g.

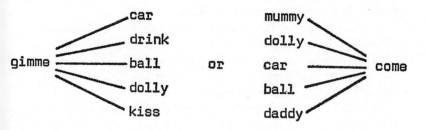

You can see how useful and how important these action words are to express all sorts of ideas, and it is well worth encouraging their development.

You do this by expanding the child's expression. He might say 'gimme', pointing to the car, or he might say 'car', meaning 'give me the car'. You can say 'gimme car' hoping that he will eventually imitate you and say the two together.

Another way is to place three or four objects that he knows and can name on the floor between you. You say 'gimme. . . .' He gives you the object and you are very pleased. Now the trick is to try to reverse the game so that *he* asks and you give. There is no easy way that we can think of to do this. You will have to look for opportunities and try various things out. The problem is to let him see that you are taking turns. Perhaps using another member of the family would help. You ask the child to give you the object, then the other members of the group asks you, then it is the child's turn. You could go behind him and ask for him— encouraging him to say it (but not too forcefully). At first he may just use the name of the object and hold his hand out. If so, you repeat 'gimme . . .' each time the other person responding after the 'gimme...'

If he likes finding hidden objects—and most children do— you can hide them under small cups or cloths and play 'gimme . . .' But remember that this finding of more than one hidden object is quite advanced and so you will need to plan the games keeping in mind his all-round level of ability. The checklist will help here.

SOCIAL-EMOTIONAL DEVELOPMENT

This is yet another major area of change for the young child in the second year of life. It is also an area that gives most parents a great deal of pleasure and frustration.

The 'product' of the development may be the 'demanding, self-willed, bossy, inconsiderate, or viewed from another angle, the 'curious, outward going, exploring, independent, interested, amusing' toddler. Whichever way you view it, few parents would say that life with the toddler is boring.

We shall discuss briefly the 'normal' pattern of development at this stage. But, of course, the handicapped baby will vary far more and you will especially need to think about how your child fits into this pattern. He may be particularly excitable or placid.

There are four main aspects.

1. Curiosity

The child becomes mobile and increasingly inquisitive. He wants to get around and explore. He wants to find out about the things around him.

At this stage he wants to *do* things with objects and people. He learns by doing. But he quickly loses interest in things unless he can do something *new* with them. Hence, he may not settle for long at any one thing and he is frequently moving on to other activities.

2. Independence

The child is now developing his own aims in the things he wants to do. Having decided on what the end-product of his activity should be, he is determined to get it, and to get it in his own way.

He is becoming increasingly independent. He wants to do things for himself although he needs the constant reassurance of mum's presence.

However, the child is often not successful in his determined pursuit of his objective. Sometimes he has not yet developed the ability to do what he wants to do, sometimes you have to prevent him from doing it when it is unacceptable or dangerous. When either of these things happen he is frustrated and may react to frustration by *temper and tantrums*. At this stage this is often the only way in which the child can release his feelings : when all his determination is centred on one objective and he cannot attain this objective, the strong feelings aroused in him have to have some release. A child of this age has very little control over his feelings and is not being deliberately naughty when he gives way to tantrums.

You will need to work out your own way of dealing with a tantrum from your knowledge of your child, but the general points to follow are :

(i) The child should not get what he wants by throwing a tantrum—if he does he is rewarded and, therefore, will do it again. When he repeats it for reward, it is no longer a normal reaction to frustration.

(ii) Punishment for tantrums is usually ineffective and may, in fact, prolong them—it gives the child attention.

(iii) Tantrums usually stop more quickly when ignored. As soon as the child has calmed down you can engage his interest in some other activity and then give him attention.

Continually meeting with frustration when he tries to achieve his objectives can lead to habitual tantrums, or to apathy. You can avoid this by guiding his play so that he achieves success. (See section on Play.)

You can also bypass some of the causes of confrontation between you and the child. For instance, you can put a fireguard round the fire so that you do not need continually to be reminding him not to go near it. At this inquisitive, exploratory stage it is useful to remove at least some of the temptations from the child, so that you do not have to bombard him with prohibitions —apart from all else, you cannot possibly follow up all your prohibitions, so the child learns to ignore your instructions.

3. Making people understand

The child now communicates his needs and feelings by a mixture of vocalisations, gestures, words, tantrums etc. He shows considerable determination in his efforts to make you understand what he wants, and often uses somewhat dramatic gestures accompanied by vocalisation.

During this stage the child is learning the value of communication in getting what he wants. Whereas the younger child confronted by a problem such as a closed door will probably bang ineffectively at it and possibly cry, the older child will come to find mum and in a mixture of gesture and vocalisation make her understand what he wants. But between these two stages there is a long period when he is trying to communicate but does not know how. It is then that he becomes frustrated.

4. A child centred world

The child's development is still totally *centred around 'me'*. He has not yet got sufficient maturity or experience to be able to see anything from another's point of view.

He views everything in terms of his own needs : if he wants an object, for instance, he must get it, and he cannot yet understand that someone else may also lay claim to it so at this stage he cannot 'share'.

He does not understand the differences between what is 'mine' and 'not mine', and he now needs to learn the rules of possession. He can be helped to appreciate the distinction between what is his and what belongs to someone else by the provision of a space or box of his own—his own 'territory'—and some things which are definitely his own.

At the beginning of this stage the main way the child distinguishes between objects and people is by the way they react to him—that is, most people do react to him, objects do not. However, in some cases animals or very young children do not react back, so do not be surprised if he treats young babies like toys! As he progresses through this stage he begins to make emotional distinctions between objects, people and animals, e.g. dolls and teddies are treated differently from bricks and cars.

Finally, to sum up, we would again like to emphasise that at this stage the child's main interest is his determined pursuit of his own aims. If his aims conflict with yours or are unattainable for him, this may lead to confrontation and frustration or apathy. This is a normal pattern at this stage of development.

For the mentally handicapped child this stage may last a long time. If the child has prolonged difficulties in communication, in achieving the end product of his play, in satisfying his needs for stimulation, in learning the rules of give and take and social behaviour, you may think he is developing behaviour problems. It is important that you try not to confuse slow development with emotional disturbance.

Before you put the awkwardness of the child down to the handicapping condition ask yourself if it is merely normal but slower development.

For further ideas about possible behaviour problems, and how you can try to deal with them, see Chapter 12.

PROBLEM SOLVING

Every day we use our knowledge to solve simple problems—you cannot reach the box on top of the cupboard so you get a chair and stand on it; you can see the sweets in the glass jar but you cannot take them out so you take the lid off, the jar is too small to put your hand in to get the sweets so you tip it up.

You probably do all these things without being aware that there is a problem being solved. The baby, however, has not yet learnt how to solve these problems or had the practice in solving them that you have.

To solve a problem we have to :

(i) recognise what it is we want to do : unless we do this we are not faced with a problem;

(ii) be unsure how we can do it : if we know what to do there is no problem. Therefore, all problem situations have some *uncertainty* about them. If you think about it, we are all faced with uncertainty every day and have to find ways of dealing with it. This is a major problem in mental handicap and it is well worth trying to teach the child to cope with it.

(iii) try something to see if it works. Usually we try applying a piece of behaviour which we have used in other situations similar to the new situation; and if it doesn't work, we try another, this is being *flexible*. Again, it is something that mentally handicapped people have difficulty with. They frequently repeat the same old behaviour, even though it is not working, and do not try out something different. Eventually they will give up and not achieve their objective—not solve the problem.

(iv) be prepared to fail, yet not be so discouraged that we give up. This means we need quite a lot of success in solving previous problems to give us the confidence and encouragement to try again. Mentally handicapped people often meet with more failures than successes, unless we help, and so they may not try and try again to solve the problem.

Therefore, it is important to plan simple problem solving games from early in life—planning them carefully to avoid too much failure—and gradually to build up the child's confidence and ability to deal with *uncertain* situations.

Games

Here are some ideas for the first simple games to play :

(*a*) Put a toy behind a transparent plastic or glass screen. Can the baby reach around it to get the toy? If not, prompt.

(*b*) Tie a toy to a piece of string and put it out of reach. Let him explore the string and learn that if he pulls it the toy will come closer. When he can do this, try attaching two toys to different coloured strings, then asking him to get one of them. Use prompts if necessary to show him which toy is attached to which string, and always make sure that you use toys that he knows and will usually get when you ask him.

(*c*) Place a toy out of reach but on a piece of paper or cloth that the baby can reach. Ask him to get the toy, and if he does not, prompt him by pulling the paper and showing him how to do it. Fade out the prompt until he can do it himself in different situations—using a different toy and cloth instead of paper etc., that is, he has understood the link between the toy and what is underneath it (item 112—Adaptive).

(*d*) Put objects that he wants into different shaped bottles or pots with lids on. Use different lids. Let him explore how to get the object out. Prompt occasionally when needed, but do not show at first what to do—if you show him you have taken away the problem.

(*e*) When he can do this, try boxes with different catches or toys such as a jack-in-the-box, where he has to find out how to get the jack to shoot up by pressing a button or lever.

(*f*) Play hiding an object in your hand and let him choose which one it is in. At first, always put it in the same hand. When he finds it three times in a row, switch to the other hand. You can also play this game with cups.

Be an opportunist

We would like to conclude this section on practical guidelines by emphasising what is probably the most important point we can make: be an opportunist! By this we simply mean look for and take any opportunity you can to teach your child. This will depend on three things:

1. Your knowledge of child development and what next step is important to your child.

2. Your skill in turning a situation into a learning game.

3. Your ability to observe your child and spot the opportunity. Particularly, this means:

(i) spotting that your child has an interest in something;

(ii) spotting the possibilities of using that 'something' in teaching the next step.

Here is an example of opportunist teaching described by Steve's mum.

> I am ironing and have a big basket full of clothes. I soon noticed that Steve loves looking at the clothes in the basket. He has a funny mischievous look on his face and smiles when I take some things out. I start to tell him who the clothes belong to, and pop socks, vests, scarves, etc. on him. Now he comes to the basket and starts trying on all sorts of things, especially Dad's vest. He is always laughing and feels it's a good game to play. Every now and then I stop and just give him a little hand to get something on when he's stuck. This is good practice for dressing. Of course, I keep telling him whose things they are and what they are called, and I hope that soon he will begin to tell me!

Remember, then, that most of the help we give the young child is done in these natural play situations, not in specially structured teaching with 'educational' toys. These do, of course, help but it is on the many opportunities that occur throughout the day that we need to capitalise. With the mentally handicapped child you just need to understand the importance of the opportunities more fully, and to step in and add that little extra help they cannot provide for themselves, so that they can gain as much as possible from their activities.

DIFFERENCES AND SIMILARITIES

Much of the first year of life is spent learning about the things which make up our everyday world. We learn that cats are different from dogs, apples are different from oranges, but that dogs and cats are like each other in a number of ways and are very different from birds; and that apples and oranges look more alike than aples and bananas.

This ability to distinguish what makes things the same or different is called discrimination and is obviously very important for learning.

To help the child learn about the differences or similarities between things, we need to think out just what makes them the same or different. Once we know the main difference between one thing and another, we can draw the child's attention to it. Again we need some sort of guiding framework.

At a simple level things can look different, feel different, taste different, smell different, sound different or do different things— a ball will roll, a brick will build, a pencil will make a mark etc. We shall call these differences between things properties. Thus the main properties of a ball are its shape—it is round— and the fact that it will roll. But it may also be large, coloured, furry, and make a sound. The main properties, i.e. roundness and rolling are common to all balls and make a ball different from a block or cube. The other properties can vary, and are not essential in learning that balls are different from other things : but they become important later on, when we need to learn about different types of balls, e.g. football, tennis ball, etc.

Therefore, nearly all the things that make up our world have many different properties but only some of these are important to identify the object or to distinguish it from other objects. Our first task, then, is to learn which are the important properties— those we need to pay attention to—and which are unimportant for the time being, and can be ignored. This ability to search or explore an object, and note the main properties, is often little developed in mentally handicapped children : their attention will often get stuck on one property and they do not switch it to note others.

We can draw two guidelines from this :

1. Always work out the main properties of the object, and draw the child's attention to them. Do this particularly when teaching him about a new object, e.g. a comb has a certain shape and combs hair.

2. When he 'knows' the object, try to teach him to explore or search out other properties in it. Sometimes he will need to pay attention to them, at other times to ignore them. For example, his cup might be the blue one and so he will have to attend to the property of colour. On the other hand he may put all the cups in one box—regardless of colour—and all the saucers in another. Thus he is ignoring the colour, and sorting objects according to their function.

(*Note:* this example is quite advanced, and would come at the end of the second year stage or later.)

If we return to the properties of things, we will find a large number, and it is worth noting how they are connected with the senses.

Hearing
We can hear differences in

    (i) the level of noise, ranging from very loud to very quiet; and
    (ii) the tone of the noise : a high note or low note.

Work on the ability to distinguish between different tones of noise, and different sounds. Also try to connect the sound to the particular object that makes it.

Vision
Things can look different in many ways. They have different shapes, colours, sizes. They can also vary according to the angle at which we look at them, and their arrangement in space, e.g. things can be on top of each other, underneath, close together, etc.

Touch
We use touch to distinguish rough from smooth, soft from hard, hot from cold. We can also 'feel' shapes and sizes.

We should not forget the senses of TASTE and SMELL. You will already have noticed the baby indicating his likes and dislikes of certain foods, and, whilst obviously making sure he eats, it is worthwhile giving him many opportunities to extend his ability to distinguish between different tastes and textures of food. Similarly, let him smell things.

Another property of objects is weight—heavy and light—so make a point of giving him objects of varying weight, especially ones which are unexpectedly heavy or light. For example, if he is playing with bits of wood, mix a few light plastic objects and a few heavy metal ones of about the same size with them. This may surprise him and turn his attention to another property of the object.

In short, try to think about the range of properties of objects and provide experience in them all. The first aim is simply to give the child plenty of experiences with the different properties: after all, if you do not realise that a property exists, you will not be likely to pay attention to it and so learn about it.

Once the child has some knowledge of properties, he can begin to discriminate between them, *or* to show that he can put objects together because they are similar.

This brings us to our third main guideline :

3. The *greater* the difference between objects, the easier the discrimination. For example, it is easier to discriminate between a ball and a teddy than between a teddy and a doll or other furry animal. Similarly, it is easier to discriminate between a square and a circle than between a square and a triangle. The circle is round but both the others have angles and straight lines.

Also : the *more* properties there are that differ between two objects, the easier will be the discrimination. For example, it will be easier to discriminate between a large, blue, round tin and a small, red, square box than between either a large box and a small box or a blue tin and a red tin, etc.

Therefore,

(i) Start with large differences and gradually work down to smaller ones;
(ii) Use objects with many different properties and gradually come down to differences in *one* property, e.g. shape, colour or size.

Finally, at this early stage, it is mainly the *shape* of objects and their uses or *functions* that are most important.

Games
Before discussing some games in detail, we would like to emphasise two points.
(*a*) When you are using a game to teach something, the child will need to know the 'rules' of the game first. If he does not, he has to learn two things at the same time—the rules, and the objective of the teaching. If, for example, you want to teach him to discriminate between circles and squares you might decide to use a sorting game—squares in one pile, circles in the other. Therefore, start the game with objects that he knows and can tell the difference between, say cars and balls, and when he has

learnt the rules of the game use it to teach new things. You should always keep this in mind when using new ways of helping him.

(b) In all the games, do not overwhelm the child by giving too many objects at once. This applies not only to different objects, but to objects that are the same as well. His span of attention will be quite short at first, and you will, in fact, need to build it up. It is worth noting how many objects he will play with—if you put five or six toys in front of him, will he play with only one or two, or will he play with them all turn by turn, or does he just sit looking bewildered? If you are putting objects in a container or posting them through a hole, or running them down a slope, how many times will he pick one up, place it, then pick up another and so on, before switching his attention or stopping?

To keep the game going and to expand his span of attention, you can use three prompts.

(i) You give the object to the child, and say 'do some more' or 'again' or 'another', etc.

(ii) You point to the object, and say 'do some more', etc.

(iii) You prompt verbally only, saying 'another' etc.

These prompts are in order of difficulty and you fade them out accordingly.

1. As we said earlier, the child needs first to learn the main properties of individual everyday things. These are usually the shape and function. You need to ask yourself, what does this thing do or what can it do? Let's take the example of roundness and rolling. Balls and cars can be pushed and will roll. At first you teach each one separately. Then you might make a slope and put the ball at the top so that it rolls down, then the car. You then take a round pencil or dowel or tube and see how this rolls. When the child is placing these things on the slope and *is anticipating that they will roll*, you can assume he has got the idea of rolling. Now put some none-round objects in the game, and ones which will not slide down the slope, e.g. a match box or square or small teddy etc. Watch to see if he places them on the slope with an expectancy that they will roll—remember, get him to place them on the slope so that he is discovering what happens, and is not passively watching you.

The progression, then, is from one familiar object to other objects that do *similar* things; and, *when this is established*, to the unexpected—objects that are *different*.

You can do the same thing with size. Start by teaching him a game of posting objects through a hole in a box. When he is happily playing it, introduce some large ones which will not go through. Remember, at first keep the differences as big as possible, and then gradually make them smaller. Always give your child time really to understand and consolidate the first steps before moving on to the discrimination.

2. The next game has already been discussed in the language section, so we will look at it only briefly here.

The idea of the game is for the child to select one object out of two or more objects. For example : place two objects that he knows on the floor, and get him to pick up or fetch the one which you want.

There are many variations to the game :
How to indicate to him which object to get. You can do this by :
(*a*) Asking for it, e.g. 'get the ball'.
(*b*) Showing him one the same and saying 'get one like this' or 'get the same' or 'get the cup—like this cup' or hold up your cup and say 'cup—you get a cup'. (You will have to explore many different ways of saying and doing this.)
(*c*) Show him a picture of the object and say 'get one like this', using real objects for him to get.

You can use prompts, such as pointing, to help your child at first.

With a very young child, when you hold up an object for him to find one the same, he will often want to get the one you are holding up. If this happens try *once or twice* to show him that you want him to get the other objects. If this does not work, do not push—change the game.

One way the game might change is this :

3. *Matching objects.* The whole idea in matching objects is simply to put two similar objects together. In the game above, your child may take the object from you and start to look at it. Try to get him to put it with the one the same.

You will probably find that it will be easier for your child to put one object or picture on or next to another, rather than just pointing to the one that is the same. Children like *doing* things.

The progression of these games is fairly straightforward.

(*a*) Always start with two choices, then gradually build up to three or four.

(*b*) Always have *one* new object in the choices, the rest being things he knows.

(By choices we mean the things he has to choose from to find the matching object.)

(*c*) Use objects first, then objects to pictures, then pictures to pictures.

(*d*) Use everyday, familiar objects.

(*e*) Use clear pictures which have only the one object on the sheet. Let's look briefly at a picture matching game.

(i) Take two pictures of objects he knows.

(ii) Place them on the floor about six inches apart.

(iii) Give him one of the *objects*, e.g. a cup, and say 'Put it on the cup'.

(iv) Give him time to respond. If he does not, prompt by pointing. If this does not work 'model' by putting it on the picture yourself, or give him a physical prompt by guiding his hand. Fade out your prompts.

(v) When he can do this with objects to pictures, use pictures to pictures.

Note: The pictures to use in these early games should be stuck on card, about 5 or 6 inches (12–15 cm) square.

4. *Sorting games.* Sorting is simply putting similar things in separate groups. The guidelines are :

(*a*) Start with familiar objects that he knows, and not too many —say about three of each.

(*b*) Use two different objects, and then three or four and so on.

(*c*) Make the same objects as identical as possible, i.e. all the same colour and size; and as different as possible from the other objects.

(*d*) It is useful to have a specified area into which he puts the sorted objects, e.g. two shallow boxes, or two trays. This helps to contain his attention. You may also find it useful to have the mixed up objects in a third box different from the other two.

One way to teach him the idea of sorting is as follows :

(i) Place three small balls and three cars in a box and mix them up.

(ii) Model the game by taking them out and placing them in two piles. Tell him what you are doing, and don't do it too quickly.

(iii) Put them back in the box and tell him to do it.

(iv) If you get no response, take out a ball, put it in his pile, then a car, saying 'car for me', and put it in your pile. Encourage him to take out an object and, if a ball, to put it in his pile, if a car, to give it to you—or better still, put it in your pile. If he does not do this—prompt him.

or

(v) Say 'get the ball' . . . 'put it here'. 'Get another ball' . . . etc. until all the balls are sorted, then repeat with the cars.

You can build on this game, using different objects, increasing numbers of objects, pictures, etc.

The order of development is roughly: shapes, colours, then sizes. However, do not rush into colours and sizes too soon, and remember that a big ball and small ball will be easier to distinguish than a light blue ball and a medium blue ball.

5. *Post-boxes and jigsaws.* Post-boxes and jig saws help to teach shape. The post-box will usually use geometric shapes, the jigsaws both geometric and real object shapes.

The guidelines are the same for post-boxes and jigsaws:

(*a*) Try to start with as few shapes as possible—preferably two.

(*b*) Use prompts—especially in helping the child to rotate the shape to fit into the slot. This is the point where children frequently fail so it is useful to say 'turn it' at the right moment.

(*c*) Start with shapes with biggest differences between them, e.g. circle and square.

Now let us use a simple formboard, as described in the appendix.

(i) Place the formboard with the circle nearest your child.

(ii) Take out the circle, but leave the triangle and square in place.

(iii) Hand it to your child and indicate to him, using prompts if necessary, to put it in.

(iv) Repeat this with the square.

(v) When you feel he has a good idea of placing these in the slots, take out the square and circle, but give him the only circle to replace. When he has done this—even with the help of prompts—give him the square.

(vi) When he can do both quite well, with you handing him one piece after the other, place them both in front of him, side by side and get him to replace them.

(vii) When he can do this, repeat the plan with the triangle. First get him to place it in the slot, then hand him first the circle then the triangle, then the square and triangle and *finally* all three.

This sounds straightforward, though your child will probably insist on many variations. However, keep the step-by-step idea in mind as a guideline.

6. *Finding games*. This is quite an advanced category but children often find them fun.

When the child can pick up and find one object hidden under another :

(i) Find two very different containers, e.g. a large, red, square tin and a small, round, blue one.

(ii) Place a new toy which he wants to explore, or a sweet, or part of a biscuit, under the large one—*while he is looking*.

(iii) Tell him to get the object.

(iv) Repeat once or twice, then place it under the small one—again while he is looking.

(v) When you think he has got the idea, i.e. when he can find the object with no mistakes—again hide the object while he is watching you, but then place a screen in front of the containers for 3–5 seconds. Remove the screen.

(vi) Without delay, tell him to find the object.

(vii) When he can do this, you can lengthen the time he has to wait.

At this stage he will probably try to pick up both containers. If you use one big one which needs both hands to pick it up— and provided he does not learn just to knock it over—this might help. You can also try holding down both tins, telling him to choose one, until he goes for one at a time. But be careful not to frustrate him and so put him off the game.

Once he has got the idea of the game—and this can take a long time, so be patient and probe him once or twice each week —you can begin to vary the containers to make it more difficult, e.g. make them both the same size, or shape, or colour. Finally, you can use two containers exactly the same, so the child has to remember the right container by its position alone.

These are just some ideas, but remember to think up others, to look for opportunities to teach him about objects, to use picture books and also to ask other parents, or teachers for their ideas.

MEMORY

We have already made the point that memory (stored representations of things and events) builds up considerably during this second year. This provides the base for complex play, imagination, recognising objects, comparing objects and events and, of course, language.

1. At first the child's immediate memory is short. If you take two cups and put a toy under one whilst the child watches, and then push them to him to find the object, he will find it. But count 5 or 10 before pushing and he is less likely to find it— especially if he has turned his attention to you, *or* you have hidden the cups behind a screen for the 10 seconds. Only by the end of the second year can he reliably remember long enough to find the object.

Gradually build up this 'memory time' with little hiding games. One variation is to change the position of the cups after you have hidden the toy (item 121—Adaptive).

2. He will gradually build up memories of where things are kept. To help this, it is worth keeping some of his favourite objects or toys always in the same place. When he has learnt this, and can always find them, you can, occasionally, put them somewhere else, in order to get him to search and explore—how to go about finding them is a little problem. It can also initiate communication—he comes to you to 'tell' you a toy is missing.

3. Unexpected, new or bizarre things or happenings seem to be more easily remembered than everyday routines. Try to use your imagination to provide memorable events occasionally.

4. When we remember something we do it by :

(i) *Recognition*—we see or hear something that is familiar : it 'jogs' our memory.

(ii) *Recall*—we pull things out of our memory bank without any 'outside' help.

Recognition memory is usually easier to use. In this second year of life, therefore, it is useful to exercise the child's memory by 'prompting' it with an object or event.

For example, if you are trying to teach the child to recognise and remember the word 'ball', it will be easiest if he can see and handle the ball. If you want him to learn 'jump', it will be easiest if he can see a jump, preferably the same kind of jump, each time. For example, make his favourite teddy jump.

The sort of progression you can build upon with a mobile child can be illustrated in hiding games. You can hide toys, or yourself, or another member of the family.

(*a*) To give the child the idea of the game, you say to a member of the family, 'go and hide'. Let the child see the person hide. Then say 'where's daddy' or 'let's find daddy' (you would emphasise the words 'hide' and 'find', and always use them in the game). Then take his hand and find daddy. Gradually let him lead you —then go by himself.

(*b*) You can hide the teddy—let a little bit be showing—and then find him. When this is achieved you hide teddy, while the child is not looking, in the same known places, but out of sight.

(*c*) You hide and call out 'find me'—keeping up little noises to attract the child.

(*d*) You can build up two or three hiding places, e.g. behind the chair, door, table. Whilst doing this, you use the words—'is he behind the chair . . . the door', etc., so building up his comprehension. Once he has learnt to understand the words, you do not need to go with him but can prompt him by saying—'the chair' or 'the door'.

(*e*) You can also try bizarre games. Once he understands the game and the words 'find teddy' or 'where's teddy gone?', you can put teddy in funny or unexpected places—up your jumper, on top of the bookshelf.

(*f*) So far this is all in one room—but now you can expand the game to other rooms.

(i) Play with a favourite toy in one room, leave the toy in a conspicuous place and start to leave the room. Then—'Oh! where's teddy—get teddy'. Once this is achieved, leave the rom and then pretend that you have lost teddy.

(ii) You can now use the same idea as in (*d*), but with a different place—'is he in the kitchen?', the bathroom, etc.

(iii) You can also try sending the child to get familiar things —his coat or his shoes. Again, you need to make sure that he knows the place where they are kept, and understands the name.

All these games are very good for developing language, as well as helping memory and teaching the child to be more independent.

GROSS MOTOR

Many parents of handicapped babies think that once the baby has taken his first steps without help, they have overcome the biggest obstacle. In some ways this is true. But the handicap— the slow learning—is there all the time and one has always to make up for it with special teaching. Therefore, once the baby is taking his first steps you will still have to try to encourage him to walk further and further, and to walk rather than crawl.

In particular, he now needs to develop better balance and co-ordination. He needs to learn about the movements of his body —when he's running, jumping, sliding, pushing things, climbing, etc. He must also become secure and confident in moving his body and using it in everyday activities. If you are not balanced and confident you move badly and you have poor posture. The result is that you look different, and this will not help a handi-capped person to lead a normal life.

We shall now make some brief points about the stages that follow on from walking. We would emphasise that this covers a long period, and the time between the different stages will appear very drawn out. A number of the parents we have worked with have found this frustrating and somewhat disheartening; they often feel that their child has just stopped developing or that they are not doing enough for him. Please do not feel discour-aged. In most cases the child is consolidating many of his skills. It is not so much that development is not taking place but that the differences between the developmental milestones are less obvious than before.

The stimulation and exercises with which you provide your child are also less obvious. Instead of the more direct exercises like pulling to sit and to stand you will need to plan more games and opportunities for the child to develop his motor skills. For example, imitation games like 'O'Grady says', access to stairs and climbing frames, making movement to music, are particularly useful, as are opportunities to pull and push toys and carry things. Remember, you will still need to use prompts often and to provide specific training for some skills.

1. Walking sideways and backwards

You can encourage the baby to do this by using a pull-along toy. At first he will just pull it along behind him. When he does, attract his attention back to it (if it is one that makes a noise this will help). Stop it and pull it back a bit so that he feels the pull on the string. Shake it to attract his attenion. When he looks back at it, encourage him to pull it again. In order to pull it along and look at it at the same time he has to walk sideways and backwards.

2. Turning and pivoting

At first you will notice that the baby can walk only in a straight line. He then needs to develop the balance to turn corners, next to turn his body on one spot and finally to pivot on one foot. Ball games and dancing will help him develop this.

3. Climbing

This demands more strength and balance than walking. The child has to lift one leg high, whilst taking all his weight on the other and keeping his balance. He then has to have the strength to push the whole of the body up with the other leg.

The teaching is similar to that for walking. You have to think of strength, balance and confidence. Use prompts to show him how to climb, at first steadying himself with his hands. Check that the height of the steps, stairs or rungs of the climbing frame are not too big for his legs : small steps at first are obviously easier —you need less strength. Also always make sure that the child feels reasonably happy. If he gets frightened, do not force him but try to make the task easier.

4. Standing on one foot

Again this is a problem of balance and coordination, and it can be some time before the child can achieve it without holding on. You will probably find one leg is better than the other, but do keep trying both. It is also an extension of climbing—one leg being lifted high up whilst the child balances on the other.

Dancing and imitation are useful games to provide practice. If you keep the child standing when taking pants off, you can provide many opportunities for standing on one leg. This is also a help for later dressing. When you do this, always link the words to the actions, e.g. 'step one, step two', or 'lift your leg', 'give me your foot'.

Like you did with walking, you will need to use prompts at first and also gradually to reduce the amount of support you give.

5. Kneeling

When the baby begins to walk without support, he is usually also able to kneel without support (item 75—Gross Motor). If you can persuade him to 'walk' a little on his knees, this exercise is very good for improving his balance and for learning how to shift his weight from one side to the other.

6. Jumping

This helps to develop the baby's muscles, as well as his balance and coordination. If possible, it is useful to use a bouncy surface such as a mattress. Hold the baby's hands and jump him up and down on the mattress—the 'spring' as he lands will push him up again and encourage him to push against it himself.

Babies jump first with one foot, then with both feet off the floor (item 81—Gross Motor), eventually jumping off a raised surface like a step with both feet (item 95—Gross Motor).

You can start this by having games of 'jumping' off a small height, like a large book. If you put three or four around the floor and play getting from one to the other—using imitation—this can be useful. Gradually you increase the height of the 'jump'.

Also take opportunities for letting the baby jump off higher things, such as chairs and beds, whilst you take most of his weight by holding his hands. This helps build confidence as well as co-ordination.

7. Running

When the baby can walk steadily and with good balance, he can begin to walk faster and then to run. Encourage this by walking and running with him, and once he can run himself, practise *stopping, starting* and *turning*.

8. Picking up objects from the floor

This is another exercise needing balance and coordination. To do this the baby has to be able to stop and start easily when walking, then he must learn to bend and pick up an object without falling over (item 89—Gross Motor). You can use games where he has to pick up sweets and toys off the floor.

Again, you can make it easier by holding his hand and by placing toys at lower and lower heights until he can get them off the floor.

At first you will find that the baby will sit down by the object rather than bend for it. You will have to model it, even sing 'picking up' songs and carrying the objects back to a box.

9. Kicking a ball

When the baby is able to balance for a second or two on one foot, he can kick a ball. In fact you can use the game of kicking a large ball to help him to obtain this balance, as, at first, you can hold his hands whilst he kicks the ball. When he can kick the ball without support, you can extend the game so that he has to walk up to it and kick it, and eventually (a lot later), to run and kick it.

10. Catching a ball

This too will come much later, but we would just like to point out at this stage that the common failure in catching a ball is not so much in coordinating the hands but in looking at the ball. Most children look at the face of the thrower. Most throwers hold the ball down by their legs—a long way from their face. Hold the ball high up near your face and stoop down. Make sure the child is looking at the ball, then gently toss toward his chin.

11. Walking on a line

Place a long piece of string in a straight line on the floor, and show the baby how you can walk along it. Encourage him to do the same, leading him if necessary at first. This will help him to walk steadily, with good balance, and to be aware of the movement of his body and placing of his feet.

12. Walking and balancing on a board or wall

This is an extension of walking along a straight line. If you can find a long plank—about 8 inches (20 cm) wide, balance it on low bricks. First he can try to stand on the plank, then to walk along with one foot on it and one foot on the ground. Later he will begin to walk on it with both feet. You can also do this along the top of a low wall.

13. Pushing and pulling

Pushing and pulling heavy objects develops the baby's muscle strength, and increases his awareness of the movement of his body and the parts he uses to move and push or pull.

14. Swings

Swinging is an activity the baby will have been used to and enjoyed for a long time. When he can balance well, he can use a playground or garden swing. The baby swings which have specially enclosed seats are best, as he cannot then fall off. Again remember to introduce him to the swing gently and slowly at first.

The activities we have described here will continue past the two year level. Swings, slides and climbing frames all give scope for different activities, and encourage confidence and balance if they are used properly with supervision. Tricycles are also very popular—at first the sort that the child scoots along with his feet on the ground, and eventually the sort with pedals can be used.

It is not just to develop strength, coordination, posture and confidence that we teach these things, but also to let the child be as normal as possible : so he can play in the park, and do what other children do.

K

FINE MOTOR

By the time the baby is into his second year, he has developed the abilities to coordinate his eye and hand, to reach and grasp, and to pick things up neatly between thumb and first finger. However, this is only the beginning, and for many years he will continue to develop more and more control over his fine motor skills and his eye-hand coordination. For example, he will gradually learn to use a pencil and gain more and more control in drawing and writing, he will learn to pour liquid from container to container with more and more accuracy. It is important to continue building up his fine motor skills by selecting carefully the toys we give him, and by teaching him how to use them.

It is very easy to overlook the importance of fine motor skills. This is because the actual skill is always being used for another purpose. The child, for example, isn't building towers with bricks because he wants to practise his fine motor skills, he's doing it because he wants to build a big tower—and then knock it down! In the section on motivation in Chapter 5, we made the point that the wanting to do something often comes before the actual doing. We also noted that, like most normal children, handicapped children know what they want to do but haven't got the skill to do it; this often causes them frustration. However, it is during this period of knowing what you want to do and trying to do, that you *practise* and hence develop the fine motor skill. Because mentally handicapped children learn slowly, their frustration at this time will presumably be greater. In the case of Down's Syndrome there is some evidence to suggest that there is a special problem with motor learning. Therefore, there is the danger that before they achieve the satisfaction of doing what they want to do, the children have become so frustrated that they have given up. You will have not only to provide toys to help develop fine motor skills, but also need to teach the skills during the course of the games. For example, if you have a toy where pegs are pushed into holes, it may be necessary to show the child how to grip the peg and also to use prompts so that he is successful at putting the peg in the hole.

It is because fine motor skills are associated with many different activities that they appear in the adaptive checklist rather than the fine motor checklist. You should look through the adaptive checklist and note the items which seem to have a large fine motor content.

We will list some of the activities that will develop during the second year, and suggest that you pay special attention to how the child is trying to do the activity in relation to his fine motor skills.

1. Balancing objects on other objects.
2. Putting objects into holes, e.g. pegboards, post-boxes.
3. Screwing and unscrewing.
4. Pouring sand or water.
5. Fine movements such as switching on light switches, turning dials, taps, door knobs/handles, telephone dials, pressing bell buttons.
6. Placing hoops on pegs, leading up to threading cotton reels on string.
7. Using crayons and paints, board and chalk.

SELF-HELP SKILLS

Doing things for *oneself* is very satisfying and helps us to be, and to *feel*, more independent. If you have experience of normal two- to three-year-old children, you will have met the 'me do it' determination which seems so important to them. It is equally important to the handicapped child.

But as we have mentioned in the section on fine motor skill development, it often happens that the child wants to do it for himself but does not have the motor skills. You will need to try to help him feel he is helping himself, and indeed to insist that he does things for himself if he is able.

You should encourage the child to do as many things for himself as possible. By the end of this time he will probably be able to feed himself fully, and should be contributing some of his own efforts in washing and dressing.

Encourage him in this by giving him as much opportunity as possible to take part in these tasks. When it is time to wash him, give him the cloth and encourage him to wipe it over his face and his hands—prompt at first if necessary. When you are dressing him, encourage him to do parts of the dressing himself—put his arm in his coat, his feet in his shoes, etc.

When you are planning to teach the child how to do a task for himself, you need to break that task down into small parts and teach one part at a time. Always try to teach the last part of the task first, so that the child gains the satisfaction of completing the task (see Chapter 5). For an example, we will describe the task of putting on a jumper. This is probably how you do it:

(i) pick up the jumper and find the back—how?—the label is at the back;

(ii) hold the jumper in front of you then pull it over your head, with the back of the jumper towards the back of your head;

(iii) pull the jumper down over your face;

(iv) holding the end of the jumper with the right hand, push the left arm up into its sleeve;

(v) pull the sleeve down so that the hand comes through;

(vi) do the same for the other arm;

(vii) pull the jumper down.

The child cannot do all this for himself at this stage—his arms may not be long enough to reach behind his head to pull the jumper over, and the sequence is in any case too complicated for him. Which parts can he do? He can probably do the last part—pull the jumper down. If he is not already doing this, prompt him to do it. When he can do this, go back one stage—push his arm just into the sleeve for him, then encourage him to push it down the sleeve and put his hand out through the end. When he can do this, go back another stage, and so on. Of course, if there are any steps that he can already do for himself, let him do them—prompt only the difficult ones.

Use this method for all the tasks you teach the child.

You should observe the way the child tries to do the task, if possible observe how other young children do it and, of course, try it yourself—there are, for example, at least four ways to take a jumper off. You will find it helpful to write down the stages of the action as we have done here—it helps to remind you that actions we have practised for years and so think of as simple are, in fact, very complicated, and that this is how they appear to the child!

The main areas to think about in this second year stage of

dressing are pulling off looser garments, e.g. hats, coats, vests; pulling up pants or pulling down the front of jumpers and vests; stepping into shoes and taking off slippers or slip-on shoes.

The child should be getting the idea of washing his hands and parts of the body, and also trying to clean his teeth and brush his hair.

In feeding, he will be using a spoon, possibly a fork and be able to drink. He can also learn to pour water into cups so that later on he will be able to get a drink for himself.

TOILET TRAINING

Toilet training is like any other task to be learnt: we need to know what behaviours the child needs to be ready to learn; how to train; and, of course, what the final behaviour is.

Let's start with this last point. Many mothers will say their child was toilet trained very early. When one questions what they mean by toilet trained, they say they had clean nappies.

But we would say that toilet training is meaningful only when the child can indicate he wants to use the pot or toilet, and 'hold' on long enough to do so. This would mean that during the day he would have only a few accidents: one or two a day wet, and one or two a week soiled. Most normal children achieve this about the age of two to two-and-a-half years. Some are earlier and some are later, and it will depend to some extent on how much effort parents have put into the training.

Because this is learnt about this age, many parents will not start to try toilet training until the child is two. There is something to be said for this, as many of us have spent long frustrating hours trying to train very young children to use the pot and seeming to get nowhere. It is also interesting to note that this is often with our first child!

If we analyse the task and try to identify its steps, we may get a better idea of what to do and what not to do.

1. The child must note a sensation in his bladder or bowel.
2. He must recognise that this signal means he wants to go.
3. He must hold on, and either (a) indicate to you that he wants to go, or (b) go to the potty and do it himself.

There is quite a lot of learning in this.

What we need to do is to teach the child to associate the signal—i.e. pressure on the bladder—with the toilet or potty. If we use the idea that the signal is more likely to be associated with the act (behaviour) if it is followed by a reward, then we need to find as many opportunities to reward the behaviour as possible.

All parents know this, but the important point is to make sure the child actually *performs* the behaviour. Many of us sit children on pots and toilets when we think they might need to go. We make them sit there for a long time, exhorting them to do something and getting increasingly frustrated. There is nothing interesting or exciting about sitting on a pot or toilet, especially when mum gets annoyed. So we are in danger of teaching the child to *avoid* the pot, because it is such an unpleasant experience.

The only way we can be fairly sure that he will perform, and we can all be happy is carefully to observe the behaviour so that we can predict when it will happen.

Let's consider bowel movements first. Many babies achieve control of bowel movements quite early in life: they become fairly regular, wait a certain time after meals and so on. If we can note their daily pattern, we are able to predict when they will perform. Now we can 'catch' the baby by putting him on the pot just in time. Many of our mothers of Down's Syndrome babies have done this, and started to sit the baby on the pot in the first year. They have had a lot of success—fewer dirty nappies, and the babies seem eventually to learn to use the pot earlier than those who have not had this experience. They have had many opportunities to learn to associate the signals, behaviours and the pot, and have been rewarded.

Using the pot to urinate is not so easy. First of all babies, take some time to control their bladders and hold on. Therefore, you really need to wait until the child shows that he can remain dry for at least an hour or so. When you think he can do this, you will need to keep a chart or record.

As you see in this example, the mother checked the child every two hours and noted whether he was wet, dry or soiled. His bowel control was well established and he performed after breakfast or his midday meal. He was also dry often enough to make it worthwhile to start training.

For example :

DAY		1	2	3	4	5	6	7	8....
TIME									
AM	7	W X	W X	W X					
	9	D U	W B	W B					
	11	W X	D U	W U					
PM	1	W B	D U	W X					
	3	D U	W X	W X					
	5	W X	W U	D U					
	7	W X	D X	W X					

State of nappy : W = Wet   D = Dry   S = Soiled
On potty : U = Urinated   B = Bowel movement   X = nothing

You will also note that using the pot first thing in the morning is often a waste of time at first, and it is better to concentrate on more productive times of the day. By noting how often the child is dry and uses the pot, it is possible to plot the progress made. This can be very encouraging, and is far more accurate than relying upon the number of nappies that have to be washed or disposed of. At first you might do this for some days without trying to use the pot. You are looking for a regular pattern. If you don't see one, you may need to try shorter time checks or alter the times you look. Then you can try the pot after each check, and again look for the pattern of times when he is most likely to perform.

At first don't keep the baby on the pot too long and, of course, try to keep him interested. If he performs you clap hands, kiss him, show what he has done and how pleased you are. If he does not perform, it is best just to ignore it and pull his pants back on without too much fuss. Similarly, ignore messes in his nappy.

Most of the handicapped babies we have been concerned with are well into their third year of life before we find reasonably long dry periods; but some have been quite well trained by two-and-a-half years of age. There are also some babies who do not take to potties at all, and it is better to forget the pot and use the toilet—using a modified seat if necessary.

By the way, don't forget that you can model this behaviour yourself by performing on the toilet.

MISCELLANEOUS

12 : Behaviour problems

Our aim in this chapter is to try to help you prevent some problems of behaviour arising at all. We have done this by asking the question, what are behaviour problems?, and then discussing ways to avoid and counteract them.

WHAT ARE BEHAVIOUR PROBLEMS?

All parents have some difficulties with their children—even the 'experts' in child psychology! The difficulties are often called discipline problems or behaviour problems, and we tend to see them as different from other things the child does. One peculiarity of behaviour problems is that what is seen as a problem for one parent may not be seen as a problem by another. For example, at a recent meeting of a parent group, one mother said she was having a terrible problem with her baby—the baby kept waking up in the middle of the night. We all nodded sympathetically, remembering the anguish of waking on a cold night to cries of despair. We asked the mother how often it happened and she replied : 'At least twice a week!' We exclaimed as one 'That's no problem, ours wake twice a night!' One mother commented that she thought all babies woke at night and you just put up with it until they grew out of it.

Let's take a second example from the same group. Another mother said that her baby would not go to sleep when put to bed. The baby cried until mum went up and cuddled her to sleep. We asked how long she cried before mum had to go up : 'Oh! a long time' was the answer. Mum was instructed by the group to put the baby to bed and time how long she cried. The next week when she returned to the group we waited for her observations. She said the baby had stopped crying and there was no problem. The first night she had cried for about ten minutes and just as mum decided to go up she had stopped. After another five minutes mum checked and the baby was asleep. The next night she cried for four minutes and the next night she did not cry at all. A number of points can be made from these simple examples.

First, we parents get particularly upset by behaviour problems and this prevents us from *seeing the problem clearly*.

Second, the extent to which we get upset is very much related to our own needs and ideas of what is acceptable behaviour.

Third, we need to find out exactly what the problem is.

The first point seems fairly straightforward. All we can do is to remind ourselves constantly that we may be overreacting and that we need to sit down calmly and think it through.

The second point is more complex. The behaviours which seem to upset us are usually ones which are inappropriate, unacceptable, dangerous or defiant : that is, the child will not do as he is asked.

Let us look at these in more detail.

1. Inappropriate behaviour

The older child, for example, eats with his fingers, grins at people, regardless of what they say, blows raspberries or grunts continually, or throws objects away as soon as they are picked up.

These behaviours are inappropriate to the age of the child—when babies blow raspberries or grin at people we are delighted; and we don't get too upset when they eat with their hands or throw toys. These behaviours are all part of his normal development, and at certain stages of the development we will even be encouraging or teaching the behaviours. They become a problem only when they are no longer appropriate to the child's present level of development. It is as though one part of the development has got stuck.

However, the fact of its being 'stuck' does not of itself make it a problem behaviour. It becomes a problem for us if it causes us some inconvenience or frustration—we get cross and angry or upset. The older child eating with his fingers upsets us because we do not like to see it : we are embarrassed at what other people might think, and we feel that we cannot take him out to eat at restaurants or with friends. The child who throws things away causes us frustration and anger : the food or cup goes on the floor, he cannot amuse himself with his toys and becomes frustrated and constantly seeks our attention; we get upset that he is not playing and learning.

In other words, when the *consequences* of the child's actions *cause us discomfort*, we begin to call it a problem behaviour.

2. Unacceptable behaviours

Many behaviours are *unacceptable* because they break the rules of household or society : for example, drawing on walls, breaking the furniture, pulling things off shelves in the shops, using bad language, pulling people's hair, taking other children's toys, being rude.

The thing to notice about these types of behaviour is that their unacceptability depends very much on *our* ideas of what is right and wrong. Some families would not be very upset by the child drawing on a wall or switching on the television without permission or using occasional swear words. Others would find all these upsetting. Once again, the child's behaviour is a problem because its *consequences upset us*.

However, the child will have to be accepted by the society in which he is to live, if he is to become as normal and independent as possible. If he has strange or unacceptable behaviours they will put other people off. People will be less likely to talk to him, take him out, let him visit them and so on. Therefore, we need to think about what behaviours are acceptable and unacceptable to other people, and not just about those which upset us.

We should also note that we are not born with the knowledge of what is acceptable and unacceptable—what the rules are. We have to learn. Mentally handicapped children learn slowly and so they will often appear to have more behaviour problems than other children. But the problem is really that the child has made a mistake in using the rules—he has not learnt them sufficiently well. If you were teaching him to put a round shape in a jigsaw and he made a mistake, you would not get annoyed—unless, of course, you felt that he was being deliberately awkward. It is because the *consequences* of making a mistake in one behaviour is so upsetting that we see this as a problem. But if we look at the behaviour in the same way as we look at a mistake in a jig-saw, we will see that each time he breaks the rules and does something unacceptable this is an opportunity to *teach him the correct behaviour*.

Looking at behaviour problems this way may help us to find the patience we all need in correcting them.

This is also true of dangerous behaviour.

3. Dangerous behaviours

We get very upset if the child does something we think is dangerous : playing with the fire or with electric fittings, running out of the house into the road, playing with sharp instruments, and so on.

Because the *consequences* of the behaviour are *dangerous for the child*, we naturally get upset. But we may overreact to the dangers, and as a result become too protective.

From the child's point of view, if he does not know what the consequences of his actions are, he is unaware of the dangers. To him, exploring the electric plug or running outside to see new things are all part of his learning and play. We are delighted when he learns how to unscrew the toy nuts and bolts—this is a step forward in manipulative skills—but when he unscrews the top of a medicine bottle we are appalled. We are pleased when he starts to explore toys by poking his fingers into small holes, or putting pegs into them, but not when he does the same thing to the electric socket !

We are faced with two difficulties.

First, we do not want to overprotect the child and teach him not to explore and be independent. This is what we would do if we constantly stop him from doing things. On the other hand we must protect him from danger.

Second, many of the things he will want to do and needs to learn at an early stage of his development, bring him into contact with possible danger. But he has not developed enough to understand the danger.

Therefore, we can protect him from obvious dangers by using gates on stairs, fireguards, and safety plugs. But also, we must take every opportunity to teach him about the dangers and the consequences of his actions. Like any of us he will have to learn how to use dangerous things safely, and how to survive in situations which could be dangerous. Because he is a slow learner this will take longer.

Let us take an actual example.

We asked the parents of John, a six-year-old boy, whether he could climb up and down stairs by himself. The parents replied that he could not and that they always carried him. We then asked what he did when placed on the stairs. (This is the first step in planning a training—find out what behaviour to build on.)

They said they didn't know—they never put him on the stairs because *he would fall down*. When asked how often he fell down, they said he never had. They had not allowed him to go on the stairs. The parents were *assuming* or guessing, that he would fall, and they were not being objective about it. We found some stairs and placed the boy on the second step. He started to cry and would not move. 'There you see,' said mum, 'he knows he can't do it.'

But again, mum is jumping to conclusions too soon. All we know so far is that if he is placed on the stairs *by himself* he starts to cry. It could be that for two or three years, every time he went near the stairs, mum or dad rushed over and picked him up saying: 'oh no! it's too dangerous'. To the boy, the consequences of going near stairs was that mum or dad picked him up and were upset. Perhaps he put two and two together and learnt that stairs were frightening.

The problem, in that case, was to teach him not to be frightened and to have confidence in himself when climbing stairs. To do this we made the following plan:

(i) Mum to sit on the third step of the stairs with John on knee—facing down—firmly held by mum.

(ii) Mum moves up and down a few steps.

(iii) Mum and John sit side by side on stairs—mum with arm around John.

(iv) Mum and John move down a step.

(v) Mum and John move up a step.

(vi) Mum and John sit side by side on stairs just holding hands.

(vii) John sits on stairs and mum kneels in front of him holding his hands. He comes down one step at a time on his bottom.

(viii) John sits on stairs, mum sitting in front of him but not touching him—encouraging him to come down on his bottom.

At each stage of the plan mum was told to talk to John or sing songs, smiling and laughing and holding him with confidence.

This then was the plan. But it did not work out quite like this.

First, mum found she got backache very quickly and dad took over.

Second, at step (ii) mum knelt at the bottom of the stairs and was joining in the singing and laughing as dad bumped up and down. John then wriggled off dad's knee and came down three steps on his bottom *on his own*!

However, our story does not finish here. Mum often took John and his younger brother to the park. The younger brother loved to go on the slides and climbing frames but—as mum said—John didn't like them. What she meant was that John never made any attempt to go on them, but would always go to the swings. After her experience with the stairs mum decided that she may have taught John not to go on the slides and climbing frames. So with younger brother showing the way and mum encouraging from the rear, she tried them. The result was that after a few weeks John was playing happily with the other children in the park, and, as mum reported some months later, was having even fewer accidents than was his brother.

We have told this story to point out how we can overreact to danger, and how we can, in fact, teach the child to be fearful. It also shows how one sets about analysing the problem to find out exactly what it is, then makes a plan to put it right. But do remember that all children are different. Some are more timid than others. Some are aware of their strengths and weaknesses; if they are unsure of their coordination, they will be apprehensive of stairs and climbing frames. It is necessary to give the child opportunities to learn and develop; to encourage this development but at the same time to work within his limitations. We must appreciate that his apprehension is often real, and we need patiently to teach him to overcome his fears as he himself feels more confident.

4. Defiance and naughtiness

Most parents find that their children are defiant at some time. By this they mean that the child does not do what they ask. How often have we stood in front of a child saying 'Pick it up and put it away' and been met with an equally determined 'no'? This defiance or stubbornness is so common that it can be thought of as part of normal development. As we said in Chapter 11, it begins to appear in the second year of life and never stops. It is at this time that we see more independence emerging. The child wants to do things himself without help. He has ideas of his own and wants to try them out, regardless of what mum or dad may want.

When the child defies mum or dad he is also testing out how far he can go, what are the rules, what will happen if. . . . Again it is the *consequences of his actions* that are important.

Similarly, he may find that throwing things into the fire is far more fun (rewarding) than tidying up his toys.

The problems arise when the child is so defiant that life becomes difficult for everyone. This usually happens because the child has *learnt not to take notice* of others. He has *learnt* how to get his own way.

Let us look at how this can happen from an example.

A mother and her two-and-a-half-year-old boy were observed at home during a typical 20 minutes. We noted what she said to the boy, what he did and what she did. During the 20 minutes she spoke to him 18 times. Six of these times she spoke in response to some communication from the child. All the other 12 times she was giving instructions to the child. Eight of these were instructions to 'sit down,' 'pick it up,' etc., and four were 'do not' instructions, such as 'do not touch the television.'

Only *once* did mum follow up the instruction by making the child do what he was told. She said 'put the cup down', and when he did not she took it from him and put it down. Only *once* did the boy actually do what mum asked. She said 'pass mummy the ash tray'. When he did this she did *not* reward him by saying 'good-boy—thank you'.

Therefore, out of 12 instructions, only one was carried out by the boy, and this was not rewarded; and only one was followed through. The *consequence* for the boy of the other ten instructions was—nothing. He carried on as before. He was *being taught to ignore the instructions*.

You may feel that this was exceptional, but try it yourself. Observe your husband or a relative with a child.

If you do give the child an instruction and he does not do it, it is important to follow up and show him or make him do what you want. For example, in tidying up, if you have said 'Put the toys in the box' and the child has not even tried to do it, you need to repeat it 'be a good boy and put the toys in the box'. If he still refuses and you are quite sure he has heard you and understands what to do, you will need to take his hand, place it on the toy, make him grasp, pick up and put it in the box. Then reward the action. 'That's a good boy, put that toy in the box'. If he does not do it voluntarily, repeat the prompting. Often the child resists this prompting, *but*, having given the instruction, it is important to make sure he carries it out.

Of course, you should always ask yourself, 'can he do the thing you want?' Small children may not have sufficient concentration to pick up a lot of toys. They do one or two but then get distracted. You can also get around many difficulties by *compromising*. For example, instead of saying 'pick up the toys', you can get down on the floor with the child and say 'let's tidy up'. Then you pick up the toy cup and hand it to the child and he puts it in the box. Note that this is the last step in a 'tidy up' plan. You can then reward him for putting the toys in the box. Therefore, he will learn that the *consequences* of putting them in when asked to, are nice. The *consequences* of not putting them in the box are nasty—mum is cross and makes him put them in the hard way. Remember that the young two-year-old often wants to help mum but doesn't necessarily like being made to do things.

Bizarre behaviours
Before summing up this section we would like to note some behaviour problems which do not fit easily into the above descriptions. Some severely mentally handicapped children develop problems such as rocking, head banging, head tapping, scratching themselves, flicking their fingers, vibrating small shiny objects in front of their eyes, making guttural noise or moaning sounds for long periods at a time, or just sitting or shaking their heads. Again, you will see that most babies do some of these things occasionally. *It is only when the behaviour becomes very common that you should think of it as a problem.* By common, we mean that you can predict when it will happen, *or* that he does it most of the time.

A most obvious characteristic of these behaviours is that the young child is not doing anything—he is not playing or looking around with interest. He seems to be totally engrossed in the behaviour itself, or 'far away'. We believe that many of these behaviours can be prevented if we teach the child the necessary skills to do things—to play, to seek out stimulation and so on. By starting the teaching from birth, before these types of behaviour problems arise, and by being on the look out for strange behaviours so that we can try to stop them becoming well established, we believe that the behaviours can be prevented with many children.

Even when the behaviours have occurred, it is possible to do something about them. Let's look at an example.

A mother of a five-year-old Down's Syndrome girl, who was very handicapped and had a severe heart condition, came to us. The girl had had a long history of hospital care and treatment, and the mother had received no advice on training methods to help her.

The first stage was to observe the child in detail. Our observations noted :

1. The child could not walk but could hitch around on her bottom. She seldom moved to get toys—only to go to mum for a cuddle or game. Therefore, she enjoyed *mum's attention*.

2. When she was given a toy, she usually reached out with her left hand, took the toy, looked at it for a brief moment, sometimes sucked it and then threw it behind her.

3. Her left hand constantly scratched her legs, neck, behind her ear, and her other hand.

4. She made loud guttural noises, especially when being fed. She would not feed herself but instead took a mouthful, threw her head back and made her loud noises until the next spoonful appeared.

Together with mum, we decided to start on two behaviours first. One was to get her not to stratch, the other to stop making grunting noises when being fed.

To teach her not to scratch, we had to find something she could do instead. This behaviour had to replace the scratching, and at the same time prevent it. It had to interest the child. The answer was to teach her to use two hands in play.

Our observations also indicated that her level of play was at the 12- to 18-months level. She never used objects imaginatively, e.g. kissing dolls or giving them drinks from cups. She would copy simple acts, such as building bricks, for short periods, and would look at pictures in books. We had, therefore, to match the play we were to teach her with her developmental level.

We decided to use large toys which needed two hands, and games which needed two hands. We used trapping and rolling a large ball to mum, large-piece jigsaws, large building blocks. We then had to progress to smaller toys. When this happened they were always handed to the girl from the right side—so she took them first with her right hand. She was then shown how to play with the toy. If she started to stratch, mum would simply hand her a toy. Whenever she scratched and was not playing, mum physically stopped her and said 'no' quite sharply. Also the scratches were treated to try to make them less irritating.

After four weeks most of the scratches on the child's legs and hands had disappeared, and the ones just behind the ears were much improved. Mum found it impossible to count the number of times the girl scratched, as she was so busy just keeping her playing, so we have no record to show a reduction in scratching.

The play of the child had certainly improved. She would concentrate for slightly longer periods, do simple jigsaws, use post-boxes, and she liked rolling the ball and hitching after it. She also went and got toys from the floor and table more often and initiated her own play.

The moaning and grunting during feeding was treated differently. It was decided that the child had learnt to moan because when she did she received food—a reward. The plan was simple. If she moaned mum turned away from her and prevented the girl from seeing the food. When the moaning stopped, mum quickly turned and put food into her mouth. She would smile and talk to the child, getting and keeping her attention. A second spoonful was produced—if the girl did not moan mum would say 'good girl' and feed her; if she did moan, mum turned away.

The first few days of trying this teaching plan were hectic. The moaning got worse and longer, and the child became very frustrated because she wanted her food. This often happens when one is trying to get rid of an unwanted behaviour. The little girl had learnt to moan to get her food. Therefore, she moaned louder and longer when suddenly she was not getting it.

Also the feeding was taking a long time, and mum often gave up the plan and fed the child as quickly as possible near the end of a mealtime. This is quite understandable, but in fact it was reinforcing the moaning. The child was learning that if she moaned long and loud, eventually she got what she wanted. It is vitally important to be *consistent* and to stick to the plan.

To avoid the moaning, which always *started with the sight of food* (the signal or cue), we decided to sneak up and not let her see the food until the first mouthful was given. Then we talked and kept her attention and got the second mouthful in as soon as she swallowed. This did not give her time to start the moaning. If she did, mum got up and walked out of the room with the food until the child stopped. Then she came back in with the food behind her back, and started again. Within a week mum had to take the food away only occasionally during the feeding.

Three points can be made :

First, we need to be consistent.

Second, we need to analyse why the plan is not working, rather than give up.

Third, and this is obvious in the play example, if we are getting rid of a behaviour we must try to put a behaviour in its place. If we just leave a space, the child will fill it with another behaviour —sometimes worse than the one you got rid of. The behaviour you put in to fill the gap should be something useful, the opposite to the unwanted behaviour. It should be so different that the unwanted behaviour cannot occur—the two are incompatible.

To sum up

1. Behaviour problems tend to get us all particularly upset, so we are in danger of overreacting and missing the important points. Therefore, always try to sit down quietly and analyse the problem. You must decide *exactly what the behaviour is*, just as you do in teaching any skill.

2. Many behaviour problems are just extremes of normal behaviour. They can get out of step in the sequence of development, or they can become predominant. Therefore, we need to think about them in terms of the *normal sequence of development*.

3. Many behaviour problems arise because the child has learned to do or not to do something. Therefore, they can be looked at in the same way as any learning problem.

4. It is the *consequence* of the behaviour for the parent *and* for the child that is particularly important. Therefore, you need to find out and examine what the consequences or rewards are for the child when he produces the behaviour.

WHAT TO DO

The first step in analysing a behaviour problem is to ask the 'can-but-won't' question. Can he do what you expect of him, but won't? If *he can't do it* then it is not so much a behaviour problem, more a case of finding out how much he can do, analysing the task, working out the plan and teaching him the next step in the skill. If he can but won't, then it is a problem of *willingness* or *motivation*. Therefore, we need to concentrate on the *consequences* of the behaviour for the child. It is still a learning problem. In 'can but won't' situations it is usually a case of changing the *consequences* and being *consistent*. Often the behaviour always occurs in the presence of a specific cue or signal.

Therefore, there are three things to look for :

CUE or SIGNAL	BEHAVIOUR or ACTION	CONSEQUENCES
sight of food	moaning	given the food
placed on stairs	crying or looking fearful	picked up and cuddled

To analyse the problem, you need to observe the child and note :

    (i) what happened just before the action or behaviour;
    (ii) exactly what the behaviour was;
    (iii) exactly what the consequences were.

Then you can try altering the signal so that the behaviour does not occur; Or change the consequences so that the association between the signal and the behaviour is altered. If you do not reward, or if you punish the behaviour, the association will be weakened. If you reward it, the association will be strengthened.

It is unlikely that you will get serious behaviour problems with the young baby, and so we will not go into further detail. But you will find some books noted in the booklist which deals with this more fully.

We shall make two final points.

1. The main reward affecting the development of behaviours is

attention. When you give the child your attention, he usually likes it. Very young children particularly want your attention and reassurance—as we said in Chapter 11. If they do not get it for everyday things, they will find behaviours which you cannot fail to pay attention to—screaming, shouting, banging the door etc. You may think that you have told them off. But if they do the action again, it may mean that they did not see this telling off as a punishment but as a reward—they got your attention.

Therefore :

(i) if you are telling him off, make sure he does understand that it is a punishment;

(ii) do not let him have to do extreme things before he gets your attention—give it to him for the everyday things you want to encourage;

(iii) try to ignore—or remove your attention from unwanted behaviours when it is possible. Note : just looking at him is giving him attention. If you are deliberately taking away your attention, turn your back and walk away, or leave the room. Of course you cannot do this for extreme or dangerous behaviours, but it is often better to ignore slightly naughty things than immediately to scold the child.

2. You do not always have to 'attack' the unwanted behaviour in a direct way.

Let's take an actual case, of the young child who runs away from you in the shop. You chase him and tell him off, *but* he keeps doing it. Therefore, your chasing him and telling him off is *rewarding to him*. He likes the consequences of his action.

You can turn your back and walk away. (This needs a lot of faith and a stout heart.) This is removing the consequences—when he comes to you, you then reward him; or

You can get around it by giving him the basket or your bag to carry, and rewarding him for being so helpful. This is an example of replacing the unwanted behaviour with a useful one.

13 : Development in Down's Syndrome babies

In this chapter we will show you the ages when the Down's Syndrome babies we have been visiting over recent years passed some of the items in the developmental checklist.

These babies have all been seen regularly by us from the early months of life, and their parents have used and developed much of the stimulation described in this book to help them.

The children on whom these figures are based are all Down's Syndrome and they have no added serious problems such as deafness, blindness or physical handicap.

We have included this chapter to give you some idea of the ages at which you can expect certain behaviours to develop, and so can aim towards helping them to develop. However, do remember that this is only a guide—if your child has a different condition or other handicaps, then you will obviously expect to find differences in his or her development.

The table below gives the number of the item in the developmental checklist so that you can refer back to your list; the earliest age at which any child attained the behaviour; the *average age* of attainment for the whole group of children; and the latest age at which any child in the group attained the behaviour. You will see that the number of babies used for each item varies. This is because the ages at which we were first able to see children varied and because all the children are not yet old enough to have attained the last behaviours in the list.

Many of the children in the group are still under three years old, and have not yet reached the last behaviours in the checklist. Therefore, we have not included any ages for these behaviours in this chapter.

To give you an idea of the possible age of attainment of a later behaviour, however, we have looked at the number of children who are already three years old who are beginning to put two or three words together (e.g. 'ball gone'—item 70 Communication Checklist).

TABLE 3   *Age of Attainment of Items of Behaviour for Down's Syndrome Babies*

SOCIAL CHECKLIST

Item No.	Description of behaviour	Earliest age	Average age	Latest age	No. of Babies
6	Smiles when touched and talked to	1½m.	3m.	5½m.	18
22	Approaches image in mirror	4m.	6½m.	10m.	37

COMMUNICATION CHECKLIST

Item No.	Description of behaviour	Earliest age	Average age	Latest age	No. of Babies
9	Vocalises to smile and talk	1½m.	4m.	8½m.	28
17	Turns to sound	4m.	7m.	11m.	36
32	Says da-da, ba-ba etc.	7m.	11m.	18m.	37
34	Reacts to 'no'	11m.	14m.	24m.	35
43	Responds to familiar words by gestures etc.	10m.	13½m.	18m.	35
51	Jabbers expressively	12½m.	18m.	30m.	35
52	Says 2 words	15½m.	22m.	30m.	25

TABLE 3 *Age of Attainment of Items of Behaviour for Down's Syndrome Babies*

GROSS MOTOR CHECKLIST

Item No.	Description of behaviour	Earliest age	Average age	Latest age	No. of Babies
11	Holds head up for 15 seconds	1½m.	3m.	5½m.	24
34	Balances head and holds it steady when swayed	3m.	5m.	8½m.	31
42	Rolls from back to front and front to back	4m.	8m.	11m.	37
45	Sits without support for one minute or more	7m.	10m.	15½m.	37
52	Sits steadily for 10 minutes or more and is well balanced	8½m.	11m.	15½m.	35
56	When lying down pulls himself up to sit	8½m.	14½m.	24m.	35
60	Pulls to standing position on furniture	10m.	16½m.	24m.	33
64	Walks with hands held	10m.	17½m.	30m.	30
66	Stands alone	15½m.	21½m.	36m.	29
71	Walks 3 or more steps without support	15½m.	24m.	42m.	27

TABLE 3 *Age of Attainment of Items of Behaviour for Down's Syndrome Babies*

FINE MOTOR CHECKLIST

Item No.	Description of behaviour	Earliest age	Average age	Latest age	No. of Babies
7	Holds cube using fingers against palm	$1\frac{1}{2}$m.	$4\frac{1}{2}$m.	7m.	30
10	Grasps cube, using thumb and fingers to hold it	4m.	$6\frac{1}{2}$m.	10m.	34
14	Can pick up object size of currant	$8\frac{1}{2}$m.	12m.	$15\frac{1}{2}$m.	35
17	Picks up object size of currant using thumb and forefinger only	12m.	20m.	36m.	31

TABLE 3   *Age of Attainment of Items of Behaviour for Down's Syndrome Babies*

ADAPTIVE CHECKLIST

Item No.	Description of behaviour	Earliest age	Average age	Latest age	No. of Babies
8	Visually follows dangling ring in circular movement	$1\frac{1}{2}$m.	3m.	$5\frac{1}{2}$m.	18
28	Grasps dangling ring	4m.	7m.	11m.	36
33	Picks up cube	$5\frac{1}{2}$m.	8m.	10m.	36
34	Holds 2 cubes	4m.	8m.	11m.	35
40	Picks up neatly and directly	7m.	10m.	14m.	37
55	Pulls ring by string deliberately	7m.	$11\frac{1}{2}$m.	17m.	36
64	Removes cloth to find hidden toy	10m.	$13\frac{1}{2}$m.	21m.	35
76	Puts cube in cup	10m.	$16\frac{1}{2}$m.	24m.	34
80	Attempts to imitate scribble	10m.	$15\frac{1}{2}$m.	21m.	35
96	Puts 3 cubes in cup	14m.	19m.	30m.	29
102	Puts a peg in pegboard two or more times	17m.	23m.	36m.	24
103	Builds a tower of 2 cubes	$15\frac{1}{2}$m.	22m.	30m.	26

There are 19 children in the group who are now three or over. Of these, ten are not yet passing this item. Of the nine children who are putting words together, the earliest age for doing this is 24 months and the latest age is three years. The average age is $28\frac{1}{2}$ months.

Appendix 1:
Starting 'school'

By the time their child is 18 months to two years old, parents ask us about starting school; should he go to nursery or playgroup? should he go full-time or part-time? how will he react to being separated from them? how old should he be before starting? should he go to a special school?

There are no easy answers to these questions. It will depend very much on the abilities and temperament of the individual child, and on the locally available services. However, we can discuss some general points which may help you to find out what is best for your child.

By the age of two to three, most handicapped children will benefit from contact with other children, and play in an organised setting such as a nursery, playgroup or special school class.

These facilities vary from area to area and you will need to find out what is available. The Local Education Authority may accept mentally handicapped children into special schools from the age of two if they have places available. You should contact your local Education Office to find out more about this. Some primary schools have special nursery units, and these usually take children from the age of three. Again, you can obtain information from the Education Office. Day nurseries, which take children of any age up to five and are mainly for children who need care during the day because of special circumstances (problems at home, mother working etc.), are administered by the Social Services Department. Many areas have playgroups, which are usually part-time and take children from two-and-a-half or three to five. These are often run by specially trained play leaders, and you can obtain information from the Pre-School Playgroups Association (see Appendix 3 for address). Although playgroups cater mainly for 'normal' children, many are willing to take handicapped children. There are also some playgroups and nurseries run by voluntary organisations such as NSMHC, which cater specially for handicapped children, and it is worth contacting your regional branch for information.

We would advise you to try to find out about all the facilities available in your area, and to visit those which may suit your child, before you finally decide where he should go.

In deciding on this you will need to think of the child's abilities, and how they will be catered for by the facility. For example, if you have a mobile, energetic Down's Syndrome two-year-old who is listening to people talk, trying to communicate with words and gestures, imitating behaviour and exploring his world with some enthusiasm, it will probably be best to keep him with normal children of a similar age for as long as possible. Hence a local playgroup would be suitable. But, of course, the local playgroup is not likely to have people trained in teaching handicapped children. The special school will, and if they have a nursery class of equally advanced children you may choose this.

On the other hand, if your child is very handicapped, is immobile, and at a much earlier developmental level, he is less likely to gain from attending a playgroup of normal children because he has not yet developed the skills and abilities to utilise the opportunities provided. He would be far better off in a special school, where the staff have greater experience in individual and specialised teaching. Your special knowledge of your child's development will help you decide. Ask yourself the question, 'does he need a different sort of stimulation from that I can provide at home?' Particularly, 'does he need to learn to play with other children in groups?' If your answer to this is yes, then you should look for some sort of provision for him. In the case of special schools and nursery units, the education department will usually make arrangements to assess the child and to advise you on which provision would suit him best, and where places are available. If you feel that your child's needs would best be suited by a playgroup, go along to your local playgroup and see the supervisor to discuss what provision can be made for him. Most playgroups are more than willing to take handicapped children, but as they usually have less staff than nurseries they may feel that they will have to make special arrangements for supervision. In this case they may ask you to stay with the child or, alternatively, they may be able to arrange for him to attend on days when the numbers of children are fairly low so that they can give him enough time.

Having decided that your child is ready for some form of school or playgroup, the question then arises of how long he attends at first. Our present experience suggests that gradual introduction of the child to the situation and part-time attendance, at least in the beginning, is most suitable. Some nurseries provide part-time sessions for young children, but in other areas the child has to attend full-time, or not at all. If this is the case you have to consider whether this will be of benefit to the child. For instance, a two-year-old who has to leave home at 8.30 am to travel to nursery and does not get back until 4.00 pm every day, may be so tired when he gets home that he misses out on any of the games he used to play with mum and the family. Again you have to consider the needs of your child and your own particular circumstances before you can make a decision.

Another question frequently raised is, how will the child react to being separated from his mother? Will be become very distressed? If he does, what should we do? Of course, all children react differently, but often the child will show some distress when he first has to leave his mother. At the age of two, normal children usually show anxiety when they are separated from their parents, but by the age of three they have overcome this, they have built up the trust that enables them to know that mum will return. Remember that the handicapped child may be less mature for his age, and so may still be anxious about separation at three or four. It is, however, a good idea to get your child used to being without you for short periods so that he is able to build up this trust. You can gradually lengthen the time you are away, to help him to do this.

When the child first starts at nursery or playgroup, it will help if you can stay with him for a time until he gets used to the situation. Then you can gradually leave him for longer and longer periods, until he is ready to join in the group for the whole session. Often you find that the child will become engrossed in play and ignore your presence for most of the time, just occasionally coming back for reassurance. At this stage you can begin to leave him, but do not make the mistake of sneaking away when he is not looking—this does not help him to build up his trust. Always tell him when you are going, and reassure him that you will be back. This may be harder to do at the time, but it is better in the long run.

Whatever you decide, we would recommend that you do try to find some facility for the child when he is about two to three years of age. In our experience this is usually a benefit for both the child and the mother.

WHEN THE CHILD STARTS SCHOOL

If the child is doing well at home and you have worked out a number of games and programmes to help his development, you will, of course, be concerned that he should continue with this progress when he starts school.

It is important that his teacher is aware of what you are doing at home, and knows the details of your programmes and games. If she does not know, then she cannot follow it up in school. Equally you need to know what your child does at school so that you can continue to help him at home.

In some cases, this communication between parent and teacher seems to break down and this is to the detriment of the child. You should make every effort to work with the teacher and maintain a good communication. The points to remember here are :

(i) Some teachers receive no training to help them work with parents and, of course, parents receive no training in working with teachers. Therefore, you will need to have patience, perseverance and tact when you set out to work with your child's teachers.

(ii) It can be very helpful to the teacher if you keep a diary of what you do with the child for her to see. If the teacher then adds notes of what the child does in school, neither of you will be 'in the dark' about what the other is doing.

(iii) Your child is not the only one the teacher has to deal with. He has to be seen as part of the classroom group, so he cannot be treated in exactly the same way as he is at home.

Some parents are reluctant to keep visiting the school, particularly if they feel that the teacher is very busy, or if they feel that their first visit was not successful. However, it takes time to establish a working relationship in any situation, so do persevere. Just as you expect some failure and frustration in helping your child, so expect some of this in working with the school. In the long run your perseverance can only benefit everybody.

Appendix 2:
Materials

Here are some diagrams of the materials and equipment mentioned in the book.

PEG BOARD

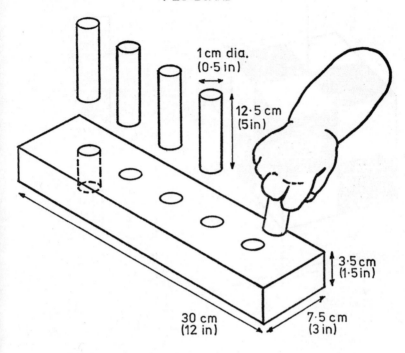

1 cm dia.
(0·5 in)

12·5 cm
(5 in)

3·5 cm
(1·5 in)

30 cm
(12 in)

7·5 cm
(3 in)

FORM BOARD

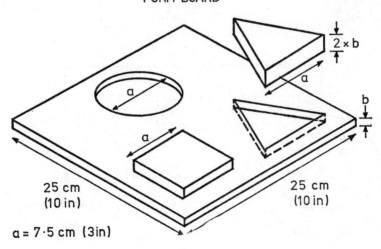

2 × b

a

b

a

a

25 cm
(10 in)

25 cm
(10 in)

a = 7·5 cm (3 in)

MOBILES

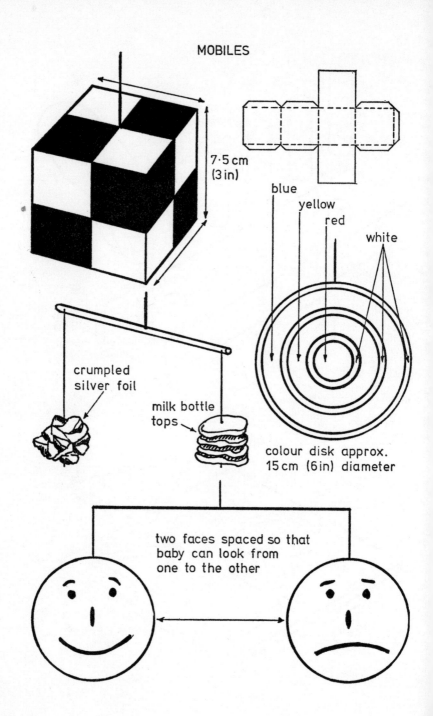

7·5 cm
(3 in)

blue
yellow
red
white

crumpled
silver foil

milk bottle
tops

colour disk approx.
15 cm (6 in) diameter

two faces spaced so that
baby can look from
one to the other

Appendix 3:
Where to look for help

*In this chapter we have given a list of sources of help, both prac-
tical and financial. We have concentrated on the help available
for young handicapped children (from birth to about two or
three years of age), but give a few suggestions for organisations
to contact when the child is older.*

WHERE TO LOOK FOR HELP

Mental handicap may be diagnosed at birth by the doctor, or the
baby's parents may be the first ones to suspect that something is
wrong. In all cases the first months are important and you will
need to seek advice and help on a number of matters.

In seeking help and advice you should insist on :

(i) Obtaining specialist assessments for your child.
(ii) Concrete suggestions on what can be done for the treatment of the child.
(iii) Access to full information about your child's condition.

Be persistent in seeking information and help, and don't be
afraid to ask doctors and therapists to explain things again and
again.

If you find it difficult to obtain help and information, do not
think that you have to fight all the battles alone. Voluntary
groups, such as the National Society for Mentally Handicapped
Children, are willing and able to help.

The first source of help to approach is your *General Prac-
titioner* or the *clinic doctor* at your local Child Health Centre.
Some health authorities have special assessment centres for handicapped children, and your doctor can refer you there if there is
one in your area, or to the *paediatrician* at a hospital. He can
advise you on any special medical problems.

Some mentally handicapped children, particularly those with

additional physical disorders, can benefit from physiotherapy at an early age. *Physiotherapists* are usually based at hospitals, and if the paediatrician feels that your baby would benefit from special exercises he can put you in touch with the physiotherapist.

If you are worried about the cause of your baby's handicap and would like more information about the risks to any other children you may have, your doctor can advise you on this and can refer you to a specialist for *genetic counselling.*

Health visitors work with doctors in general practice, and are experienced in giving help to parents of young babies. They can be contacted at local Child Health Clinics and will visit you at home to discuss general problems. They can also put you in touch with other sources of advice.

Much of the practical help available to parents of young handicapped children is obtained through the *Social Services Department.* However in many areas the department is not automatically informed of the birth of a handicapped child, so we would advise you to contact the area office of the department *yourself*—you do not need to go through your doctor. You can find the address and telephone number of the nearest office in the telephone book, under the name of your local authority and then listed under Social Services Department—Area Office. If you ring or call at your local area office, you can arrange to see a social worker who can tell you about the services the department is able to provide. Your doctor or health visitor can also give you the address of the social services office. Although you may not feel that you need help immediately, it is advisable to contact the social worker so that you can be aware of the help that is available, and you will know what to do should you need help in a crisis. Many local authorities have a leaflet listing all the services, both statutory and voluntary, which are available.

The Social Services Department may be able to help with the provision of a *home-help* to assist with day-to-day household tasks during particularly difficult times in the family, and to arrange *holidays* for the mentally handicapped child or *short-term care* in an emergency.

There are many *aids* to help the handicapped child, and you can obtain a number of items on loan from the Social Services Department. Small items, such as special cutlery and non-slip mats, can be provided as well as the larger items such as special chairs and baby walkers, safety harnesses, baby buggies and larger buggies for the older child.

Sometimes adaptations can be made to your home to make life easier for the handicapped child and his family. Alterations such as building ramps and widening doors to make access easier for wheelchairs can be carried out.

For the older child who is incontinent, plastic pants, disposable nappies, incontinence pads and rubber sheets can be obtained free, and there may also be a free laundry service to help parents. You can obtain information about this from your health visitor.

Help with *transport* to play groups or day nurseries can be arranged through the Social Services Department, and if your child has to visit hospital frequently, or he is in hospital and you have difficulty with transport to visit him, the *hospital social worker* can help you.

FINANCIAL AID

1. Attendance Allowance

This is a benefit paid to parents caring for a mentally handicapped child who requires frequent attention. There are two rates of allowance—a higher rate for children requiring continuous day and night supervision, and a lower rate for those requiring supervision either day *or* night. These allowances are paid for children *over two years of age* and are based on a doctor's assessment of the child.

If you think you are eligible for the allowance, contact your local office of the Department of Health and Social Security, or ask your health visitor. More information about the allowance can be obtained in the leaflet NI 205.

2. Mobility Allowance

This is an allowance to help pay for transport for the severely disabled to help them to get about. It is obtainable only for children over five and is explained in leaflet NI 211 from the Department of Health and Social Security.

Sometimes tax relief on car licences can be obtained for parents of a child under the qualifying age for the Mobility Allowance.

Special badges giving parking advantages for cars in which the disabled child is a passenger can be issued to anyone who receives the Mobility Allowance or the tax relief on car licences.

There are two schemes for assisted purchase of cars for recipients of the Mobility Allowance. Enquire about these at your Social Security Office.

3. The Family Fund

This is a voluntary fund to help families caring for a severely mentally or physically handicapped child under 16. It does *not* replace the statutory provisions made by the services, and is intended to help with particular problems which are not covered by the services.

The help can be in the form of goods, services or a grant of money for some definite purpose related to the care of the child. This fund usually applies only to children over the age of two, but it may consider younger children in exceptional circumstances.

The address to write to is :

The Family Fund, Beverly House, Shipton Road, York. Y03 6RB.
Tel. 0904 29241.

A useful leaflet containing information about these benefits and services, and where to apply, is leaflet HB1 *Help for handicapped people* from your Social Security office.

OTHER ORGANISATIONS

1. National Society for Mentally Handicapped Children

Pembridge Hall, 17 Pembridge Square, London W2 4EP.
Tel. 01–229–8941/01–727–0536.

This society can provide many forms of help for you and your child. Many branches have regular meetings for parents, some run special playgroups, social clubs, residential hostels, holidays etc. They also have facilities for short-term care. You can obtain the address of your local branch from the telephone book, or contact the headquarters at the address above.

2. Toy Libraries Association

Sunley House, 10 Gunthorpe Street, London E1 7RW.
   Tel. 01–247–1386.

Toy libraries are now operating in many areas, often linked with
groups of the NSMHC. The libraries are centres where you can
borrow toys for your handicapped child, and also meet other
parents and obtain advice and support. The libraries are usually
run on a sessional basis once a week, and children can visit the
library with their parents and play together during the sessions.

3. Pre-School Playgroup Association

Alford House, Aveline Street, London SE11 5DS.
   Tel. 01–582–8871.

The association gives advice on the setting up and running of
playgroups, and information on playgroups in your area. It encourages groups to make provisions for handicapped children,
and has a register of Opportunity Groups—playgroups where
handicapped and normal children can play together and mothers
of handicapped children can meet each other. These groups are
open to babies from birth, so that handicapped babies can benefit from play situations as soon as possible. The association also
publishes some leaflets on handicapped children and playgroups.

4. Voluntary Council for Handicapped Children

National Childrens' Bureau, 8 Wakley Street, London EC1V
7QE.

The Voluntary Council was set up to provide a forum for
multidisciplinary discussion for professionals and parents in the
care and education of handicapped children. It provides comprehensive information on handicap, and a useful booklet—*Help
Starts Here* by Phillippa Russell, herself a parent, is available free
of charge.

5. Other specialist organisations

National Society for Autistic Children, 1a Golders Green Road,
London NW11 8EA.
   Tel. 01–458–4375.

Royal National Institute for the Blind,
  224 Great Portland Street, London W1N 6AV.
  Tel. 01–388–1266.
Royal National Institute for the Deaf,
  105 Gower Street, London WC1E 6AV.
  Tel. 01–387–8033.
Down's Children's Association,
  Quinborne Community Centre, Ridgeacre Road, Birmingham, B32 2TW.
  Tel. 021–427–1274.
British Epilepsy Association,
  3–6 Alfred Place, London WC1E 7ED.
  Tel. 01–580–2704.
Spastics Society,
  12 Park Crescent, London W1N 4EQ.
  Tel. 01–636–5020.
Association for Spina Bifida and Hydrocephalus,
  30 Devonshire Street, London W1N 2EB.
  Tel. 01–935–9060/01–486–6100.
Scottish Society for Mentally Handicapped Children,
  69 West Regent Street, Glasgow G2.
  Tel. 041–331–1551.

For further information about services and organisations for handicapped children, we advise you to consult the book *A Handbook for Parents with a Handicapped Child* by Judith Stone and Felicity Taylor, published by Arrow Books, £2.50. This is a comprehensive guide to all the facilities available.

TOYS AND EQUIPMENT

Toy suppliers who will send catalogues and have mail order facilities
  Abbott Toys, 741 Wigmore Street, London W.1.
  Early Learning Centre, 173 King's Road, Reading RG1 4EX.
  E.S.A. (Educational Supply Association), P.O. Box 22, Harlow, Essex CM19 SAY. Two catalogues useful to parents of handicapped children are (i) *Play Specials*, (ii) *Extra Specials* (for older children).

Escor Toys, Grovely Road, Christchurch, Hants. BH23 3RQ.

James Galt and Co., P.O. Box 2, Cheadle, Cheshire.

Gazelle Toys Ltd., Snedshill Trading Estate, Oakengates, Telford, Shropshire.

(Special light aluminium toys, e.g. baby walkers.)

Learning Development Aids, Park Works, Norwich Road, Wisbech, Cambs. PE1 32AX.

(Special books and toys for children with learning difficulties.)

Mothercare, Cherry Tree Road, Watford, Herts. WD2 5SH.

Booklist

General development
Babyhood by Penelope Leach, Penguin Books, 1975.

Motor development and physical handicap
Exercises for Your Baby, by J. Levy, Collins, 1973.
Handling the young Cerebral Palsied Child at Home, by Nancie Finnie, Heinemann Medical Books, 1974.
Motor Development in Children: Normal and Retarded by Britta Holle, Blackwell, 1976.

Mental handicap
Mental Handicap—A Brief Guide by Brian Kirman, Crosby, Lockwood, Stables, 1975.
Mental Handicap by Brian Kirman and Joan Bicknell, Churchill Livingstone, 1975.
   (A more detailed book on the medical aspects of handicap, aimed mainly at professionals, but useful if you want to go into the subject in depth.)
The Special Child (second edition) by Barbara Furneaux, Penguin Books, 1973.
   (Mainly about special education and schools.)
Educating Mentally Handicapped Children, Pamphlet 60, Department of Education and Science, HMSO, London, 1975.
Parents and Mentally Handicapped Children by Charles Hannam, Penguin Books, 1975.
   (An account of how a number of families coped with their mentally handicapped child.)
A Handbook for Parents with a Handicapped Child by Judith Stone and Felicity Taylor, Arrow Books, 1977.
   (A directory of help available to parents of physically or mentally handicapped children.)
The Child with Down's Syndrome (Mongolism) by D. Smith and A. Wilson, Saunders, 1973.
Judith: teaching our mongol baby by W. W. Smith, NSMHC Pamphlet.
   (Written by a parent.)

The Story of Nigel Hunt, by Nigel Hunt, Darwen Finlayson, 1967.

(Written by a Down's Syndrome boy.)

Play

Play with a Purpose for the Under-Sevens by E. Matteson, Penguin Books, 1965.

Baby Learning through Baby Play by Ira Gordon, Sidgwick and Jackson, 1973.

Child Learning through Child Play by Ira Gordon, Sidgwick and Jackson, 1973.

Choosing Toys and Activities for Handicapped Children by Gill Morris, Toy Libraries Association.

Play Helps: Toys and Activities for Handicapped Children by Roma Lear, Heinemann Health Books, 1977.

(Some good ideas for games if you check them against your child's development. A very useful booklist.)

Spontaneous Play in Early Childhood (from birth to seven years) by Mary D. Sheridan, NFER Publishing Company, 1977.

Language

Teaching the Retarded Child to Talk—a guide for parents and teachers by Julia S. Molloy, University of London Press, 1965.

Let Me Speak by Dorothy Jeffree and Roy McConkey, Souvenir Press, 1976.

Behaviour and behaviour problems

Children and Parents—Everyday Problems of Behaviour by Hermann A. Peine and Roy Howarth, Penguin Books, 1975.

(This book deals with behaviour problems in 'normal' children, but it is also applicable to handicapped children at the same level of development. There are some useful examples of progress charts.)

Isn't It Time He Outgrew This—Or a Training Program for Parents of Retarded Children by Victor L. Baldwin, H. D. Bud Fredericks, Gerry Brodsky, C. C. Thomas, Illinois, USA.

(May be difficult to get here, but worth asking your library if they can get it.)